NO RESERVATIONS REQUIRED

A guide to dining at home.

Assistance League
of Marshalltown, Iowa

The cookbook committee appreciates
the enthusiastic participation
of the membership in testing the recipes for this book.

COOKBOOK COMMITTEE:

Barbara Headley & Linda Blum, Co-Chairmen
Laura Allen
Barbara Beichley
Joan Boyce
Tanya Davison
Deb Keefe
Abby Kersbergen
Maureen Lyons
Linda McGregor
Marty Nordmann

Library of Congress Catalog Card Number: 92-81276
ISBN 0-9632850-0-9

WIMMER BROTHERS
Memphis   Dallas

"Man does not live by bread alone."

The world's greatest restaurants have always understood this truth. Your home is your family's "restaurant." You share your home and its warm hospitality with your friends, family and the people you choose to bring into your family's inner circle.

The symbols of the table – food, fellowship, and a feeling of festive thanksgiving, provide an ambiance valued by our members. Assistance League cookbooks have a reputation of excellence that matches America's ★★★★ restaurants. We have tested these recipes with culinary care. The result is a remarkable collection, a treasury perhaps, of recipes you can prepare with confidence knowing each has been proven in restaurants like yours.

Founded in 1938, Assistance League fosters civic involvement through volunteer service and financial support to our community. This is League's fourth cookbook (1966 "Cookbook," 1976 "Cornerstones," and 1982 "Second Helping"). Recipes were contributed by active, associate, and sustaining members. Proceeds will be returned to the Marshalltown community through future Assistance League projects.

This cookbook is an invitation to share the comfort of your home with those you love and enjoy. Your lifestyle, like those of your friends and neighbors, is fast-paced and upbeat. Relax; enjoy cooking. Treasure the conversations and laughter that ring from your restaurant!

If indeed it is true man does not live by bread alone, nowhere is it more evident than where you live, love and eat together, and where there are *No Reservations Required*.

The Cookbook Committee
September, 1992

Assistance League is, as always, very grateful
to businesses in our city who support our volunteer efforts.
Without their support, we would not be able
to contribute so generously to our community.

Marilyn Downs, *Chapter Illustrations*

Annette's Hallmark, *Sales*

As You Like It, *Sales*

Bob's Furniture Shoppe, *Sales*

McGregor Furniture Company, *Storage*

Shearlock Combs, *Sales*

Willard's Furs & Fashion, *Sales*

TABLE OF CONTENTS

Before the Feast　　Appetizers & Beverages......................7

Soup d'Jour　　Soup & Sandwiches.........................25

Salad Bar　　Salads & Dressings 35

Bread Basket　　Breads, Coffee Cakes & Muffins.......55

The Tea Room　　Brunch & Ladies' Luncheon 77

Entrees　　Poultry, Beef & Pork 103

Catch of the Day　　Fish & Shellfish..............................151

From the Grill　　Barbecue & Marinades 159

On the Side　　Vegetables, Pasta & Rice 169

The Cookie Tray　　Bars, Cookies & Candy.......................189

The Dessert Cart　　Cakes, Pies & Desserts...................215

Index　　...243

Before The Feast

BANANA BREAKFAST SHAKE

2 cups skim milk
½ cup plain low-fat yogurt
1 Tbsp. vanilla
2 tsp. ground nutmeg
1 cup nonfat dry milk
1 medium banana,
    peeled, cut into chunks
1 (6 oz.) can frozen orange juice
    concentrate, thawed, undiluted

Yield: 4 cups

Place all ingredients in a blender; cover and blend for 10 seconds at high speed until well mixed and slightly frothy. Pour into glasses and serve.

Carrie Barr (Mrs. Paul)

STRAWBERRY SMOOTHIE

Children love this "healthy" drink on a hot summer day!

2 medium-sized bananas
1 cup frozen whole strawberries
2 to 2 ½ cups pineapple juice

Yield: 4 cups

Peel ripe bananas and place in a plastic bag; seal and freeze until solid or overnight. Break frozen bananas and place in blender. Add strawberries and pineapple juice; process on high until well blended. The texture will be thick like a shake. Leftover smoothie may be frozen into popsicles or try mixing with lemon-lime soda for a slushy drink.

Marilyn Downs (Mrs. Jim)

CHRISTMAS TEA

10 cups water, divided
6 regular-sized tea bags
3 cinnamon sticks
15 whole cloves
2 cups sugar
1 (3 oz.) pkg. cherry gelatin
1 (8 oz.) bottle lemon juice
1 (12 oz.) can frozen orange juice,
    prepared
1 (46 oz.) can pineapple juice

Yield: 1 ½ gallons

Bring 6 cups of water to a boil in a medium saucepan; add tea bags and steep 5 minutes. Discard tea bags. In large pot, combine remaining 4 cups of water, cinnamon sticks and cloves; bring to boil. Reduce heat and simmer 20 minutes. Add tea and remaining ingredients; increase heat and bring to boil. Serve immediately. Store in a sealed container in refrigerator, will keep 3 to 4 weeks. Reheat to serve.

Deb Keefe (Mrs. Kevin)

CHAMPAGNE PUNCH

3 cups pineapple juice
1 (6 oz.) can frozen orange juice
    concentrate, thawed
    and undiluted
1 (6 oz.) can frozen lemonade
    concentrate, thawed
    and undiluted
4 cups water
2 (750 ml.) bottles champagne
orange slices

Yield: 20 cups

Combine juices and water in a large pitcher; chill thoroughly. Just before serving, transfer to punch bowl. Carefully pour champagne down side of bowl; stir gently. Garnish with orange slices.

Variation: Substitute 1 quart lemon-lime soda for one of the bottles of champagne for a sweeter, lighter taste.

Maureen Lyons (Mrs. Ken)

ICED MARGARITAS

1 (6 oz.) can frozen lemonade
   concentrate, thawed, undiluted
1 oz. orange-flavored liqueur
2 oz. tequila
¾ cup water
lime slices
margarita salt
crushed ice

Yield: 6 glasses

Moisten rim of glasses (champagne glasses work well) with a slice of lime and dip rim in margarita salt. Combine lemonade, orange-flavored liqueur, tequila and water in blender; add ice until blender is full. Blend on high speed until thick and frothy. Pour into prepared glasses and serve.

Cathy Frost (Mrs. Curt)

YELLOW BIRDS

1 (6 oz.) can frozen orange juice
   concentrate, thawed, undiluted
1 ½ cups pineapple juice
1 to 1 ½ cups light rum
¾ cup creme de banana
2 ¼ cups water

Yield: 6-7 cups

Combine all ingredients in a pitcher; stir well. Serve over ice.

Pat Shobe (Mrs. Richard)

ORANGE SHERBET COOLER

½ cup club soda
1 ½ cups orange juice
2 cups orange sherbet
3 oz. vodka or to taste
fresh strawberries for garnish

Yield: 4-5 cups

Combine all ingredients in blender; cover and blend 15 seconds. Pour into glasses and garnish with a strawberry on rim of glass.

Madelyn Irvine (Mrs. Stephen)

APRICOT-ALMOND GRANOLA

4 cups old-fashioned rolled oats
1 cup nonfat dry milk
1 cup chopped dried apricots
½ cup wheat germ
½ cup slivered almonds
2 tsp. cinnamon
1 to 1 ½ cups brown sugar,
    firmly packed
¼ cup water
¾ cup margarine, melted
2 tsp. vanilla

Yield: 9 cups

Combine oats, dry milk, apricots, wheat germ, almonds and cinnamon in large bowl. In small saucepan, mix brown sugar and water; bring to full boil. Remove from heat and cool slightly. Stir in margarine and vanilla. Pour syrup into oat mixture; stir until moistened. Spread onto ungreased 15x10-inch jelly roll pan. Bake 2 to 2½ hours at 200°F or until dry, stirring every 30 minutes. Cool. Store in airtight container. Can be served as a snack or as a cereal.

Jayne Hager Dee (Mrs. Eric)

HIKER'S BIRDSEED

Great for a snack on the road.

4 cups honey nut doughnut-shaped
    oat cereal
2 ¼ cups (16 oz.) "M&M's"® plain
    chocolate candies
1 cup raisins
¾ cup dry-roasted peanuts

Yield: 8 cups

Combine all ingredients in large bowl or self-sealing plastic bag. Serve by the handful or by the bowl.

Linda McGregor (Mrs. Robert)

PARTY PRETZELS

4 to 4 ½ cups flour, divided
1 pkg. active dry yeast
2 Tbsp. sugar
2 ½ Tbsp. salt, divided
1 cup milk
½ cup water
2 Tbsp. vegetable oil
2 eggs, lightly beaten
non-stick vegetable cooking spray

Toppings:
coarse salt
Parmesan cheese
poppy seed
sesame seed
dill seed

Yield: 48 small or 12 large pretzels

Combine 1 ½ cups flour, yeast, sugar, and 1 ½ teaspoons salt in a large bowl. In medium saucepan, heat milk, water and oil to 120° to 130° F. Add to dry ingredients and beat 2 minutes at low speed. Increase to high and beat 2 minutes more. Stir in enough additional flour to make a soft dough. Knead dough on floured surface until smooth and elastic, about 5 minutes. Place in bowl coated with non-stick vegetable spray; spray top of dough also. Cover and let rise until doubled in size, 30 to 40 minutes.

Punch dough down; divide into number of pretzels desired. Roll into a 12-inch rope and form into pretzel shape. Cover shaped pretzels; let rest 5 to 10 minutes.

Bring 2 quarts water and remaining salt to boil in large pot. Reduce heat to simmer. Place 4 or 5 small pretzels or 1 large pretzel in water; cook 20 seconds, turning once to cook on both sides. Remove and drain on wire rack. Repeat with remaining pretzels.

Place pretzels on cookie sheet coated with non-stick vegetable spray. Brush tops with beaten egg and sprinkle with desired topping. Bake 35 minutes at 350° or until golden brown. Cool before serving.

Betsy Macke (Mrs. Mark)

PEANUT BUTTER POPCORN

1 cup sugar
1 cup light corn syrup
1 cup creamy peanut butter
1 tsp. vanilla
4 quarts popped corn

Yield: 4 quarts

Bring sugar and syrup to a boil in a heavy saucepan; boil 30 seconds, stirring constantly. Remove from heat. Add peanut butter and vanilla; stir until blended. Pour over popped corn; mix well. Spread on cookie sheet to cool.

Variation: Substitute a favorite dry cereal for part of the popped corn.

Barbara Beichley (Mrs. Duane)

SUGAR AND SPICE COCKTAIL NUTS

1 lb. large pecans or
    English walnuts (or ½ lb. each)
1 egg white
1 tsp. water
½ cup sugar
1 tsp. cinnamon
¼ tsp. salt

Yield: 1 pound

Beat egg white and water until frothy, but not stiff. Add nuts and mix until well coated. Combine sugar, cinnamon and salt. Add this mixture to the nuts; stir well. Pour onto large buttered baking sheet and bake 20 to 30 minutes at 300° F, stirring every 8 to 10 minutes. This recipe can easily be doubled.

Heidi Krabbe (Mrs. Stephen)

CREAMY CHICKEN-FILLED TURNOVERS

Filling:
2 Tbsp. butter or margarine
2 Tbsp. onion, chopped
1 ½ cups chicken, cooked,
    shredded
1 (3 oz.) pkg. cream cheese,
    softened
¼ tsp. dried thyme
¼ tsp. pepper
3 Tbsp. white wine or chicken broth

Pastry:
1 ⅓ cups flour
½ tsp. salt
½ tsp. paprika
½ cup butter or margarine
2 to 4 Tbsp. ice water

Yield: 30 turnovers

Melt butter in skillet; add onion and cook over medium heat until softened, 4 to 5 minutes. Stir in remaining filling ingredients. Continue cooking, stirring occasionally until cream cheese is melted and heated through, 2 to 3 minutes; set aside. In medium bowl, combine flour, salt and paprika; cut in butter until crumbly. Stir in water and shape into ball. On lightly floured surface, roll out dough to ¹⁄₁₆-inch thick. Cut with a floured 2 ½-inch round cookie cutter. Place 1 teaspoon filling on half of each circle; fold other half over and press edges with a fork to seal. Place turnovers on ungreased cookie sheets. Bake15 to 20 minutes at 375°F or until golden brown. These can be made ahead, frozen and baked as needed.

Ann Meiners (Mrs. Gerald)

TORTILLA CRISPS
These make a delightful accompaniment for soup or a salad.

5-6 (7-inch) flour tortillas
¼ cup butter, softened
1 Tbsp. dried parsley
½ tsp. leaf oregano
⅛ tsp. garlic powder
⅛ tsp. onion powder
¼ cup Parmesan cheese, grated

Yield: 30-36 pieces

Mix all ingredients except tortillas and Parmesan cheese. Spread about 1 tablespoon mixture on each tortilla. Sprinkle Parmesan cheese on top. Cut each tortilla into 6 wedges. Place on baking sheet. Bake 12 to 15 minutes at 350°F or until crisp and golden brown.

Anne Booth (Mrs. Richard)

CRAZY CORN NACHOS

1 Tbsp. vegetable oil
½ cup red pepper, diced
½ cup onion, finely chopped
¾ cup whole kernel corn, drained
1 (4 oz.) can diced green chilies
1 cup dairy sour cream
1 (8 oz.) pkg. cream cheese, softened
1 to 2 tsp. chili powder
cayenne pepper to taste
salt to taste
freshly ground pepper to taste
tortilla chips
4 slices bacon, fried and crumbled
2 cups (8 oz.) Monterey Jack cheese,
    shredded

Yield: 6-8 servings

Heat oil in large skillet and saute red pepper, onion and corn until soft. Stir in green chilies; remove from heat. In medium bowl, blend sour cream, cream cheese and spices. Fold mixture into sauteed vegetables. Place chips in a single layer on large baking sheet. Top each chip with a teaspoon of vegetable mixture. Sprinkle crumbled bacon and cheese on top. Broil 2 to 3 minutes or until cheese melts. Serve immediately.

Suzanne Brown (Mrs. Gregory)

BURRITO ROLL-UPS

2 (8 oz.) pkgs. cream cheese,
    softened
1 (6 oz.) can pitted ripe olives,
    drained and chopped
1 (4 oz.) can diced green chilies,
    undrained
½ cup onion, chopped
1 (18 oz.) pkg. 10-inch flour tortillas
salsa

Yield: 7 dozen

Combine cream cheese, olives, chilies and onion; mix well. Spread about 1 heaping tablespoon of cream cheese mixture on each tortilla. Tightly roll tortillas and wrap in waxed paper; chill 8 hours. Slice each roll into seven 1-inch pieces and serve with salsa.

Variation: Combine 1 (1 oz.) package dry ranch salad dressing mix with cream cheese; add ½ cup diced celery. Substitute 2 finely diced green onions for the chilies and ½ cup diced green pepper instead of onion; stir into cream cheese mixture. Continue with directions above.

Lenora Brown (Mrs. Stanley)
Pat Shobe (Mrs. Richard)

KITTEN'S BISCUITS

¼ cup shortening
2 cups self-rising flour
¾ cup milk
1 lb. raw sausage

Yield: 32 biscuits

Cut shortening into flour in small bowl with pastry blender or fork until crumbly; add milk and mix well. Knead briefly on floured surface, adding flour if needed so dough is not sticky. Roll out on floured surface to a 8x16-inch rectangle and about ¼-inch thick. Crumble raw sausage and spread over dough. Roll up jelly-roll style. Cut roll into ½- inch thick slices. Place on ungreased cookie sheet. Bake 18 to 20 minutes at 425°F.

Marki McKibben (Mrs. Larry)

PARTY WEDGES

1 (8 oz.) pkg. cream cheese, softened
½ cup dairy sour cream
1 Tbsp. onion, grated
2 tsp. milk
½ tsp. garlic salt
¼ tsp. pepper
1 (2.5 oz.) pkg. dried beef, finely chopped
¼ cup green pepper, finely chopped
10 crepes, homemade or purchased
stuffed green olives, sliced

Yield: 16-20 wedges

Combine cream cheese, sour cream, onion, milk, garlic salt and pepper until smooth. Stir in dried beef and green pepper. Lay 2 crepes side-by-side; spread each with 2 to 3 tablespoons of beef mixture. Repeat layers making 2 stacks, each 5 crepes high. Garnish top layer with sliced green olives. Refrigerate at least 1 hour. Cut into 8 to 10 wedges per stack.

Jean Brennecke (Mrs. Allen)

16

VEGETABLE PIZZA SQUARES

2 (8 oz.) tubes refrigerated
    crescent rolls
1 (8 oz.) pkg. cream cheese,
    softened
¾ cup mayonnaise
1 ½ Tbsp. dry ranch dressing mix
1 cup carrots, chopped
1 cup cauliflower flowerets
1 cup broccoli flowerets
1 (4 oz.) can sliced black olives,
    drained
¾ cup (3 oz.) Cheddar cheese,
    shredded
¾ cup (3 oz.) mozzarella cheese,
    shredded

Yield: 40-50 squares

Press crescent rolls into ungreased 10x15-inch jelly roll pan. Bake 10 minutes at 400°F. Cool. Combine cream cheese, mayonnaise and dressing mix; spread onto cooled crust. Arrange vegetables and cheeses evenly over the top. Chill until ready to serve. Cut into squares. To serve warm, bake 4 to 6 minutes at 375°F.

Variation: For a Mexican version, prepare crust as directed above. Combine cream cheese and mayonnaise only and spread on cooled crust. Top with 1 (10 oz.) jar mild taco sauce. Instead of vegetables, substitute 1 small chopped green pepper; 1 (4 oz.) can diced green chilies; 1 small chopped onion; and 1 small chopped tomato. Arrange these on top of taco sauce. Sprinkle 2 cups (8 oz.) shredded Cheddar cheese on top.

Linda Blum (Mrs. Daniel)
Barbara Headley (Mrs. Michael)

ALL-DAY MUSHROOMS

3 lb. fresh mushrooms
½ cup margarine
1 ½ tsp. garlic salt or to taste
⅛ cup parsley flakes

Yield: 3 pounds

Wipe mushrooms with damp paper towel or cloth. Melt margarine in slow cooker. Add mushrooms, garlic salt and parsley. Cook on high 2 to 3 hours; reduce setting to low and continue cooking 4 to 8 hours. Serve on platter or spear mushrooms right out of slow cooker with cocktail picks.

Lorraine Schultz (Mrs. Ed)

ASPARAGUS ROLL-UPS

18 slices firm-textured white bread
1 (2 ½ oz.) jar blue cheese spread
1 (3 oz.) pkg. cream cheese,
    softened
18 fresh or canned asparagus spears,
    cooked
½ cup butter or margarine,
    melted

Yield: 54 appetizers

Remove crusts from bread slices; discard crusts. Flaten each slice with rolling pin. Combine blue cheese spread and cream cheese. Spread one side of each bread slice with cheese mixture. Place asparagus spear along one edge of bread slice and roll up jelly-roll style. Place melted butter in a shallow dish. Dip each roll in butter until completely covered; place on baking sheet. Freeze until firm. Cut each roll into thirds. Place in a tightly covered container. Keep frozen until ready to bake. Place frozen roll-ups on a cookie sheet; bake 20 minutes at 350°F or until browned.

Jolene Jebsen (Mrs. Darrell)

BAKED MUSHROOMS

36 (1 lb.) medium to large
    mushrooms
1 ½ cups seasoned croutons,
    crushed
½ cup onion, finely chopped
½ cup dairy sour cream
⅓ cup Parmesan cheese, grated
¼ cup butter or margarine,
    melted
½ tsp. garlic salt

Yield: 36 appetizers

Wipe mushrooms with a damp paper towel or cloth. Remove stems and finely chop. Reserve caps. Mix chopped stems with rest of ingredients. Fill each cap with stuffing mix. Place on large baking sheet and bake 20 to 25 minutes at 325°F.

Susan Chadderdon

B.L.T. IN A BITE

2 pints cherry tomatoes
1 ½ lb. bacon,
    cooked, crumbled
½ cup green onion, diced
½ cup mayonnaise

Yield: 40-50 appetizers

Wash and cut off stem end of each tomato; remove pulp from tomatoes with a narrow spoon. Turn upside down on paper towels to drain 30 minutes. Combine bacon, green onion and mayonnaise; fill each tomato with bacon mixture. Refrigerate until ready to serve.

Joan Boyce (Mrs. Steven)

CUCUMBER SANDWICHES

1 (8 oz.) pkg. cream cheese, softened
1 (0.7 oz.) pkg. dry Italian
    dressing mix
1 loaf (44 slices) party rye bread
1 to 2 cucumbers, thinly sliced
dill weed

Yield: 44 appetizers

Combine cream cheese and dry Italian dressing mix in a small bowl. Spread on rye bread slices. Top each with a cucumber slice and sprinkle dill weed on top for garnish.

Mary Kenagy (Mrs. Dean)

SAUCY CHICKEN WINGS

2 to 3 lb. chicken wings
1 cup water
1 cup lemon juice
1 cup soy sauce
1 cup dark brown sugar,
    firmly packed

Yield: 6-8 servings

Cut wings into 3 pieces and discard wing tips. Place rest of chicken pieces in a 9x13-inch baking dish. Mix remaining ingredients and pour over chicken; cover and refrigerate overnight. Preheat oven to 350°. Bake 45 to 60 minutes; baste often with sauce.

Mary Kenagy (Mrs. Dean)

19

MANDARIN CHICKEN BITES

4 chicken breast halves,
    skinned and boned
1 ¾ cups chicken broth
¼ cup soy sauce
1 Tbsp. Worcestershire sauce
1 lb. fresh spinach leaves,
    rinsed and stemmed
8 cups boiling water
2 (16 oz.) cans mandarin oranges,
    drained

Curry Dip:
¼ cup mayonnaise
¼ cup dairy sour cream
2 tsp. curry powder
2 Tbsp. chutney, chopped
1 tsp. freshly grated orange peel

Yield: 4 dozen pieces

Combine chicken breasts, broth, soy sauce and Worcestershire in a 10-inch skillet. Heat to boiling over medium heat; cover and reduce heat; simmer until chicken is fork tender, about 15 to 20 minutes. With slotted spoon, remove chicken from broth and let cool slightly. Cut chicken into 1-inch cubes. Place spinach in colander; pour boiling water over leaves. Drain quickly and set aside to cool. Place a cube of chicken at stem end of spinach leaf and wrap around chicken so that chicken still shows on sides. Secure end of leaf with a toothpick. Refrigerate at least 1 hour. Recipe can be prepared up to this point one day ahead. To serve, place one mandarin orange at the end of each toothpick. Serve with curry dip. To prepare dip, blend all ingredients; place in jar and refrigerate until ready to serve.

Suzanne Brown (Mrs. Gregory)

CARAMEL APPLE DIP

28 caramels, unwrapped
½ cup margarine
1 (14 oz.) can sweetened
    condensed milk
apple slices
cake cubes

Yield: 3-4 cups

Combine caramels, margarine and sweetened condensed milk in microproof bowl. Microcook on low setting until caramels and margarine are melted. Mix thoroughly and keep warm in a fondue or slow cooker on low setting. Serve with apple wedges, pound cake or angel food cake cubes.

Nancy Hartliep (Mrs. Gill)

CINNAMON FRUIT DIP

1 (8 oz.) pkg. cream cheese,
*   softened*
⅔ cup brown sugar, firmly packed
1 Tbsp. cinnamon
1 tsp. vanilla
few drops of milk

Yield: 2 cups

Mix cream cheese, brown sugar, cinnamon and vanilla; adding small amounts of milk, until dip is smooth and creamy. Serve with fruit slices. Especially good with apples.

Lynn Hall (Mrs. David)

CHEESEY FRUIT DIP
Serves a large group.

2 cups creme de coconut
1 lb. pasteurized processed
*   cheese spread, cut into chunks*
1 (8 oz.) container frozen
*   whipped topping, thawed*

Yield: 8 cups

Combine creme de coconut and cheese in a blender; blend until smooth. Pour into bowl and fold in whipped topping. Serve with fresh fruit. Tasty with apples, grapes and peaches.

Patty Bowman (Mrs. Jim)

CREAMY ORANGE DIP

1 (6 oz.) can frozen orange juice
*   concentrate, thawed, undiluted*
1 ¼ cups milk
1 (3.5 oz.) pkg. vanilla instant
*   pudding*
¼ cup dairy sour cream
fresh pineapple half

Yield: 3 cups

Combine orange juice, milk and pudding mix in a small bowl. Beat with electric mixer until smooth. Stir in sour cream. Chill 2 hours. Just before serving, hollow out pineapple half; cut leftover pineapple into chunks and set aside. Spoon dip into hollowed-out pineapple. Place on platter and surround with a colorful variety of fresh fruit, including pineapple chunks.

Madelyn Irvine (Mrs. Stephen)
21

THE BIG DIPPER

1 ½ lb. pork sausage, mild or hot
1 ½ lb. ground beef
1 (2 lb.) box pasteurized processed
    cheese spread, cut into chunks
2 (4 oz.) cans chopped green chilies
1 (12 oz.) can tomato paste
1 (15 oz.) can tomato sauce
10 jalapeno peppers,
    chopped or to taste
jalapeno juice to taste
tortilla chips

Yield: 10 cups

Brown sausage and ground beef; drain fat. In slow cooker, combine meats and remaining ingredients. Cook on high until cheese melts, stirring occasionally. Reduce heat to low. Serve with tortilla chips.

Madelyn Irvine (Mrs. Stephen)

HOT CHEESE AND PEPPERONI PLEASER

2 cups (8 oz.) mozzarella cheese,
    shredded
2 cups (8 oz.) Cheddar cheese,
    shredded
1 ½ cups mayonnaise or
    salad dressing
1 (4 oz.) can chopped green chilies,
    drained
1 green pepper, chopped
1 medium onion, chopped
1 ½ oz. pepperoni, sliced
1 (4 oz.) can sliced ripe olives, drained
assorted firm crackers, chips or
    fresh vegetables

Yield: 36 appetizers

Combine all ingredients, except pepperoni and olives, in a shallow baking dish or pie plate. Arrange pepperoni and olives on top. Bake about 25 minutes at 325°F or until bubbly. This also works well in slow cooker on low heat. Serve with rye chips, crackers of choice or assorted fresh vegetables.

Marilyn Dodd (Mrs. Charles)
Abby Kersbergen (Mrs. Dan)

BACON-ALMOND CRACKER SPREAD

1 (6 oz.) container cream cheese
*   with chives*
1 cup dairy sour cream
2 to 3 Tbsp. chili sauce
2 Tbsp. green onions, chopped
hot pepper sauce to taste
1 lb. bacon, fried and crumbled
1 (2 oz.) pkg. slivered almonds

Yield: 3 cups

Combine all ingredients except bacon and almonds; mix well. To toast almonds, place in skillet over medium-high heat 3 to 5 minutes, stirring frequently. Add bacon and toasted almonds to dip. Serve with choice of crackers.

Jane Norris (Mrs. David)

BEEFED-UP CHEESE BALL

1 (8 oz.) pkg. cream cheese,
*   softened*
1 cup (4 oz.) Cheddar cheese,
*   shredded*
1 (3 oz.) pkg. dried beef, diced
2 green onions, diced
6 stuffed green olives, sliced
few drops Worcestershire sauce

Yield: 1 cheese ball

Combine all ingredients. Form into large ball shape; refrigerate until ready to serve. Serve with choice of crackers.

Rena Heleniak (Mrs. Bruce)

HOT GOUDA CHEESE

1 (4 oz.) tube refrigerated
    crescent rolls
3 Tbsp. Dijon-style mustard
7 oz. round of Gouda cheese
1 egg white
2 Tbsp. sesame seed or poppy seed

Yield: 10-12 wedges

Flatten crescent rolls, pressing seams together making a square. Spread with mustard and place the cheese in the center. Pull edges of dough to the top of the cheese and press together. Place cheese in oven proof dish with seams down. Brush lightly with egg white. Sprinkle with sesame seed or poppy seed. Bake 20 minutes at 350°F or until brown. Let cool 10 minutes. Serve with plain crackers, apple or pear wedges.

Nancy Veldy (Mrs. John)

BAKED BRIE WITH ALMONDS AND CHUTNEY

1 lb. round of Brie
1 (2 oz.) pkg. sliced almonds
1 (8 oz.) jar peach chutney,
    or raspberry or apricot preserves

Yield: 12-15 hors d'oeuvre

Slice off top rind; cut Brie in half horizontally. Place almonds on top of lower half. Replace top half and cover with chutney. Bake 10 minutes at 275°F or until cheese is just soft. Serve with light crackers or French bread.

Carrie Barr (Mrs. Paul)

24

Soup d'Jour

CANADIAN CHEESE SOUP

½ cup onion, minced
½ cup carrots, minced
½ cup celery, minced
6 Tbsp. butter, melted
1 ½ cups flour
12 cups chicken broth, heated
½ lb. bacon
6 cups (1 ½ lb.) American cheese,
    shredded
2 cups heavy cream
⅛ tsp. baking soda
½ tsp. liquid smoke
¼ tsp. Worcestershire sauce
⅛ tsp. pepper
salt to taste

Yield: 12-15 servings

Saute onions, carrots and celery in butter until soft in a large stock pot. Add flour and stir well. Add hot chicken broth and cook 3 minutes. Add bacon and stir. Blend in cheese, simmer until cheese melts. Mix cream and baking soda; add to soup. Remove from heat and add liquid smoke, Worcestershire, pepper, and salt.

Ann Collison (Mrs. Mark)

PROVOLONE-CHEDDAR VEGETABLE SOUP

2 Tbsp. onion, chopped
1 Tbsp. butter
1 cup frozen corn
½ cup broccoli, chopped
¼ cup carrot, shredded
¼ cup water
1 (10 ¾ oz.) can cream of potato
    soup, undiluted
1 cup milk
¼ cup (1 oz.) Cheddar cheese,
    shredded
1 oz. Provolone cheese,
    cut into cubes
⅛ tsp. pepper

Yield: 4 servings

Saute onion in butter until tender, but not brown in medium saucepan. Add corn, broccoli, carrot and water. Bring to a boil; reduce heat. Cover and simmer 10 minutes until vegetables are tender. Stir in cream of potato soup, milk, cheeses and pepper. Cook and stir over medium heat until cheese melts and soup is heated through.

Mary Holmer (Mrs. Tom)

BEER CHEESE SOUP

8 chicken-flavored bouillon cubes
8 cups boiling water
1 cup celery, finely chopped
1 cup carrot, finely chopped
½ cup onion, finely chopped
1 cup flour
1 cup butter, melted
1 cup beer
4 cups (16 oz.) Cheddar cheese,
    shredded

Yield: 12 servings

Dissolve bouillon in boiling water. Add celery, carrot and onion to broth and boil until almost tender, about 10 minutes. Mix flour and butter; stir into broth. Cook and stir until thickened; boil 1 minute. Reduce heat; add beer and cheese. Mix until smooth and cheese melts. Heat just to serving temperature.

Jayne Hager Dee (Mrs. Eric)

CHEESE AND VEGETABLE SOUP

¼ cup onion, chopped
1 cup celery, thinly sliced
2 Tbsp. margarine
3 medium potatoes, thinly sliced
4 cups chicken broth, divided
1 cup carrots, thinly sliced
1 ½ cup cauliflower, chopped
1 ½ cup broccoli, chopped
¼ cup water
1 ½ cups milk
1 Tbsp. dried parsley
salt to taste
pepper to taste
1 cup (4 oz.) Cheddar cheese,
    grated
4 oz. pasteurized process
    cheese spread, cubed

Yield: 5-6 servings

In Dutch oven, saute onion and celery in margarine until transparent. Add potatoes and 2 cups of chicken broth; cook until potatoes are tender. Combine carrots, cauliflower, broccoli and water in a microproof bowl. Cover and microcook 4 minutes on high; stir and repeat. Drain vegetables and add to soup. Add remaining 2 cups of chicken broth, milk, parsley, salt and pepper. Heat, but do not boil. Add cheeses. Stir until cheese melts.

Jolene Jebsen (Mrs. Darrell)

27

CABBAGE, CARROT AND CARAWAY SOUP

*Wonderful with a hearty dark bread, toasted and
sprinkled with a bit of Parmesan cheese.*

2 cups potatoes, peeled, diced
5 cups water
1 Tbsp. vegetable oil
1 cup onion, chopped
1 ½ tsp. caraway seed
1 tsp. salt
¼ tsp salt-free seasoning
2 cups carrots, pared, sliced
½ cup celery, diced
4 cups (1 lb.) cabbage, chopped
1 large beet or 1 (8 oz.) can
    chopped beets, undrained
⅛ tsp. pepper
½ tsp. dried dill or 1 Tbsp. fresh
    snipped dill
1 cup tomato puree

Yield: 10 servings

Cook potatoes in water until tender, 10 to 15 minutes in a large saucepan. Drain and reserve the cooking water. In a Dutch oven, heat the oil and saute onion until translucent. Add the caraway seed, salt, salt-free seasoning, carrots, celery, cabbage and the reserved cooking water. Bring to boil, reduce heat, cover and simmer until vegetables are tender, about 20 minutes. Cook beet in ½ cup water until tender. Remove from saucepan and reserve liquid. Remove outer beet skin and chop. Add beet liquid, chopped beets, potatoes, pepper, dill and tomato puree to soup. Cover and simmer 30 minutes.

Kay Sinning (Mrs. James)

CABBAGE AND BLUE CHEESE SOUP

½ cup butter
2 large onion, chopped
2 bay leaves
¾ lb. green cabbage, shredded
1 Tbsp. caraway seed
5 cups chicken stock
2 cups (8 oz.) blue cheese, crumbled
1 cup heavy cream
pepper
1 Tbsp. sherry

Yield: 6 servings

Melt butter in stock pot; add onion and bay leaves. Cook 15 minutes then add cabbage and caraway seed. Cook 5 minutes and add chicken stock. Bring to a boil; reduce heat and simmer 15 minutes. Soup may be refrigerated at this point for later use. Add blue cheese and cream. Do not boil. Season with pepper and sherry. Remove bay leaves before serving.

Betsy Macke (Mrs. Mark)

SHARING VEGETABLE SOUP

This cooks for 6 hours, but well worth the time.
Share some with a friend!

3 to 4 lb. country style beef ribs
3 quarts water
1 Tbsp. seasoned salt
pepper to taste
9 ribs celery, sliced
2 large onion, chopped
3 (14 oz.) cans whole tomatoes
1 lb. carrots, pared, sliced
1 cup pearl barley, regular or quick

Yield: 30 servings

Place ribs and water in a large stock pot. Add seasoned salt and pepper. Bring to boiling point, reduce heat, cover and simmer 2 hours. Add celery, onions and tomatoes; simmer 2 more hours. Remove ribs. Cut meat into bite-size pieces; discard bones and fat. Return meat to stock pot and add carrots and barley; simmer 2 more hours. This soup reheats well.

Jeanette Allison (Mrs. A. F.)

MINESTRONE

1 medium onion, diced
1 large rib celery, diced
1 medium carrot, diced
¼ small head of cabbage, chopped
¼ lb. fresh green beans, cut into
    1-inch pieces
1 (28 oz.) can whole tomatoes
2 cups water
½ tsp. dried oregano
2 Tbsp. crushed basil
1 (10.5 oz.) white kidney beans,
    drained
½ cup elbow macaroni

Yield: 8 servings

Combine all ingredients except white kidney beans and macaroni in a stock pot and simmer until vegetables are tender, about 1½ to 2 hours. Add macaroni and kidney beans and simmer until macaroni is tender.

Terry Norris (Mrs. John W., Jr.)

HEARTY BEEF SOUP

1 ½ lb. ground beef
1 cup flour
½ cup margarine, melted
4 cups hot water
1 cup tomatoes, chopped
2-3 carrots, pared, sliced
1 onion, chopped
1 rib celery, sliced
1 (10 oz.) box frozen
   mixed vegetables
4 Tbsp. beef-flavored bouillon
   granules

Yield: 8 servings

Brown ground beef and drain. Set aside. Spray a heavy saucepan with non-stick vegetable spray. Add flour and margarine, mix well. Add water slowly, stirring constantly. Add remaining ingredients. Simmer on low heat 1 hour 30 minutes. Stir occasionally, as soup might stick to pan.

Sharon Miriovsky (Mrs. Michael)

CHEESY WILD RICE SOUP

1 cup cooked wild rice
10 slices bacon, cooked, crumbled
1 Tbsp. onion, minced
3 (10 ¾ oz.) cans cream of
   potato soup, undiluted
4 cups milk
3 cups (12 oz.) Cheddar cheese,
   shredded

Yield: 8-9 servings

Combine rice, bacon, onion, cream of potato soup, milk and cheese in large saucepan. Stir well and let stand 15 to 30 minutes. Return to medium heat and simmer 30 minutes.

Jinx Hill (Mrs. Michael)

VIKING STEW

2 lb. lean chuck roast,
    cut into 1-inch pieces
⅓ cup flour
4 slices bacon
1 Tbsp. sugar
1 onion, cut into fourths
2 cloves garlic, minced
1 (15 oz.) can tomato sauce
2 cups dry Burgundy wine
1 cup beef broth
2 bay leaves
⅛ tsp. dried thyme
⅛ tsp. crushed basil
2 carrots, sliced
2 ribs celery, sliced
2 large potatoes, cubed
1 cup fresh mushrooms, sliced
1 cup fresh broccoli,
    cut into small pieces
1 cup zucchini or green beans, sliced
1 green pepper, cut in strips
2-4 Tbsp. flour (optional)
½ cup water (optional)

Yield: 8 servings

Season beef with salt and pepper. Dredge beef in flour; set aside. Fry bacon in large heavy pot until crisp. Remove bacon and crumble; brown beef in remaining bacon drippings. Sprinkle sugar over beef; add bacon, onion, garlic, tomato sauce, wine, broth, bay leaves, thyme and basil. Cover and simmer 1 hour 30 minutes. Remove bay leaves. Add vegetables and continue to simmer uncovered until vegetables are tender, 45 to 60 minutes. If desired, stew can be thickened by mixing 2 to 4 tablespoons flour with ½ cup water; stir into stew. Heat to boiling, stirring frequently until thick.

Marty Nordmann (Mrs. Brian)

CLAM CHOWDER

2 slices bacon, chopped
¼ cup onions, chopped
1 ¼ cups water
½ tsp. salt
1 ½ cup potatoes, peeled, cubed
2 (6.5 oz.) cans clams
1 Tbsp. butter
2 cups half and half

Yield: 5 servings

Fry bacon and onions until onions are translucent in a 2-quart saucepan. Add water, salt and potatoes. Boil slowly without lid 15 minutes. Add 1 can drained clams and 1 can with juice. Add butter and half and half. Simmer 5 minutes.

Betsy Macke (Mrs. Mark)

31

MEXICAN CORN CHOWDER

½ cup onion, chopped
1 Tbsp. butter or margarine
2 cups potatoes, peeled, diced
1 cup water
½ tsp. crushed basil
2 cups milk
2 (16 oz.) cans cream-style corn
1 (14.5 oz.) can whole tomatoes,
   drained, chopped
1 (4 oz.) can chopped green chilies,
   undrained
½ cup sweet red pepper, diced
½ tsp. salt
⅛ tsp. pepper
1 cup (4 oz.) sharp Cheddar cheese,
   shredded

Saute onion in butter in a large saucepan. Add potatoes, water and basil. Cover and continue cooking on medium heat until potatoes are tender. Remove from heat. In 3-quart casserole, combine milk, corn, tomatoes, green chilies, red pepper, salt and pepper. Add cooked onion and potato mixture. Bake 50 minutes at 350°F. Add cheese and bake 10 minutes. This may also be mixed in a slow cooker and heated on low for several hours.

Susan Malloy (Mrs. Patrick)

Yield: 10 servings

THREE BEAN CHILI CHOWDER

1 ½ cups onion, chopped
1 green pepper, chopped
2 Tbsp. margarine
1 (15 ½ oz.) can kidney beans,
   undrained
1 (15 oz.) can black beans or
   great northern beans, undrained
1 (15 oz.) can pinto beans, undrained
1 (28 oz.) can whole tomatoes
1 cup chicken broth
¾ to 1 cup picante sauce

Garnishes:
Cheddar cheese, shredded
Monterey Jack cheese, shredded
green onions, sliced
dairy sour cream

Saute onion and green pepper in margarine until tender. Add rest of ingredients, except garnishes. Bring to a boil; reduce heat and simmer 10 minutes. Garnish with Cheddar and Monterey Jack cheese, green onions and sour cream.

Madelyn Irvine (Mrs. Stephen)

Yield: 8 servings

MOM'S EASY VICHYSSOISE

1 (10 ¾ oz.) can cream of
potato soup, undiluted
1 (10 ½ oz.) can chicken broth
1 (10 ¾ oz.) can, filled with milk
1 (8 oz.) pkg. cream cheese, softened
1 Tbsp. fresh chives, chopped

Yield: 6 servings

Place all ingredients, except chives, in blender. Mix well. Pour into a saucepan and simmer just until warm. Add chives and chill 4 hours. Serve cold.

Ann Collison (Mrs. Mark)

ITALIAN BEEF

1 (4 lb.) arm or rump roast
3 cups hot water
3 beef-flavored bouillon cubes
1 tsp. salt
3 Tbsp. sugar
½ tsp. pepper
1 tsp. dried oregano
1 tsp. crushed basil
1 Tbsp. dried parsley
⅛ tsp. garlic salt
2 bay leaves

Yield: 8-10 servings

Place roast in medium-size roasting pan. Combine remaining ingredients and pour over roast. Bake covered 3 hours at 350°F. Remove roast and discard bay leaves. Slice roast thinly and serve on hard rolls with reserved cooking liquid.

Margaret Gervich (Mrs. Douglas)
Linda McGregor (Mrs. Robert)

KING BOREAS BARBECUE

2 lb. ground beef
2 cups onion, chopped
¾ cup ketchup
½ cup sweet pickle relish
⅛ tsp.hot pepper sauce
⅛ tsp. steak sauce
½ cup water
1 Tbsp. mustard

Yield: 10-12 servings

Brown ground beef, drain. Place ground beef and remaining ingredients in a slow cooker. Cover and cook on low for 3 to 4 hours. Serve on buns.

Helene Christensen (Mrs. Lyle)

HEALTHY HEROES

¾ cup fresh mushrooms,
    thinly sliced
½ cup cucumber,
    seeded and chopped
1 Tbsp. green onion, sliced
1 clove garlic, minced
2 Ibsp. balsamic vinegar
⅛ tsp. pepper
1 hoagie bun
2 lettuce leaves
2 oz. ham, thinly sliced
2 oz. turkey breast, thinly sliced
4 slices tomato
¼ cup (1 oz.) part-skim
    mozzarella cheese, shredded

Yield: 2 servings

Combine mushrooms, cucumber, green onion, garlic, balsamic vinegar and pepper. Let stand 30 minutes. Slice bun in half lengthwise; pull out soft bread inside of top and bottom, leaving a shell. Spoon one-half of mushroom mixture into each half of bun. Cover with a lettuce leaf. Top with ham, turkey, tomato slices and cheese. Cut open-face sandwich in half to serve.

Pat Shobe (Mrs. Richard)

Salad Bar

PARMESAN CHEESE DRESSING

1 ⅓ cups vegetable oil
½ cup white vinegar
¼ cup Parmesan cheese,
  freshly grated
.1 Tbsp. sugar
2 tsp. salt
1 tsp. celery salt
½ tsp. ground white pepper
½ tsp. dry mustard
¼ tsp. paprika
1 clove garlic, minced

Yield: 2 cups

Combine all dressing ingredients in blender or jar with lid and shake well. Refrigerate until ready to use.

Julie Squiers (Mrs. Richard)

GRANDMA'S POTATO SALAD DRESSING

1 cup sugar
4 Tbsp. flour
3 Tbsp. mustard
2 Tbsp. water
¼ cup vinegar
¼ cup margarine
4 heaping Tbsp. salad dressing
celery seed (optional)

Yield: 2 cups

Combine sugar and flour in a saucepan. Add mustard, water and vinegar; bring to a boil. Add margarine and stir until melted. Stir in salad dressing, 1 tablespoon at a time, until well blended. Add celery seed if desired. Cool and pour over potato salad.

Laura Allen

AVOCADO SALAD DRESSING

2 cups mayonnaise
2 ripe avocados, mashed
1 Tbsp. vinegar
1 Tbsp. Dijon-style mustard
1 ½ Tbsp. lemon juice
2 Tbsp. sugar or 1 Tbsp. honey
1 Tbsp. onion, grated
salt to taste
pepper to taste

Yield: 2 ½ cups

Combine all ingredients in food processor. Process until mixed. Refrigerate in jar with tight-fitting lid.

Joanne Shive (Mrs. Thomas)

AVOCADO AND BEAN SALAD

¼ cup vegetable oil
2 Tbsp. vinegar
2 Tbsp. lemon juice
1 Tbsp. sugar
½ tsp. chili powder
¼ tsp. salt
⅛ tsp. garlic salt
⅛ tsp. pepper
1 (15 oz.) can garbanzo beans, drained
¾ cup kidney beans, drained
2 Tbsp. green onions, sliced
2 avocados

Yield: 4-6 servings

Combine all ingredients except avocados. Chill thoroughly. At serving time, spoon beans into 2 avocados halved lengthwise and seeded, or arrange with peeled avocado slices.

Cindy Mack (Mrs. Tom)

SOUR CREAM COLESLAW

1 large head cabbage
1 green pepper
1 onion

Dressing:
1 cup dairy sour cream
1 cup mayonnaise
3 Tbsp. vinegar
1 tsp. celery seed
¾ to 1 cup sugar
salt (optional)

Yield: 12-15 servings

Shred cabbage. Chop pepper and onion. Combine dressing ingredients and pour over cabbage mixture. Cover and refrigerate until ready to serve.

Marge Solley (Mrs. Larry)

CABBAGE PATCH SALAD

1 (1 lb.) bag shredded cabbage
    and carrots
4-6 green onions, sliced
1 green pepper, chopped
½ cup slivered almonds
½ cup sunflower seed
1 (3 oz.) pkg. chicken-flavor
    dried oriental noodles,
    crushed, uncooked

Dressing:
½ cup vegetable oil
4 Tbsp. sugar
4 Tbsp. cider vinegar
chicken seasoning packet
    from oriental noodles

Yield: 10 servings

Combine cabbage, onions, green peppers, almonds, sunflower seed and noodle chunks. Combine dressing ingredients and pour over vegetables. Toss to coat and serve immediately.

Laura Allen
Betsy Macke (Mrs. Mark)

APPLE HARVEST COLESLAW

It is nice to have a salad that can be prepared ahead.

1 Golden Delicious or
 Granny Smith apple, diced
4 cups cabbage, finely shredded
1 carrot, pared, finely diced
½ green pepper, finely diced
2 Tbsp. onion, finely diced

Dressing:
⅓ cup mayonnaise
2 Tbsp. white vinegar
2 tsp. milk
1 ½ tsp. Dijon-style mustard
⅛ tsp. sugar
salt
pepper

Yield: 6 servings

Combine apples, cabbage, carrot, green pepper and onion. In a separate bowl, combine mayonnaise, vinegar, milk, mustard and sugar. Blend well and toss with apple cabbage mixture. Salt and pepper to taste. Cover and refrigerate about 4 hours. Toss several times before serving. Can make 24 hours ahead and will keep 3 to 4 days.

Maxine Welp (Mrs. William)

CHINESE CABBAGE SALAD

1 large head Napa cabbage, shredded
4-6 green onions, sliced

Topping:
2 (3 oz.) pkgs. dried oriental noodles,
 crushed, uncooked
½ cup margarine
½ cup sesame seed
1 (3 oz.) pkg. slivered almonds
3 Tbsp. sugar

Dressing:
1 cup oil
½ to ¾ cup vinegar
¼ cup red wine vinegar
2 Tbsp. soy sauce

Yield: 10-12 servings

Combine cabbage and onions. Refrigerate covered until ready to use. Use oriental noodles; discard seasoning packet. Melt margarine, sesame seed, almonds, sugar and noodle chunks in a skillet; brown lightly. Let stand at room temperature to cool, stirring occasionally. Topping may be made days in advance. Just before serving, combine dressing ingredients and toss with cabbage and onion mixture. Topping is served separately and sprinkled on top of each serving as desired.

Jane Bauer (Mrs. Robert)

HOT CABBAGE SALAD

3 slices bacon
¼ cup onion, chopped
6 cups (1 ½ lb.) coarsely
    shredded cabbage
2 Tbsp. water
¼ tsp. salt
¼ tsp. sugar
⅛ tsp. pepper
1 Tbsp. cider vinegar
1 Tbsp. dill, finely snipped,
    fresh or frozen (optional)

Yield: 8 servings

With scissors, cut the bacon into small pieces and saute in a large skillet over medium-high heat until three-fourths done—about 2 minutes. Add the onion and continue cooking another minute until the onion browns slightly. Add cabbage, water, salt, sugar and pepper. Saute and toss about 2 to 3 minutes but do not allow the cabbage to become overcooked. It should be slightly wilted but still crisp. Add vinegar and dill; toss again. Serve immediately.

Kindera Severidt (Mrs. Dean)

CLASSIC SPINACH SALAD

4-5 slices bacon
¼ cup onion, chopped
2 Tbsp. brown sugar
1 ½ tsp. vinegar
⅛ tsp. dry mustard
⅛ tsp. paprika
½ bunch spinach leaves, washed,
    dried, torn into bite size pieces

Yield: 6 servings

Fry bacon; remove from skillet and crumble. Add onion, brown sugar, vinegar, mustard and paprika to bacon drippings. Cook until boiling. Add crumbled bacon to spinach leaves. Pour hot dressing over leaves and toss well. Serve immediately.

Sally Becker (Mrs. R.B.)

SPINACH SALAD SUPREME

1 bunch fresh spinach
1 orange, peeled and sliced
½ avocado, peeled and sliced
*   in crescents*
1 oz. Swiss cheese, cut into
*   julienne strips*
½ small red onion, sliced and
*   separated into rings*
4 pitted prunes, cut in half
8 walnut halves (optional)

Dressing:
½ cup vegetable oil
¼ cup lemon juice
¼ tsp. Italian seasoning
¼ tsp. garlic powder
1 tsp. salt
¼ tsp. pepper
¼ tsp curry powder
¼ tsp. dried parsley flakes

Yield: 6 servings

Wash, dry and tear spinach into bite-size pieces. Combine spinach, orange, avocado, cheese, onion and prunes. Combine dressing ingredients. Just before serving, toss salad with dressing. Garnish with walnuts if desired.

Linda Blum (Mrs. Daniel)

OVERNIGHT SALAD

1 head lettuce, broken into
*   small pieces*
1 head cauliflower, cut into
*   small pieces*
½ large sweet onion,
*   finely chopped*
½ cup bacon bits
2 cups salad dressing
⅓ cup sugar
Parmesan cheese

Yield: 10-12 servings

Layer all ingredients in order listed in large bowl. Sprinkle Parmesan cheese on top. Do not stir. Seal and refrigerate overnight. Toss salad at serving time.

Lucy Grossman (Mrs. R.C.)

CHILLED ASPARAGUS WITH DIJON VINAIGRETTE

20 fresh asparagus stalks, trimmed
¼ cup water

Vinaigrette:
1 Tbsp. green onion, finely chopped
¼ tsp. sugar
⅛ tsp. water
2 Tbsp. white wine vinegar
1 tsp. Dijon-style mustard

Yield: 4-5 servings

In a 12x8-inch (2-quart) microproof dish, combine water and asparagus, arranging flower ends toward center and stalk ends toward outside edge. Cover with microproof plastic wrap. Microcook on high 3 to 5 minutes or until asparagus is tender-crisp, rotating dish one-half turn halfway through cooking; drain. To cook asparagus by conventional method, bring ½ cup water to a boil in a large skillet; add asparagus. Reduce heat; cover and simmer 5 to 6 minutes or until tender-crisp. Drain. Place asparagus in a shallow bowl or a glass pie pan. In a jar with a tight-fitting lid, combine vinaigrette ingredients and shake well. Pour vinaigrette over asparagus; toss to coat. Cover and refrigerate 2 to 3 hours, tossing occasionally.

Pat Johnson (Mrs. Craig)

CHEESY BROCCOLI SALAD

3 cups broccoli flowerets
6 slices bacon, cooked, crumbled
1 cup red onion, chopped
½ cup (2 oz.) Cheddar cheese,
   shredded

Dressing:
1 cup mayonnaise
2 Tbsp. white vinegar
¼ cup sugar

Yield: 6 servings

Place broccoli, bacon, onion and Cheddar cheese in a large bowl. Combine dressing ingredients; pour over salad and toss. Serve chilled.

Marge Zeigler (Mrs. Ralph)

42

BERNIE'S BROCCOLI SALAD

1 large bunch broccoli,
cut into flowerets
½ cup green pepper, finely chopped
1 cup green onions, finely chopped
1 cup red grapes, halved
1 cup green grapes, halved
1 cup celery, chopped
½ lb. bacon, cooked, crumbled
¾ cup nuts, chopped

Dressing:
1 cup salad dressing
⅓ cup sugar
1 tsp. vinegar

Yield: 6-8 servings

Combine broccoli, green pepper, green onions, grapes, celery, bacon and nuts. Combine dressing ingredients and toss lightly with broccoli mixture. Serve chilled.

Variation: Alternate dressing; ½ cup mayonnaise, ⅔ cup sugar and 1 tablespoon vinegar.

Ellen Block (Mrs. W.S.)
Noel Lund (Mrs. Ted)

BROCCOLI RAISIN SALAD

1 bunch broccoli,
cut into flowerets
½ cup red onion, chopped
1 cup celery, chopped
1 lb. bacon, cooked, crumbled
½ cup sunflower seed
½ cup raisins

Dressings:
¾ cup mayonnaise
¼ cup sugar
2 Tbsp. vinegar

Yield: 12 servings

Combine salad ingredients in a large mixing bowl. Set aside. Combine dressing ingredients. Pour dressing over salad and stir to blend. Serve chilled.

Variation: Omit celery and substitute golden raisins for dark raisins.

Dee Peterson (Mrs. Robert)
Sally Robertson, (Mrs. James)

43

RAW VEGETABLE SALAD

This salad is attractive as well as tasty.

2 cups cherry tomatoes, halved
2 cups fresh broccoli pieces
½ lb. mushrooms, sliced
1 medium green pepper, cut in strips
1 medium onion, cut in rings

Combine vegetables in large bowl. Combine dressing ingredients. Pour over fresh vegetables, coating thoroughly. Cover and refrigerate overnight.

Dressing:
1 (0.7 oz.) pkg. dry Italian
   salad dressing mix
⅔ cup vegetable oil
½ cup vinegar
1 Tbsp. dill weed
2 Tbsp. water

Fran Hermanson (Mrs. Paul)

Yield: 15 servings

BROCCOLI CAULIFLOWER SALAD

1 bunch broccoli
1 small head cauliflower
½ lb. fresh mushrooms, sliced
1 (8 oz.) can water chestnuts,
   drained and sliced
1 (3 ½ oz.) can pitted ripe olives,
   drained and sliced
1 (8 oz.) bottle Italian salad dressing
20 lettuce leaves
cherry tomatoes

Cut broccoli and caulifower into bite-size pieces. Combine all ingredients, except tomatoes. Cover and refrigerate overnight. Drain and serve on lettuce leaves with garnish of tomatoes.

Joan Ballard (Mrs. Dale)

Yield: 10 servings

44

CAULIFLOWER SUPREME SALAD

3 cups cauliflower, chopped
5 green onions and tops, sliced
1 cup celery, chopped
1 (2 oz.) can ripe olives,
*   drained and chopped*

Dressing:
½ cup dairy sour cream
½ cup mayonnaise
1 (0.7 oz.) pkg. Italian dry
*   salad dressing mix, use only half*

Yield: 8 servings

Combine cauliflower, green onions, celery and olives. Pour one-half of dry salad dressing mix into bowl. Add sour cream and mayonnaise; mixing well. Pour over vegetables and toss lightly. Refrigerate until ready to serve.

Evy Wells (Mrs. Rodney)

CUCUMBERS WITH SOUR CREAM

3 large cucumbers, thinly sliced
½ large red onion, thinly sliced

Dressing:
1 cup dairy sour cream
2 Tbsp. sugar
2 tsp. salt
⅛ tsp. pepper
2 tsp. paprika
2 tsp. mustard
1 tsp. salt-free herb seasoning
¼ cup vinegar

Yield: 4-6 servings

Combine dressing ingredients and blend thoroughly. Pour over cucumbers and onions; refrigerate several hours.

Elaine Graeff (Mrs. Dan)

DILLED TOMATOES
Heart healthy!

2-4 tomatoes, peeled or unpeeled
2 Tbsp. onion, grated
¼ cup olive oil
¼ cup red wine vinegar
1 Tbsp. celery, chopped
1 Tbsp. fresh dill or 1 tsp. dried dill
cucumbers, sliced (optional)
lettuce leaves (optional)

Yield: 2-4 servings

Slice tomatoes. Combine onion, olive oil, vinegar, celery and dill; pour over tomatoes. Marinate in covered container at least 3 hours. Serve on platter with sliced cucumbers or on a bed of lettuce. Keeps in refrigerator several days.

Linda Bloom (Mrs. Michael)

NEW POTATO SALAD VINAIGRETTE
The walnuts give this salad a nutty flavor.

6-8 (¾ lb.) small new potatoes
3 cups water
2 medium tomatoes, cut into wedges
½ red onion, sliced
¼ cup green onions, sliced
¼ cup walnut pieces

Dressing:
¼ cup vegetable oil
3 Tbsp. walnut oil or olive oil
2 Tbsp. cider vinegar
2 Tbsp. finely chopped fresh tarragon
¼ tsp. salt
⅛ tsp. pepper

Yield: 8 servings

Combine potatoes and water in a medium saucepan. Bring to a boil; reduce heat. Cover; simmer 10 to 15 minutes or until tender. Drain; cool slightly. To microcook potatoes, combine potatoes and 2 tablespoons water in a 2-quart microproof casserole. Microcook on high 5 to 7 minutes or until tender, stirring once during cooking. Drain. Combine tomatoes, red onion, green onions and walnuts in a large bowl; toss gently. Combine all dressing ingredients. Pour dressing over tomato mixture; toss to coat. Cut warm potatoes into quarters. Add to tomato mixture; toss to coat. Serve immediately.

Pat Johnson (Mrs. Craig)

CALICO SALAD

1 (8 oz.) can white shoepeg
(small kernel) corn, drained
1 (8 oz.) can tiny peas, drained
1 (8 oz.) can French cut green beans,
drained
1 ½ cups carrots, pared, sliced
1 cup celery, chopped
½ cup onion, chopped
1 green pepper, chopped

Marinade:
½ cup vegetable oil
½ cup sugar
¾ cup vinegar
1 tsp. salt
1 tsp. celery seed

Yield: 12 servings

Combine marinade ingredients, except for celery seed, and boil 3 minutes. Cool and add celery seed. Combine vegetables in a large bowl. Pour cooled marinade over vegetables. Cover and refrigerate overnight. This salad keeps well in the refrigerator for several days.

Noel Lund (Mrs. Ted)

MIXED VEGETABLE SALAD

2 (10 oz.) pkgs. frozen mixed
vegetables, cooked,
drained, cooled
3 cups celery, diced
1 small onion, finely chopped
1 (16 oz.) can red kidney beans,
drained and washed
salt
pepper

Dressing:
½ cup white vinegar
2 Tbsp. flour
⅔ cup sugar
2 tsp. dry mustard

Yield: 12-15 servings

Bring dressing ingredients to a boil and stir for 3 minutes. Cool. Combine vegetables in a large bowl. Pour dressing over vegetables; stir well. Salt and pepper to taste. Refrigerate overnight before serving. This salad will keep up to 10 days in refrigerator.

Verda Stief (Mrs. Charles)

NUTTY WILD RICE SALAD

½ cup wild rice
2 cups canned beef bouillon,
    undiluted
1 cup frozen peas
2 ribs celery, thinly sliced
    on diagonal
4 green onions, sliced
½ cup slivered almonds, toasted
lettuce cups (optional)

Dressing:
2 Tbsp. red wine vinegar
1 Tbsp. soy sauce
1 tsp. sugar
¼ cup vegetable oil
2 tsp. sesame oil

Yield: 4 servings

Cover rice with cold water to a depth of 1-inch above rice in a medium saucepan. Heat to boiling. Drain water from rice and add bouillon. Simmer covered until liquid is absorbed, about 1 hour. Combine all dressing ingredients. While rice is still warm, toss with dressing; cool. Combine rice, peas, celery, green onions and almonds in a medium bowl. Toss well. Refrigerate until ready to serve. Serve in small lettuce cups or a lettuce-lined bowl.

Sue Miller (Mrs. Lewis)

POLYNESIAN RICE SALAD
Great with grilled meats or chicken.

½ cup vegetable oil
¼ cup cider vinegar
2 Tbsp. soy sauce
½ tsp. salt
1 cup celery, thinly sliced
¼ cup green onion tops, thinly sliced
3 cups cooked long-grain rice,
    cooled to room temperature
1 (8 ½ oz.) can water chestnuts,
    drained, sliced
1 cup fresh mushrooms, sliced
1 (11 oz.) can mandarin oranges,
    drained
lettuce (optional)

Yield: 6 servings

Combine salad oil, vinegar, soy sauce, salt, celery and onion. Stir in rice; toss well. Fold in water chestnuts, mushrooms and oranges just until blended. Chill thoroughly and serve in a lettuce-lined bowl.

Gayle Boyd (Mrs. James)

SUMMER PASTA SALAD

1 (10 oz.) pkg. small ring macaroni
2 tomatoes, diced
¼ cup celery, diced
¼ cup green onion, diced
½ cup cucumber, diced
¼ cup sweet pickle relish
½ cup (2 oz.) Cheddar cheese,
*   shredded*
1 cup salad dressing

Yield: 12-15 servings

Cook macaroni according to package directions. Rinse and cool. Add remaining ingredients; toss and chill.

Linda McGregor (Mrs. Robert)

MARINATED VEGETABLE-PASTA SALAD

1 bunch broccoli, cut into flowerets
½ head cauliflower, chopped
1 (16 oz.) can artichoke hearts,
*   drained and quartered*
1 (16 oz.) can sliced black olives,
*   drained*
½ pint cherry tomatoes, halved
8 oz. fresh mushrooms, sliced
4 oz. spiral pasta, cooked, cooled
1 (8 oz.) bottle zesty Italian
*   salad dressing*

Yield: 12-16 servings

Combine all ingredients until coated with dressing and serve immediately.

Carrie Barr (Mrs. Paul)

ROTINI SALAD

This salad can be made ahead. It's even better the second day!

1 (16 oz.) pkg. tri-colored rotini
1 medium cucumber, diced
1 (4 oz.) jar pimento, drained,
  chopped
1 (4 ½ oz.) can black olives,
  drained, chopped
1 medium red or white onion,
  chopped
2-3 ribs celery, chopped

Dressing:
1 cup vegetable oil
1 cup vinegar
1 cup sugar
1 Tbsp. dry mustard
parsley flakes to taste
garlic powder to taste
lemon pepper to taste

Yield: 12 servings

Cook rotini according to package directions; drain. Combine rotini, cucumber, pimento, black olives, onion and celery in a large bowl. Combine dressing ingredients. Pour over rotini mixture. Serve chilled.

Tommie Warrington (Mrs. R.D.)

CREAMY HAM SALAD

1 cup mayonnaise
2 Tbsp. cider vinegar
1/8 tsp. pepper
1 cup ham,diced
1 cup frozen peas, unthawed
1 cup celery, diced
1/2 cup red onion, chopped
1 Tbsp. dried dill weed
4 oz. spiral macaroni, cooked

Yield: 4 servings

Combine mayonnaise, vinegar and pepper. Add remaining ingredients and toss to coat with dressing. Chill well. May be made the day before serving.

Terry Norris (Mrs. John W., Jr.)

50

RED, RED SALAD

1 (6 oz.) pkg. raspberry gelatin
2 cups boiling water
1 (10 oz.) pkg. frozen raspberries,
   thawed
1 (16 oz.) can jellied cranberry sauce

Yield: 8-10 servings

Dissolve gelatin in water. Add raspberries and cranberry sauce. Whip until smooth. Pour into a serving bowl and chill until firm.

Barbara Beichley (Mrs. Duane)

CRUNCHY VEGGIE GELATIN

1 (3 oz.) pkg. lime gelatin
2 cups carrots, grated
½ cup celery, chopped
1 small onion, chopped
1 (8 oz.) container frozen
   whipped topping, thawed
1 cup mayonnaise
1 (8 oz.) container small curd
   cottage cheese
⅛ tsp. salt

Yield: 12 servings

Prepare gelatin according to package directions and refrigerate one hour until syrupy. Add carrots, celery and onion. In a separate bowl, combine whipped topping and mayonnaise. Fold into gelatin mixture. Add cottage cheese and salt; stir well. Chill until firm.

Joan Heddens (Mrs. J.D.)

NORTHWEST SALAD

Fun to serve over the 4th of July.

2 (3 oz.) pkgs. raspberry gelatin,
    divided
2 cups hot water, divided
1 (10 oz.) pkg. frozen raspberries,
    thawed
1 cup half and half
½ cup sugar
1 (¼ oz.) envelope unflavored gelatin
¼ cup cold water
1 cup dairy sour cream
1 tsp. vanilla
1 (16 oz.) can blueberries,
    undrained

Yield: 12 servings

Dissolve 1 package raspberry gelatin in 1 cup hot water. Stir in raspberries. Pour into an 8-cup mold. Refrigerate until firm. Combine half and half with sugar in a saucepan; heat through. Soften unflavored gelatin in cold water. Stir into warm cream mixture until gelatin dissolves. Remove from heat; stir in sour cream and vanilla. Cool mixture; pour over first layer and refrigerate until firm. Dissolve remaining package of raspberry gelatin in remaining cup hot water. Add blueberries and juice; stir to combine. Cool and pour over second layer. Chill until firm. Recipe can be doubled and made in a 9x13-inch pan.

Marty Nordmann (Mrs. Brian)

ORANGE COOLER SALAD

Looks nice in clear bowl!

1 (3 oz.) pkg. orange gelatin
1 cup hot water
1 pint orange sherbet
1 banana, sliced
1 cup mandarin oranges, drained

Yield: 9-12 servings

Dissolve gelatin in hot water. Add sherbet and stir until dissolved. Fold in bananas and oranges. Chill until firm.

Barbara Beichley (Mrs. Duane)

MARINATED FRESH FRUIT SALAD

4 cups cantaloupe balls
1 (13 ½ oz.) pineapple chunks,
  drained or fresh pineapple
2 cups seedless green grapes
4 cups watermelon balls
1 (6 oz.) can frozen lemonade
  concentrate, thawed, undiluted
¼ cup orange marmalade

Combine fruit in bowl. Combine lemonade and marmalade; pour over fruit. Stir gently. Chill at least 2 hours, or overnight, before serving.

Pat Johnson (Mrs. Craig)

Yield: 12 servings

FROZEN PEACH SALAD

1 (15 oz.) can sliced peaches
1 cup miniature marshmallows
1 (3 oz.) pkg. cream cheese,
  softened
¼ cup sugar
¼ tsp. salt
1 cup cherry or vanilla yogurt
1 (15 oz.) can dark sweet cherries,
  pitted and drained.

Drain peaches, reserving ½ cup juice. Combine peach juice and marshmallows in a small saucepan. Stir over low heat until melted. Cool slightly. Beat cream cheese until smooth in a mixing bowl. Add sugar and salt; beat until fluffy. Add marshmallow mixture and yogurt; mix until smooth. Add cherries and peaches. Freeze in individual cups.

Yield: 9 servings

Caroline Larson (Mrs. Ronald)

HOLIDAY CRANBERRY SALAD

1 lb. cranberries
1 cup sugar
1 cup miniature marshmallows
2 cups frozen whipped topping,
  thawed
sugar to taste
1 cup crushed pineapple, drained

Grind the cranberries. Stir in sugar and marshmallows. Fold in whipped topping and sweeten to taste. Add pineapple and stir. Refrigerate until firm or overnight.

Barbara Beichley (Mrs. Duane)

Yield: 10-12 servings

53

WATERMELON CHERRY COMPOTE

A colorful and delicious fruit salad for a summer luncheon.

6 cups watermelon,
    cubed and seeded
2 cups fresh sweet cherries, pitted
1 cup fresh blueberries
1 (10 oz.) package frozen
    strawberries, thawed
2 Tbsp. lime juice
¾ cup club soda, chilled

Yield: 8-10 servings

Combine watermelon, cherries, and blueberries in a large bowl; chill 3 hours. Combine strawberries and lime juice in blender and process until smooth; chill. Combine strawberry mixture and club soda; drizzle over fruit. Serve immediately.

Pat Shobe (Mrs. Richard)

ORANGE TAPIOCA SALAD

2 (3 oz.) pkgs. vanilla
    tapioca pudding
1 (20 oz.) can pineapple tidbits
1 (11 oz.) mandarin oranges
12-15 marachino cherries, halved
2 medium-size bananas, sliced

Yield: 10-12 servings

Drain pineapple and oranges into a measuring cup. Add water to make 3 cups liquid. Cook pudding according to package directions, using juice instead of milk. Cool. Add fruit and chill. May be made one day ahead if bananas are added just before serving.

Linda Blum (Mrs. Daniel)

Bread Basket

WHOLE WHEAT BISCUITS
So good with homemade soup or stew.

1 cup flour
½ cup whole wheat flour
2 Tbsp. sugar
2 ½ tsp. baking powder
½ tsp. salt
3 Tbsp. vegetable oil
½ cup milk

Yield: 8 biscuits

Preheat oven to 400°F. Combine dry ingredients; set aside. Combine oil and milk; stir into dry ingredients until just moistened. Turn dough out onto floured surface. Knead 3 to 4 times. Roll dough to ½-inch thick. Cut with 2 ½-inch biscuit cutter. Place on ungreased baking sheet. Bake 12 to 15 minutes. Serve warm.

Barbara Headley (Mrs. Michael)

WHOLE WHEAT BANANA BREAD

½ cup butter or margarine,
   softened
¾ cup sugar
2 eggs
1 cup flour
1 tsp. baking soda
½ tsp. salt (optional)
1 cup whole wheat flour
3 large ripe bananas,
   mashed (1 ½ cups)
1 tsp. vanilla
½ cup walnuts, chopped

Yield: 1 loaf

Preheat oven to 350°F. Cream butter and sugar until light and fluffy. Add eggs, one at a time, beating well after each addition. Sift flour, baking soda and salt; stir in whole wheat flour. Add to creamed mixture, blending well. Fold in mashed bananas, vanilla and walnuts. Pour mixture into greased 9x5x3-inch pan. Bake for 50 to 60 minutes or until a toothpick inserted in center comes out clean. Cool in pan for 10 minutes, remove and cool on wire rack.

Linda Casady (Mrs. William)

GOLDEN BANANA LOAVES

½ cup butter or margarine
1 cup sugar
1 egg
1 cup ripe bananas, mashed
½ cup sour milk or buttermilk
2 cups flour
1 tsp. baking soda
½ tsp. salt
3 cups crispy rice cereal squares,
  divided, measure then crush
3 Tbsp. brown sugar
3 Tbsp. melted butter or margarine

Yield: 2 loaves

Preheat oven to 350°F. Cream butter and sugar; add egg. Stir in bananas and sour milk. Sift flour, soda and salt. Add to banana mixture and stir in ¾ cup cereal. Pour into two 8x4x2½-inch buttered loaf pans. Make topping by mixing remaining cereal; brown sugar and butter. Sprinkle over batter. Bake 35 minutes or until toothpick inserted in center comes out clean. Cool in pan 15 minutes before removing. May also use one 9x5x3-inch loaf pan and bake 55 to 60 minutes.

Kirstan Condit (Mrs. Rick)
Lynn Hall (Mrs. David)

PEACH BREAD

Peach Butter is a delicious accompaniment and can be made
by simply mixing peach jam and softened butter!

2 ¼ cups peach puree
  (6-8 medium peaches or
  2 (15 oz.) cans of peaches,
  drained)
1 ½ cups sugar
½ cup shortening
2 eggs
2 cups flour
1 tsp. cinnamon
1 tsp. baking soda
1 tsp. baking powder
¼ tsp. salt
1 tsp. almond extract
1 cup pecans, chopped (optional)

Yield: 2 loaves

Preheat oven to 325°F. Place peaches in blender and puree. Measure 2 ¼ cups. Set aside. Cream sugar and shortening. Add eggs and mix well. Add peach puree, dry ingredients, and almond extract; mix thoroughly. Stir in nuts. Pour into two 9x5x3-inch greased loaf pans. Bake 50 to 60 minutes.

Linda Blum (Mrs.Daniel)

57

PUMPKIN SWIRL BREAD

Dough:
1 ¾ cups flour
1 ½ cups sugar
1 tsp. baking soda
1 tsp. cinnamon
½ tsp. salt
¼ tsp. ground nutmeg
1 cup canned pumpkin
½ cup margarine, melted
1 egg, lightly beaten
⅓ cup water

Filling:
I (8 oz.) pkg. cream cheese, softened
¼ cup sugar
1 egg, beaten

Yield: I loaf

Preheat oven to 350°F. Combine filling ingredients; mix well. Set aside. Combine dry ingredients in large bowl. Combine pumpkin, margarine, egg and water in separate bowl. Add to dry ingredients mixing until just moistened. Reserve 2 cups pumpkin batter and place remaining batter into two 9x5x3-inch greased and floured loaf pans. Pour cream cheese mixture over pumpkin batter; top with reserved pumpkin batter. Cut through batters with a knife to create swirl effect. Bake 1 hour and 10 minutes or until toothpick inserted in center comes out clean. Cool 5 minutes, remove from pan to cool further.

Barbara Headley (Mrs Michael)

STRAWBERRY BREAD

Bread:
2 (10 oz.) pkgs. frozen strawberries,
*   thawed*
3 cups flour
1 tsp. baking soda
1 tsp. cinnamon
1 tsp. salt
2 cups sugar
1 ¼ cups vegetable oil
4 eggs, well beaten
1 tsp. red food coloring (optional)

Strawberry Spread:
½ cup reserved strawberry juice
1 (8 oz.) pkg. cream cheese, softened

Yield: 2 loaves
58

Preheat oven to 350°F. Drain thawed strawberries, reserving ½ cup juice for topping. Pour remaining juice back into strawberries. Set aside. With spoon, mix dry ingredients together; make a well in the center. Add thawed strawberries, vegetable oil and beaten eggs. Mix well. Stir in food coloring. Pour into two 9x5x3-inch greased and floured loaf pans. Bake 1 hour. Cool 1 hour before removing bread from pans. Blend reserved strawberry juice and cream cheese. Spread on cooled sliced bread.

Deb Keefe (Mrs. Kevin)

GERMAN SOUR CREAM TWISTS

3 ½ cups flour
1 tsp. salt
1 cup butter or shortening
1 pkg. active dry yeast
¼ cup warm water (105°F to 115°F)
¾ cup dairy sour cream
1 whole egg and 2 yolks,
    well beaten
1 tsp. vanilla
2 cups sugar, divided

Yield: 60 twists

Sift flour and salt in bowl. Cut in butter; set aside. Dissolve yeast in water. Mix sour cream, eggs and vanilla in large bowl. Add flour mixture and yeast mixture; mix well. Cover with damp cloth and refrigerate for at least 2 hours. Preheat oven to 375°F. Roll one-half the dough on floured board to about 8x16-inches. Sprinkle with ⅓ cup sugar. Fold ends toward center overlapping at center. Sprinkle with ⅓ cup sugar; roll to 8x16-inches. Sprinkle with ⅓ cup sugar; fold ends towards center overlapping at center and roll ¼-inch thick. Cut strips 1x4-inches long. Twist ends in opposite directions making a horseshoe shape. Repeat with remaining dough. Keep dough refrigerated when not using. Lightly spray cookie sheet with non-stick vegetable spray. Bake 15 minutes. Remove from pan immediately.

Ruth Carpenter (Mrs. Ralph)

SARAH'S ROLLS

Can use food processor for this recipe.

1 cup milk
1 pkg. active dry yeast
¼ cup sugar
1 tsp. salt
¼ cup butter, melted
2 eggs
3 ½ to 4 cups flour, divided

Yield: 2 dozen rolls

Heat milk to 105°F to 115°F. Stir in yeast, sugar and salt. Let stand 5 minutes. Stir in butter, eggs and one-half of the flour. Beat 5 minutes. Stir in remaining flour. Knead until smooth on floured surface. Place in lightly greased bowl and turn to coat entire surface. Cover and let rise in warm draft-free place until almost doubled in bulk, about 1 hour. Punch down. Shape into desired shapes (clover leaf, crescent, etc.). Place on lightly greased baking pan and let rise until double. Preheat oven to 375°F and bake 15 to 18 minutes or until lightly browned.

Kathy Briggs (Mrs. Terrence)

60

QUICK CINNAMON ROLLS

2 pkgs. active dry yeast
½ cup warm water
*   (105°F to 115°F)*
1 ¼ cups buttermilk
2 eggs
5 ½ cups flour, divided
½ cup butter or margarine,
*   softened*
½ cup sugar
2 tsp. baking powder
2 tsp. salt

Cinnamon Roll Filling:
2-3 Tbsp. soft butter, divided
2-3 tsp. cinnamon
½ cup sugar

Yield: 24 rolls

Dissolve yeast in water in large mixing bowl. Add buttermilk, eggs, 2 ½ cups flour, butter, sugar, baking powder and salt. Blend 30 seconds on low speed, scraping sides and bottom of bowl. Beat 2 minutes on medium speed. Stir in remaining 3 cups flour. Dough should remain soft and slightly sticky. Knead 5 minutes or about 200 turns on lightly floured board. Place in lightly greased bowl and turn to coat entire surface. Cover and let rise in warm draft-free place until almost doubled, about 1 hour. Dough is ready to bake if slight dent remains when touched. Divide dough. Roll one-half of dough into a 12x7-inch rectangle. Spread one-half of butter onto dough. Mix cinnamon and sugar. Sprinkle one-half onto buttered surface. Roll up, beginning at wide side. Seal well by pinching edge of dough. Cut into twelve slices. Place in a greased 9x1 ½-inch round baking pan leaving a small space between each slice. Repeat steps with remaining half of dough. Preheat oven to 350°F and bake 25 minutes. Top with confectioners sugar icing.

Joan Ballard (Mrs. Dale)

61

SWEDISH CHRISTMAS TEA RING

Dough:
2 pkgs. active dry yeast
½ cup warm water
(105°F to 115°F)
1 ½ cups scalded milk
1 cup sugar
½ cup butter or margarine
2 large eggs, lightly beaten
6 ½ to 7 cups flour, sifted, divided
2 tsp. salt

Filling:
¼ cup butter, divided
½ cup sugar, divided
1 Tbsp. cinnamon, divided
nuts (optional)
raisins (optional)
2 Tbsp. butter, melted, divided

Glaze:
1 ½ cups confectioners sugar
1 tsp. vanilla
3-4 Tbsp. milk
maraschino cherries, sliced
(optional)

Yield: 2 rings

Dissolve yeast in warm water. Scald milk. Add sugar and butter to milk. Cool. Add eggs to cooled milk mixture. Pour into yeast mixture. Add one-half of the flour, about 3 ½ cups and blend by hand until smooth. Add remaining flour and salt. If dough is sticky, add a little more flour. Knead until smooth and elastic. Place in lightly greased bowl and turn to coat entire surface. Cover and let rise in a warm draft-free place until almost doubled in bulk, about 1 hour. Punch down and let rise until double in size again, about 30 minutes. Remove dough from bowl and cut into two sections. Roll each section into a 9x15-inch rectangle. Cover with one-half butter, sugar and cinnamon. Raisins and nuts may also be added. Roll up tightly, beginning at the wide side. Stretch dough slightly to even out. Bring ends of the dough together in a circle and seal by overlapping a layer of dough over the opposite end of the roll. Cut in toward the center of the ring, but not clear through, at 1 to 1½-inch intervals. After cutting all the way around the ring, lift and twist slices and lay them on their sides. Place on buttered, round pizza pan. Baste with one-half of butter and let rise 15 to 30 minutes. Preheat oven to 350°F and bake 30 to 35 minutes. Let cool. Frost with butter icing or glaze, and decorate with sliced maraschino cherries.

Pauline Hartman (Mrs. Bob)

THREE LOAF WHITE BREAD

**2 ¾ cups warm water
(105°F to 115°F)
2 pkgs. active dry yeast
3 Tbsp. sugar
1 Tbsp. salt
2 Tbsp. shortening
6 ½ cups flour, divided**

Yield: 3 loaves

Pour water into a big bowl, add yeast and let stand a few minutes. Stir to dissolve. Add sugar, salt, shortening and 3 cups of the flour. Beat 2 minutes with mixer and add the remaining 3 ½ cups flour. Beat by hand until smooth. Place in lightly greased bowl and turn to coat entire surface. Cover and let rise in warm draft-free place until almost doubled in bulk, about 1 hour. Punch down. Beat a minute or so. Shape into 3 loaves and put into three 8½x4½x2½-inch greased loaf pans. Let rise until even with top of pans. Preheat oven to 350°F and bake 25 to 30 minutes.

Joynell Raymon (Mrs. Larry)

FOOD PROCESSOR WHOLE WHEAT BREAD

1 tsp. plus 1 Tbsp. brown sugar
¼ cup warm water (105° to 115°F)
1 pkg. active dry yeast
1 ½ cups whole wheat flour,
*   divided*
1 ¼ to 1 ½ cups all-purpose flour
1 tsp. salt
3 Tbsp. butter, softened
¾ cup warm water
*   (105°F to 115°F)*
1 Tbsp. melted butter (optional)

Yield: 1 loaf

In a small bowl combine 1 teaspoon brown sugar and water. Sprinkle on yeast. Stir to dissolve and set aside until foamy, 5 to 10 minutes. With metal blade in place, add to the processor bowl the whole wheat flour, 1 ¼ cups all-purpose flour, remaining brown sugar, salt and butter. Process 5 seconds. Add yeast mixture and blend, using 3 or 4 on/off turns. Let the processor run and slowly pour water through feed tube. Process 60 seconds. Dough should be smooth and moist but not wet. If additional flour is necessary, add 2 tablespoons at a time and process 10 seconds after each addition. Remove dough to a lightly floured board and knead several minutes. Form into a ball and place in buttered bowl, turning to coat all surfaces. Cover and let rise until doubled, about 1 hour and 30 minutes. Punch down dough. Knead on floured board several minutes. Cover and let rest 10 minutes. Shape into a loaf and place in 8½x4½x2 ½-inch greased loaf pan. Cover and let rise until doubled, about 1 hour. Preheat oven 375°F (350°F for glass pan) and bake 40 to 45 minutes. Loaf is done if it sounds hollow when tapped. Brush with melted butter, if desired. Cool on rack.

Cindy Mack (Mrs. Tom)

ENGLISH MUFFIN BREAD

2 ½ to 3 cups flour, divided
1 pkg. active dry yeast
1 ¼ cups water
1 Tbsp. sugar
¾ tsp. salt
cornmeal

Yield: 1 loaf

Combine 1 cup flour and yeast in a large bowl. In saucepan, heat water, sugar and salt to 115°F to 120°F, stirring to dissolve sugar. Add to dry ingredients. Beat at low speed with electric mixer 30 seconds, scraping bowl. Beat 3 minutes at high speed. By hand, stir in enough remaining flour to make soft dough. Shape into ball. Place in lightly greased bowl turning to coat entire surface. Cover and let rise in warm draft-free place until almost doubled in bulk, about 1 hour. Punch down, cover, and let rest 10 minutes. Grease a 1-quart casserole or 8x4x2½-inch loaf pan. Sprinkle top with cornmeal. Cover and let rise until double. Preheat oven to 400°F and bake 40 to 45 minutes. Cover loosely with aluminum foil if top browns too quickly. Remove from pan immediately.

Linda Blum (Mrs. Daniel)
Lorraine Schultz (Mrs. Ed)

JAM AND CREAM CHEESE LOAF

½ cup warm water
(110°F to 115°F)
1 pkg. active dry yeast
2 ½ cups buttermilk biscuit
baking mix
1 egg beaten
½ cup plus 1 Tbsp. sugar, divided
1 (8 oz.) pkg. cream cheese,
softened
1 Tbsp. lemon juice
½ cup jam or preserves

Yield: 10-12 servings

Dissolve yeast in water in mixing bowl. Stir in buttermilk biscuit baking mix, egg and 1 tablespoon sugar; mix well. Turn onto surface dusted with additional biscuit mix. Knead gently 20 strokes. Place dough on center of a greased cookie sheet. Roll to 14x9-inch rectangle. Combine cream cheese, ½ cup sugar and lemon juice; spread mixture lengthwise down center third of rectangle. Make 3-inch long cuts at 1-inch intervals on both long sides. Fold strips at an angle over filling. Cover; chill overnight. Preheat oven to 350°F and bake 20 to 30 minutes. Spoon jam down center of loaf. Bake additional 5 minutes. Cool 10 minutes.

Joan Boyce (Mrs. Steven)

BLUEBERRY CRUMB COFFEE CAKE

Crumb Topping:
4 Tbsp. margarine, softened
½ cup flour
2 Tbsp. sugar

Cake:
1 ¾ cups flour
2 tsp. baking powder
¼ tsp. cinnamon
1 cup margarine
⅔ cup sugar
¼ cup milk
3 eggs, lightly beaten
1 tsp. grated lemon peel
1 (8 oz.) pkg. walnuts, chopped
1 pint fresh blueberries, divided

Yield: 12 servings

Preheat oven to 350°F. To prepare crumb topping, melt margarine in saucepan over medium heat; stir in flour and sugar. Stir until mixture forms a soft dough. Remove from heat and set aside to cool. Grease and flour a 9-inch springform pan. Combine flour, baking powder and cinnamon; set aside. Cream margarine and sugar. Combine milk and eggs. Stir dry ingredients alternately with liquid ingredients into sugar mixture. Fold in lemon peel, nuts and one-half of blueberries. Spoon into prepared pan. Sprinkle top with remaining blueberries. Crumble the topping and sprinkle on top of blueberries. Bake 60 to 65 minutes. Serve warm or cool.

Tommie Warrington (Mrs. R.D.)

LADY LEE COFFEE CAKE

This recipe freezes well.

Filling:
1 cup brown sugar, firmly packed
3 tsp. cinnamon
½ cup nuts, chopped
2 Tbsp. flour

Batter:
1 (18.25 oz.) box yellow, lemon,
  or butter pecan cake mix
1 (3.5 oz.) pkg. instant
  vanilla pudding
¾ cup water
¾ cup vegetable oil
4 eggs
1 tsp. vanilla
1 tsp. butter flavoring

Frosting:
1 cup confectioners sugar
2 Tbsp. milk
½ tsp. vanilla
½ tsp. butter flavoring

Yield: 3 9-inch cakes

Preheat oven to 350°F. Mix filling ingredients and set aside. Prepare batter with electric mixer in order of ingredients given, adding eggs one at a time. Divide two-thirds batter evenly between three 9x1½-inch greased and floured cake pans. Reserve one-third batter for later use. Sprinkle filling and then rest of batter. Batter may not cover top. Bake 30 minutes. Cool 10 minutes. Combine frosting ingredients and blend until smooth. Drizzle frosting over top of cakes.

Sally Walberg (Mrs. Ron)

68

PINEAPPLE BUNDT COFFEE CAKE

1 (10 oz.) jar maraschino cherries,
 drained
⅓ cup margarine, softened
½ cup brown sugar, firmly packed
1 cup crushed pineapple, drained
1 (18.25 oz.) box yellow cake mix
1 (3.5 oz.) pkg. instant
 vanilla pudding
¼ cup vegetable oil
1 cup dairy sour cream
¾ cup hot water
4 eggs
1 tsp. vanilla
1 tsp. butter flavoring
¼ cup sugar
1 tsp. cinnamon
1 cup pecans, chopped

Preheat oven to 350°F. Arrange maraschino cherries in bottom of greased bundt pan. Mix margarine, brown sugar and crushed pineapple; spoon over and around cherries. Combine cake mix and pudding. Add vegetable oil, sour cream and water to dry ingredients; blend well. Add eggs, one at a time, beating well. Add vanilla and butter flavoring; beat again. Pour one-half batter over cherries and pineapple layer. Combine sugar, cinnamon and pecans. Sprinkle over batter. Cover with remaining cake batter. Bake 50 minutes. Cool 5 minutes. Loosen and invert onto plate.

Yield: 16 servings

Sally Robertson (Mrs.James)

POPPY SEED BUNDT CAKE

1 cup butter
1 ½ cups sugar
4 eggs, separated
1 cup dairy sour cream
1 tsp. baking soda
2 cups sifted flour
3 tsp. vanilla
2 oz. poppy seed

Preheat oven to 350°F. Cream butter and sugar. Add egg yolks; beat well. Add sour cream and soda; beat well. Add flour and vanilla; beat well. Stir in poppy seed. In separate bowl, beat the 4 egg whites until soft peaks form and fold into batter. Pour into greased bundt pan. Bake 60 minutes.

Yield: 16 servings

Carole Weber (Mrs. Delano)

SOUR CREAM COFFEE CAKE WITH HONEY NUT TOPPING

Batter:
2 cups flour, sifted
1 tsp. baking soda
1 tsp. baking powder
½ cup butter
½ cup margarine
1 cup sugar
2 eggs
1 cup dairy sour cream

Topping:
6 Tbsp. butter
6 Tbsp. brown sugar
6 Tbsp. heavy cream or half and half
3 Tbsp. honey
½ cup walnuts, chopped
2 tsp. cinnamon

Yield: 9 servings

Preheat oven to 375°F. Sift flour, baking soda and baking powder. Cream butter and margarine in large bowl until fluffy. Gradually add sugar and then eggs one at a time, beating after each addition. Stir dry ingredients into batter, alternately with sour cream. Turn into a greased and floured 9x9x2-inch baking pan. Bake 40 minutes. Cool 10 minutes then turn onto wire rack to cool completely. In small saucepan, melt butter. Stir in sugar, cream and honey. Bring to a boil, stirring constantly. Cook 10 minutes until thick and creamy. Blend in nuts and cinnamon. Cool 5 minutes before spreading on cake.

Jinx Hill (Mrs. Michael)

RASPBERRY CREAM CHEESE COFFEE CAKE

Batter:
2 ½ cups flour
¾ cup sugar
¾ cup butter
½ tsp. baking powder
½ tsp. baking soda
¼ tsp. salt
¾ cup dairy sour cream
1 egg
1 tsp. almond extract

Filling:
1 (8 oz.) pkg. cream cheese,
  softened
¼ cup sugar
1 egg
½ cup raspberry jam

Topping:
½ cup sliced almonds

Yield: 16 servings

Preheat oven to 350°F. Combine flour and sugar; cut in butter using a pastry blender until mixture resembles coarse crumbs. Remove 1 cup crumbs for topping. To remaining crumb mixture, add baking powder, soda, salt, sour cream, egg and almond extract; blend well. Spread batter over bottom and 2-inches up side of greased and floured 9-inch springform pan. Batter should be ¼-inch thick on sides. Combine cream cheese, sugar and egg; blend well. Pour over batter in pan. Carefully spoon jam evenly over cheese filling. Combine 1 cup of reserved crumb mixture and almonds; sprinkle over top. Bake 50 to 60 minutes or until cream cheese filling is set and crust is a deep golden brown. Cool 15 minutes. Remove sides of pan. Serve warm or cool.

Abby Kersbergen (Mrs. Dan)

FRUIT AND HONEY MUFFINS

4 eggs
1 quart buttermilk
1 cup vegetable oil
1 ½ cups applesauce
1 cup honey
5 cups flour
5 tsp. baking soda
2 Tbsp. cinnamon
2 tsp. nutmeg
2 cups dried fruit
1 cup raisins
1 (16 oz.) box bran flakes
½ cup bran (optional)
coconut (optional)

Yield: 4-5 dozen

Mix all ingredients in a large bowl. Refrigerate in a closed container at least 24 hours. Fill muffin cups three-fourths full. Preheat oven to 350°F and bake 20 minutes.

Linda Casady (Mrs. William)

REFRIGERATOR WHEAT GERM MUFFINS

4 ½ cups flour
4 ½ cups wheat germ
1 ¼ cups sugar
1 cup brown sugar, firmly packed
5 tsp. baking soda
2 tsp. salt
4 eggs, beaten
1 quart buttermilk
1 cup vegetable oil

Yield: 6 dozen

Mix dry ingredients, add remaining ingredients. Stir until well blended. Store covered in refrigerator up to 4 weeks. Preheat oven to 400°F. Fill greased muffin cups two-thirds full. Bake 12 minutes. Two cups of batter will make one dozen muffins.

Jolene Jebsen (Mrs. Darrell)

SUGAR AND SPICE MUFFINS

1 ¾ cups flour
1 ½ tsp. baking powder
½ tsp. salt
½ tsp. nutmeg
⅓ cup vegetable oil
¾ cup sugar
1 egg
¾ cup milk

Topping:
⅔ cup melted butter or margarine
¾ cup sugar
1 tsp. cinnamon

Yield: 1 dozen muffins or 36 mini-muffins

Preheat oven to 350°F. Sift flour, baking powder, salt and nutmeg; set aside. Beat vegetable oil, sugar, egg and milk. Add liquid to dry ingredients. Stir to blend. Fill well-greased muffin cups about one-half full. Do not use paper cupcake liners. Bake 12 to 15 minutes, whether using regular or mini-muffin cups. Remove immediately from pans. While hot, dip each muffin in melted butter then roll in sugar and cinnamon mixture.

Ann Meiners (Mrs. Gerald)

MORNING GLORY MUFFINS

2 cups flour
1 cup sugar
2 tsp. baking soda
1 tsp. cinnamon
½ tsp. salt
2 cups carrots,
    peeled and finely shredded
½ cup raisins
½ cup walnuts, coarsely broken
½ cup coconut
1 tart apple, peeled,
    cored and chopped
3 eggs
⅔ cup vegetable oil

Yield: 18 muffins

Preheat oven to 350°F. Grease or line 18 muffin cups. Place flour, sugar, baking soda, cinnamon and salt in a large bowl, stirring to blend well. Stir in shredded carrots, raisins, walnuts, coconut and chopped apple until all ingredients are well mixed. In a separate bowl, mix eggs and oil until blended. Add liquid ingredients to dry ingredients, mixing just until moistened. Do not over mix. Batter will be stiff. Divide batter evenly between prepared muffin cups. Bake 20 to 25 minutes or until a toothpick inserted into the center comes out clean. Cool 5 minutes in pan; remove and cool.

Valois Brintnall (Mrs. Lee)
Lenora Brown (Mrs. Stanley)
73

RHUBARB MUFFINS

2 eggs, lightly beaten
¼ cup vegetable oil
½ cup plain yogurt
1 tsp. vanilla
1 ¾ cups fresh rhubarb, chopped
1 cup sugar
2 cups flour
2 tsp. baking powder
½ tsp. baking soda
½ tsp. salt
¼ tsp. cinnamon
¼ tsp. grated orange peel
¼ tsp. mace or nutmeg

Yield: 18 muffins

Preheat oven to 375°F. Mix eggs, vegetable oil and yogurt well. Add rhubarb. Combine dry ingredients in separate bowl. Fold liquid ingredients into dry ingredients until moistened. Spray muffin cups with non-stick vegetable spray. Fill one-half to three-fourths full. Bake 18 to 20 minutes or until golden brown.

Barbara Headley (Mrs. Michael)

GLAZED JAM PUFFS
Great for Sunday morning treat!

2 cups buttermilk biscuit baking mix
2 tsp. sugar
¼ cup butter or margarine,
    softened
⅔ cup milk
12 tsp. jam

Frosting:
1 cup confectioners sugar
½ tsp. vanilla
1 Tbsp. water
⅛ tsp. salt

Yield: 12 servings

Preheat oven to 450°F. Place buttermilk biscuit baking mix into mixing bowl. Add sugar and mix. Add butter and mix with fork or pastry cutter until crumbly. Add milk; stir until soft dough forms. Place 1 tablespoon of dough in paper-lined muffin cup. Top with 1 teaspoon of jam. Drop 1 tablespoon of dough over jam. Bake 10 to 15 minutes until golden brown. While baking, combine confectioners sugar, vanilla, water and salt; blend well. Remove from pan immediately and frost while warm. Serve warm.

Margaret Gervich (Mrs. Douglas)

74

MAGIC MARSHMALLOW CRESCENT PUFFS

¼ *cup sugar*
1 tsp. cinnamon
2 (8 oz.) tubes refrigerated
 crescent rolls
⅓ *to* ½ *cup margarine, melted*
16 large marshmallows
¼ *cup nuts, chopped (optional)*

Icing:
½ *cup confectioners sugar*
2 to 3 tsp. milk
½ *tsp. vanilla*

Yield: 16 servings

Preheat oven to 375°F. Combine sugar and cinnamon. Set aside. Separate 2 tubes crescent rolls into 16 triangles. Dip a marshmallow in melted butter, then in sugar-cinnamon mixture. Place marshmallow on inside end of triangle. Fold corners over marshmallows and roll toward point, completely covering marshmallow and squeezing edges of dough to seal. Dip pointed side in butter and place buttered side down in greased deep muffin cups. Repeat with remaining marshmallows. Place pan on a cookie sheet during baking. Bake 10 to 15 minutes or until golden brown. While baking, combine confectioners sugar, milk and vanilla; blend until smooth. Remove puffs from muffin cups immediately and drizzle with icing. Sprinkle with nuts. Serve warm.

Kindera Severidt (Mrs. Dean)

POPPY SEED WAFFLES

Serve with lemon yogurt and lemon peel.

2 eggs, lightly beaten
2 cups buttermilk biscuit baking mix
2 (8 oz.) cartons lemon yogurt
¼ cup vegetable oil
2 Tbsp. poppy seed

Yield: 8 4-inch waffles

Lightly grease grids of waffle iron and preheat. Combine eggs, buttermilk biscuit baking mix, yogurt, oil and poppy seeds. Stir until just combined. Will be slightly lumpy. Pour 1½ cups batter onto bottom grid of waffle iron. Bake 4 to 5 minutes. Repeat with remaining batter.

Abby Kersbergen ((Mrs. Dan)

GINGERBREAD WAFFLES

2 eggs
⅓ cup sugar
½ cup molasses
6 Tbsp. shortening
½ cup hot water
2 cups flour
1 tsp. ginger
1 tsp. baking soda
1 tsp. cinnamon

Apple Cider Sauce:
2 cups apple cider
2 Tbsp. cornstarch
½ cup sugar
½ cup butter
1 ½ cups light corn syrup
5 Tbsp. lemon juice
½ tsp. nutmeg
¼ tsp. ginger

Yield: 12 4-inch waffles
        3 cups sauce

Beat eggs until light and lemon-colored. Add sugar and beat again. Add molasses and beat. Melt shortening in hot water. Sift dry ingredients. Pre-heat waffle iron. Add shortening mixture to the egg mixture alternately with dry ingredients. Beat thoroughly. Pour 1 ½ cups batter onto bottom grid of waffle iron. Bake 3 to 4 minutes. Repeat with remaining batter. Serve immediately with warm applesauce or Apple Cider Sauce. To prepare sauce, dissolve cornstarch in a little of the apple cider. Mix all the ingredients in a large saucepan. Cook over medium heat until thickened, stirring constantly. Serve warm.

Sauce variation: Serve over ice cream or apple, pumkin or mince pie.

Barbara Headley (Mrs. Michael)

The Tea Room

OVEN CHEESE FONDUE

May prepare the night before. Also good as a side dish with meat.

**1 clove garlic, minced
1 tsp. dry mustard, divided
⅔ cup butter, softened, divided
2 small loaves French bread
3 Tbsp. onion, chopped
⅓ cup flour
1 ½ cups non-dairy creamer
1 tsp. salt
1 tsp. paprika
3 cups boiling water
1 cup dry white wine
3 egg yolks, well-beaten
3 cups (12 oz.) Swiss cheese,
   shredded**

Yield: 6-8 servings

Blend garlic, ½ teaspoon mustard and ⅓ cup butter. Cut bread into ¼-inch slices. Spread butter mixture on bread slices. Line bottom and sides of earthenware or glass Dutch oven with enough of bread slices to cover, buttered side down. Melt remaining ⅓ cup butter in heavy saucepan over medium heat until frothy. Add onion and cook until golden. Whisk in flour; add non-dairy creamer, remaining ½ teaspoon mustard, salt and paprika. Add boiling water. Stir, increasing heat to medium high. Boil until thick. Remove from heat; blend in wine, egg yolks and cheese. Return to heat and blend well. In Dutch oven, alternate layers of cheese sauce and bread, ending with bread, buttered side up. Bake covered 50 minutes at 350°F or until brown and bubbly.

Patty Bowman (Mrs. Jim)

BRUNCH CASSEROLE
Great for overnight guests.

4 cups white bread or French bread,
    cubed
2 cups (8 oz.) Cheddar cheese,
    shredded
10 eggs, lightly beaten
4 cups milk
1 tsp. dry mustard
1 tsp. salt
¼ tsp. onion powder
⅛ tsp. pepper
8 to 10 slices bacon,
    cooked and crumbled
½ cup mushrooms, sliced
½ cup tomato, peeled, chopped

Yield: 12 servings

Arrange bread cubes in a greased 9x13-inch baking pan. Sprinkle with cheese. Beat eggs, milk, dry mustard, salt, onion powder and pepper. Pour evenly over cheese and bread. Sprinkle with bacon, mushrooms and tomato. Cover and chill up to 24 hours. Bake uncovered 1 hour at 325°F or until set. Tent with foil if becomes too brown before eggs are set.

Valois Brintnall (Mrs. Lee)

THIS IS STRATA!

12 slices bread, cubed
2 cups ham, cubed
12 oz. sharp pasteurized
    process cheese slices
6 eggs
3 ½ cups milk
2 tsp. onion, minced
½ tsp. salt
¼ tsp. dry mustard
1 cup fresh bread crumbs
½ cup butter, melted

Yield: 12 servings

Layer bread cubes, ham and cheese slices in a 9x13-inch baking pan. Beat eggs, milk, onion, salt and dry mustard; pour over layers. Cover with aluminum foil; refrigerate overnight. Before baking, sprinkle with bread crumbs; pour melted butter over crumbs. Bake 1 hour 30 minutes at 325°F.

Janet Mead (Mrs. Ed, Jr.)

HAM AND EGG CASSEROLE

8 oz. Virginia or regular ham,
   thinly sliced
12 hard-cooked eggs, thickly sliced
6 Tbsp. butter
1 or 2 scallions, minced
6 Tbsp. flour
3 cups milk, heated
1 tsp. salt (optional)
¼ tsp. pepper (optional)
1 cup (4 oz.) Swiss cheese,
   shredded

Yield: 8 servings

In a greased 2-quart baking dish, arrange ham slices, then egg slices. Melt butter with scallions in a saucepan. Gradually blend in flour; remove from heat; stir in milk. Return to heat; stir until thick. Add salt and pepper if desired. Pour over egg slices; sprinkle with Swiss cheese. Bake 15 minutes at 375°F or until cheese bubbles and melts to a golden color. Serve over toast points or toasted English muffins.

Denise Johnson (Mrs. Dan)

SEAFOOD BRUNCH

1 (7 ½ oz.) can crab meat,
   drained , flaked
½ cup celery, chopped
¼ cup onion, chopped
¾ cup mayonnaise
⅛ tsp. cayenne pepper
12 slices white bread,
   crusts trimmed
½ cup butter, softened
4 cups (16 oz.) Swiss cheese,
   shredded
5 eggs
3 cup milk
1 tsp. salt
⅛ tsp. pepper
¼ tsp. dry mustard

Yield: 8 servings

Toss crab with celery and onion; blend in mayonnaise and cayenne. Spread both sides of bread with butter. Place one-half of bread in a 9x13-inch baking pan. Arrange one-half of crab mixture and one-half of Swiss cheese over bread. Repeat layering ending with bread. Beat milk, salt, pepper and dry mustard. Pour over layers; top with remaining one-third of Swiss cheese. Let stand one hour or refrigerate covered up to 24 hours. Bake uncovered 1 to 1 hour and 15 minutes at 325°F.

Jolene Jebsen (Mrs. Darrell)

EGG AND SAUSAGE BREAKFAST

3 cups (12 oz.) Cheddar cheese,
    shredded, divided
12 eggs, lightly beaten
⅛ tsp. cayenne pepper
1 ½ cups half and half
    or heavy cream
½ cup onion, chopped
¼ cup green pepper, chopped
2 (4 oz.) cans sliced mushrooms
2 (12 oz.) pkg. plain breakfast
    sausage, browned,drained

Yield: 8-10 servings

In a greased 9x13-inch baking pan, layer 1½ cups of Cheddar cheese, beaten eggs, cayenne, half and half, onion, green pepper, mushrooms, browned sausage and remaining 1½ cups of Cheddar cheese. Refrigerate overnight. Bake 30 to 40 minutes at 325°F until middle is firm.

Caroline Larson (Mrs. Ronald)

CRESCENT SAUSAGE AND CHEESE SQUARES

1 (8 oz.) tube refrigerated
    crescent rolls
1 (8 oz.) pkg. brown and serve
    sausages, sliced
2 cups (8 oz.) Monterey Jack cheese,
    shredded
4 eggs, lightly beaten
¾ cup milk
½ tsp. salt
¼ tsp. pepper
¼ tsp. oregano

Yield: 6-8 servings

Separate crescent rolls into two large rectangles. Place in ungreased 9x13-inch baking pan; press over bottom and ½-inch up sides to form crust. Seal perforations. Place sliced sausage over crust; sprinkle with cheese. This can be prepared up to this point ahead of time; cover and refrigerate. Combine eggs, milk, salt, pepper and oregano. Pour over Monterey Jack cheese. Bake 20 to 25 minutes at 425°F until golden brown.

Linda McGregor (Mrs. Robert)

EGGS TAHOE

1 clove garlic, minced
½ medium onion, chopped
¼ cup butter
¼ cup flour
2 cups milk, heated
1 (7 oz.) can green chilies
½ tsp. salt
¼ tsp. pepper
2 Tbsp. butter
10 eggs
8 (10-inch) flour tortillas
1 ½ cups (6 oz.) Cheddar cheese,
  shredded
1 ½ cups (6 oz.) Monterey Jack
  cheese, shredded
2 cups dairy sour cream
2 tomatoes, chopped
2 avocados, sliced
salsa (optional)
jalapeno peppers (optional)

Yield: 8-12 servings

Saute garlic and onion in ¼ cup butter in a large skillet over high heat. Stir in flour. Add heated milk and whisk constantly until thickened. Add chilies, salt and pepper; remove from heat. In another large skillet, scramble eggs in 2 tablespoons butter. Spoon 2 tablespoons of sauce and one-eighth of the eggs on each tortilla. Roll up and place seam side down in a 9x13-inch baking pan. Spoon remaining sauce over tortillas. Sprinkle with Cheddar and Monterey Jack cheese. Bake 15 to 20 minutes at 350°F . Top tortillas with sour cream, tomatoes and avocado slice. May serve with salsa and jalapeno peppers.

Patty Bowman (Mrs. Jim)

FRITTATA

Excellent served with fruit for a brunch.

¾ *cup green pepper, chopped*
1 ½ *cups mushrooms, sliced*
1 ½ *cups zucchini, chopped*
¾ *cup onion, chopped*
1 *cup ham, cubed*
1 *clove garlic, minced*
3 *Tbsp. vegetable oil*
6 *eggs, beaten*
¼ *cup half and half*
1 *(8 oz.) pkg. cream cheese, diced*
1 ½ *cups (6 oz.) Cheddar cheese,*
   shredded
2 *cups bread, cubed*
1 *tsp. salt*
¼ *tsp. pepper*

Saute green pepper, mushrooms, zucchini, onion, ham and garlic in oil until zucchini is crisp and tender; cool slightly. Beat eggs with half and half; add cream cheese, Cheddar cheese, bread, salt, pepper and vegetables. Mix well. Pour into well-greased 10-inch springform pan. Bake 1 hour at 350°F or until center is set. Cool 10 minutes before cutting.

Mid Lander (Mrs. Chuck)

Yield: 8 servings

ITALIAN ZUCCHINI PIE

This is a delicious meatless main dish.

4 *cups zucchini, thinly sliced*
1 *cup onion, chopped*
¼ *cup margarine*
½ *cup parsley, chopped or*
   2 *Tbsp. dried parsley*
½ *tsp. salt*
½ *tsp. pepper*
¼ *tsp. garlic powder*
¼ *tsp. basil*
¼ *tsp. oregano*
2 *eggs, beaten*
2 *cups (8 oz.) mozzarella cheese,*
   shredded
1 *(9 or 10-inch) unbaked pie shell*
2 *tsp. mustard*

Cook and stir the zucchini and onion in margarine for 10 minutes. Stir in parsley, salt, pepper, garlic, basil and oregano. Combine beaten eggs with mozzarella cheese; stir into zucchini mixture. Spread bottom of pie shell with mustard. Pour zucchini mixture into crust. Bake 18 to 20 minutes at 350°F.

Betty Collison (Mr. David)

Yield: 6 servings

BACON AND EGG LASAGNA

12 lasagna noodles,
     cooked and drained
1 lb. bacon, cut in 1-inch strips
1 cup onion, chopped
1/3 cup bacon drippings
1/3 cup flour
1/2 tsp. salt
1/4 tsp. pepper
4 cups milk
12 hard-cooked eggs, sliced
2 cups (8 oz.) Swiss cheese,
     shredded
1/3 cup Parmesan cheese,
     grated
2 Tbsp. parsley, chopped

Yield: 12 servings

Cook bacon until crisp in a large skillet; drain, reserving 1/3 cup drippings. Set bacon aside. Saute onions in bacon drippings until tender. Add flour, salt and pepper; stir until a paste forms. Add milk; cook and stir until mixture comes to a boil and is thickened. Spoon a small amount of white sauce into bottom of greased 9x13-inch baking pan. Divide lasagna noodles, bacon, white sauce, eggs and Swiss cheese into thirds; layer in pan in order given. Sprinkle with Parmesan cheese. Bake 25 to 30 minutes at 350°F or until thoroughly heated. Sprinkle with parsley. Let stand 10 minutes before serving. This recipe can be completely prepared the day before serving. Assemble, cover and refrigerate. Bake covered 25 minutes at 350°F . Uncover, bake 15-20 minutes longer or until hot.

Nancy Wilson (Mrs. David)

FRUITED CHICKEN SALAD

4 cups chicken, cooked and cubed
1 (15 oz.) can pineapple tidbits,
    drained
1 cup celery, chopped
1 (11 oz.) can mandarin oranges,
    drained
½ green pepper, chopped
¾ cup seedless grapes
2 Tbsp. onion, grated
½ cup green olives, chopped
1 cup mayonnaise
½ tsp. curry powder
1 Tbsp. mustard
1 (15 oz.) can chow mein noodles

Yield: 8 servings

Combine all ingredients except noodles; chill overnight. Add noodles before serving.

Eleanor Handorf (Mrs. Wilmer)

BEST-EVER CHICKEN SALAD

5 cups chicken, cooked and cubed
2 Tbsp. vegetable oil
2 Tbsp. orange juice
2 Tbsp. vinegar
1 tsp. salt
3 cups cooked rice
1 ½ cups small seedless grapes
1 ½ cups celery, sliced
1 (15 oz.) can pineapple chunks,
    drained
1 (11 oz.) can mandarin oranges,
    drained
1 cup slivered almonds, toasted
½ cup mayonnaise

Yield: 8-10 servings

Combine chicken, vegetable oil, orange juice, vinegar and salt in a large bowl. Let stand 30 minutes to allow flavors to blend. Add rice, grapes, celery, pineapple, oranges, almonds and mayonnaise; toss gently.

Pat Shobe (Mrs. Richard)

CHICKEN AND SNOW PEA SALAD IN A TARRAGON VINAIGRETTE

Must use fresh snow peas—frozen won't be crisp enough.

⅓ cup white wine tarragon vinegar
3 Tbsp. Dijon-style mustard
1 Tbsp. sugar
1 tsp. salt
1 tsp. garlic, minced
1 tsp. dried tarragon
½ tsp. pepper
½ tsp. crushed red pepper flakes
⅔ cup safflower oil
5 cups cooked wild rice
3 cups chicken, cooked and cubed
1 cup celery, sliced
½ cup parsley, chopped
½ cup green onions, sliced
½ lb. fresh snow peas
½ cup slivered almonds, toasted

Yield: 10 servings

Combine vinegar, mustard, sugar, salt, garlic, tarragon, pepper, and red pepper flakes. Whisk oil slowly into vinegar mixture; set aside. In large bowl, combine rice, chicken, celery, parsley and green onion. Pour vinegar dressing over rice mixture; toss to coat. Refrigerate covered several hours or overnight. Remove ends and strings from snow peas. Blanch in boiling water 30 seconds; plunge into ice water; drain. Pat dry. Cut diagonally into 1-inch pieces. Chill. Immediately before serving, toss salad with snow peas and almonds.

Pat Latham

CHICKEN ARTICHOKE SALAD

May be served warm or cold.

1 (6.9 oz.) pkg. chicken-flavored
    rice mix
¼ tsp. curry powder
½ cup mayonnaise
2 green onions, chopped
½ green pepper, chopped
8 green olives, sliced
3 to 4 chicken breasts, skinned
    and boned, cooked and cubed
2 (6 oz.) jars marinated
    artichoke hearts
lettuce leaves (optional)

Yield: 6 servings

Prepare rice mix according to package directions. Chill if serving cold. Blend curry and mayonnaise. Add rice mixture, onions, pepper, olives and chicken. Drain and chop artichokes, reserving ¼ cup of liquid. Add artichokes and reserved liquid. If serving cold, chill; serve on lettuce leaves. If serving hot, bake covered 35 to 45 minutes at 350°F or microcook covered on medium-high 10 to 12 minutes.

Nancy Veldey (Mrs. John)

ITALIAN SALAD

Can be made early in the day for a quick summer supper.

1 (16 oz.) pkg. small macaroni shells,
  cooked
4 oz. hard salami, chopped
½ lb. Provolone cheese, cubed
½ lb. pepperoni stick, chopped
3 tomatoes, chopped
2 green peppers, chopped
1 onion, chopped
3 ribs celery, chopped
1 (0.6 oz.) envelope Italian
  dressing mix

Combine macaroni, salami, cheese, pepperoni, tomatoes, pepper, onion and celery. Prepare dressing mix according to package directions. Toss with macaroni mixture. Chill.

Laura Allen

Yield: 8-10 servings

PASTA SALAD ITALIANO

Can be may a day ahead.

1 cup broccoli, chopped
1 cup cauliflower flowerets
½ cup mushrooms, sliced
1 (8 oz.) can sliced water chestnuts
1 carrot, chopped
¼ cup green or black olives, sliced
1 cup cherry tomatoes, halved
1 (8 oz.) bottle Italian dressing
1 (8 oz.) pkg. spaghetti or rotini,
  cooked, drained and chilled
¼ cup Parmesan cheese, grated
¼ cup bacon bits (optional)

Combine broccoli, cauliflower, mushrooms, water chestnuts, carrot, olives, and tomatoes in a medium bowl; pour dressing over and toss. Cover and marinate in refrigerator at least 3 hours. Drain; reserving marinade. Combine marinade with noodles; toss lightly. Place noodles in salad bowl and toss with vegetables. Sprinkle with Parmesan cheese and bacon bits.

Marcia Ward (Mrs. Curtis)

Yield: 8-10 servings

GARDEN LINGUINE

A colorful use of fresh vegetables—a true celebration of summer!

2 Tbsp. olive oil
½ cup butter
2 carrots, cut in julienne strips
¾ cup green onions, chopped
2 cloves garlic, minced
½ lb. fresh mushrooms, sliced
1 medium zucchini, sliced
1 cup snow peas,
    cut in half diagonally
1 lb. fresh asparagus,
    trimmed, sliced
½ cup chicken broth
1 cup heavy cream
2 Tbsp. fresh basil,
    minced or 1 tsp. dried basil
2 Tbsp. fresh parsley, minced
¼ tsp. salt
¼ tsp. pepper
9 oz. linguine, cooked al dente,
    drained
1 cup·Parmesan cheese,
    freshly grated, divided

Yield: 4 main-dish servings;
    6-8 side-dish servings

Heat oil and butter in a large skillet. Add carrots; simmer 2 minutes. Add green onions, garlic, mushrooms, zucchini, snow peas and asparagus. Simmer until tender. Remove vegetables with slotted spoon; set aside. To skillet, add broth, cream, basil, parsley, salt and pepper. Simmer to thicken slightly. Add ½ cup Parmesan cheese to sauce; stir to blend. Return vegetables to sauce. Stir briefly to reheat; do not boil. In a heated serving dish, toss linguine with vegetable mixture and remaining ½ cup Parmesan cheese. Serve immediately.

Suzanne Brown (Mrs. Gregory)

MEAT AND VEGETABLE FETTUCINE SALAD

1 lb. cauliflower flowerets
¼ lb. snow peas, strings removed
1 lb. zucchini, cut into ¼-inch strips
2 red peppers, cut into slivers
2 large carrots, coarsely shredded
1 medium red onion,
    quartered and thinly sliced
¾ lb. cooked beef, pork, poultry,
    or seafood, thinly sliced (optional)
½ lb. spinach fettucine,
    broken, cooked al dente

Dressing:
¼ cup fresh parsley, minced
¼ cup fresh basil, minced
    or 1 Tbsp. dried basil
1 clove garlic, crushed
¼ cup olive or vegetable oil
¼ cup chicken broth
⅓ cup red wine vinegar
4 tsp. Dijon-style mustard
2 tsp. sugar
¼ tsp. salt
⅛ tsp. pepper

Yield: 6 servings

Blanch or steam cauliflower and snow peas until tender-crisp. In a large bowl, combine cauliflower, peas, zucchini, red pepper, carrots, onion, meat and fettucine. Mix dressing ingredients; pour over salad. Toss well. Chill one hour or more before serving. May be made a day ahead.

Kay Sinning (Mrs. James)

TORTELLINI SALAD

1 (9 oz.) pkg. cheese tortellini,
    cooked and cooled
1 cup ham, cut into julienne strips
¾ cup frozen baby peas, thawed
2 oz. Swiss cheese, cubed
2 Tbsp. green onions, minced
1 Tbsp. parsley, minced
1 (8 oz.) bottle ranch-style dressing

Yield: 6 servings

Toss all ingredients together in a bowl; chill.

Susan Chadderdon

HAM MOUSSE

An old favorite for salad luncheons.

1 (¹⁄₄ oz.) envelope unflavored gelatin
1 Tbsp. cold water
1 (10 ³⁄₄ oz.) can beef consomme
¹⁄₂ cup salad dressing
²⁄₃ cup celery, diced
1 Tbsp. onion, chopped
1 Tbsp. pimento, chopped
1 Tbsp. green pepper, chopped
1 cup baked ham, chopped
4 hard-cooked eggs, chopped

Yield: 6-8 servings

Dissolve gelatin in cold water. Bring consomme to boil in saucepan; add gelatin. Stir until dissolved; cool to lukewarm. Add remaining ingredients. Pour into greased 1-quart mold and chill 4 to 6 hours. Unmold and serve on lettuce leaves. May garnish with additional slices of hard-cooked egg, parsley or stuffed olives.

Dorothy Apgar (Mrs. Patton)

SALMON AVOCADO MOUSSE

Colorful and attractive; unmolds easily.

1 (¹⁄₄ oz.) envelope unflavored gelatin
1 cup cold water
2 Tbsp. sugar
2 Tbsp. fresh lemon juice
1 Tbsp. white wine vinegar
2 Tbsp. onion, grated
¹⁄₂ tsp. salt
2 Tbsp. horseradish
1 (16 oz.) can red salmon,
      drained, flaked
¹⁄₂ cup mayonnaise
¹⁄₂ cup ripe olives, chopped
¹⁄₂ cup celery, chopped

Dressing:
1 large avocado, mashed
¹⁄₂ cup dairy sour cream
¹⁄₈ tsp. salt
lettuce leaves

Yield: 6 servings

Soften gelatin in water in a saucepan. Stir over low heat until dissolved. Add sugar, lemon juice, vinegar, onion, salt and horseradish; chill until almost set. Fold in salmon, mayonnaise, olives and celery. Pour into greased 1-quart mold; chill until set. Combine avocado, sour cream and salt. Unmold mousse. Serve on lettuce leaves with dressing drizzled over slices.

Maxine Eckles (Mrs. Kenneth)

CREPES ALMONDINE

¾ cup salad dressing
3 Tbsp. flour
½ tsp. salt
⅛ tsp. pepper
1 ½ cups milk
1 cup (4 oz.) Swiss cheese, shredded
2 cups chicken, cooked and cubed
1 cup celery, chopped
2 Tbsp. pimento, chopped
2 Tbsp. green onions, sliced
¾ cup slivered almonds,
    toasted, divided
10 to 12 non-dessert crepes

Yield: 5-6 servings

Combine salad dressing, flour, salt and pepper in a saucepan. Gradually add milk. Cook, stirring constantly, until thickened. Add cheese; stir until melted. Stir in chicken, celery, pimento, green onion and ½ cup of the almonds. Fill crepes; roll up and place seam side down in 9x13-inch baking dish. Bake 20 minutes at 350°F. Sprinkle remaining ¼ cup almonds on top; bake 5 minutes.

Jinx Hill (Mrs. Michael)

SHRIMP SALAD SANDWICHES

Attractive, yet simple to make—a nice ladies' luncheon entree.

1 (4 oz.) can tiny shrimp
2 Tbsp. celery, chopped
1 Tbsp. fresh chives, minced
2 Tbsp. mayonnaise
1 to 1 ½ Tbsp. lemon juice to taste
1 tsp. Worcestershire sauce
½ tsp Dijon-style mustard
¼ tsp. caraway seed
16 thin cucumber slices
8 slices whole wheat bread, toasted
4 tomato slices
1 cup alfalfa sprouts

Yield: 4 servings

Rinse shrimp; drain thoroughly. Combine shrimp, chives, mayonnaise, lemon juice, Worcestershire, mustard and caraway; stir well. Cover and chill 1 hour. Arrange 4 slices of cucumber on each of 4 slices of toasted bread. Top each with one-fourth of the shrimp mixture, one tomato slice and one-fourth of the sprouts. Cover with remaining bread. Serve immediately.

Pat Shobe (Mrs. Richard)

HOT TUNA SALAD ROLLS

Filling mixture may also be served cold as a summertime salad.
Try using pita bread instead of hoagies.

1 (12 oz.) can tuna, drained, flaked
1 cup celery, chopped
1 cup frozen baby peas
1 cup (4 oz.) Swiss or
    Monterey Jack cheese, shredded
¾ cup mayonnaise or salad dressing
1 Tbsp. dried parsley or
    ¼ cup fresh parsley, chopped
6 hoagie buns
¼ cup butter or margarine, melted

Combine tuna, celery, peas, cheese, mayonnaise and parsley. Cut a thin slice from top of each bun; set tops aside. Hollow out roll bottoms, leaving a thick shell. Brush inside with butter. Fill with tuna mixture and cover with reserved tops. Wrap each bun separately with aluminum foil. Bake 15 minutes at 400°F. Unwrap and serve.

Yield: 6 servings

Barbara Headley (Mrs. Michael)

CHEESY CRAB-STUFFED POTATOES

Our tester's comment "Yummy! Yummy!"

4 medium baking potatoes
vegetable oil
1 cup (4 oz.) Cheddar cheese,
    shredded
½ cup butter, melted
½ cup half and half
¼ cup onion, diced
½ tsp. salt
¼ tsp. cayenne pepper
1 (6 oz.) can crab meat,
    drained, flaked
paprika

Coat potato skins with vegetable oil; prick skins. Bake 1 hour at 350°F. Let cool to touch. Cut potatoes in half lengthwise. Carefully scoop out pulp into a mixing bowl, leaving shells intact. Set shells aside. Add cheese, butter, half and half, onion, salt, cayenne and crab meat. Mash with potato masher or use electric mixer. Refill shells with potato mixture; sprinkle with paprika. Bake 15 to 20 minutes at 425°F.

Yield: 4 servings

Dotty Goodman

92

SAN DIEGO BEACH-BAKED POTATOES

Very colorful—good for a luncheon or light supper.

4 medium-large baking potatoes
1 (7 oz.) can corn kernels, undrained
1 (4 oz.) can chopped green chilies,
  undrained
¼ cup pimentos, chopped
1 cup (4 oz.) Cheddar cheese,
  shredded
1 tsp. garlic powder

Yield: 4 servings

Prick potatoes; bake 1 hour at 400°F or microcook on high approximately 20 minutes. Cut a thin slice off top, scoop out pulp, leaving shells intact. Mash potatoes with fork; add remaining ingredients. Refill shells with potato mixture; sprinkle with additional shredded cheese, if desired. Bake 10 minutes at 400°F or microcook on medium approximately 3 minutes or until heated through.

Martha-Ellen Tye (Mrs. Joe B.)

FRESH ASPARAGUS SOUFFLE

1 lb. fresh asparagus, chopped
¼ cup margarine
¼ cup flour
½ tsp. dried thyme
½ tsp. red pepper sauce
¼ tsp. salt
1 ¼ cups milk
4 eggs, separated,
  room temperature
¾ to 1 cup Parmesan cheese,
  grated
¼ tsp. cream of tartar

Yield: 4 servings

Steam asparagus in medium saucepan until tender-crisp. Drain; set aside. In same pan, melt butter. Blend in flour, thyme, red pepper sauce and salt; cook 1 minute. Gradually stir in milk. Cook over medium heat until thickened; simmer 1 minute. In medium bowl, beat egg yolks; quickly stir in sauce. Add Parmesan cheese and asparagus; mix well. Cool slightly. In large bowl, beat egg whites with cream of tartar until stiff but not dry. Fold in sauce mixture. Pour into greased 1½-quart souffle dish. Bake 40 to 45 minutes at 375°F or until golden brown. Serve immediately.

Kathy Briggs (Mrs. Terrence)

SPINACH SOUFFLE

Even non-spinach eaters enjoy this.

1 (10 oz.) pkg. frozen spinach
1 Tbsp. onion, grated
2 eggs
½ cup dairy sour cream
½ cup Parmesan cheese, grated
1 Tbsp. flour
1 Tbsp. butter or margarine, melted
salt
pepper

Yield: 4 servings

Cook or microcook frozen spinach and onion in a small amount of water until thawed. Drain well; squeezing out excess water. Beat eggs; add sour cream, Parmesan cheese, flour and butter. Salt and pepper to taste. Stir in spinach and onion. Bake in greased 1-quart casserole dish 25 to 30 minutes at 350°F or until center is set. Do not over bake or it will separate.

Ann Meiners (Mrs. Gerald)

CHEESE SOUFFLE

More foolproof than most souffles.

½ lb. sharp Cheddar cheese, diced
2 Tbsp. butter
¼ cup flour
¼ tsp. dry mustard
½ tsp. salt
1 cup milk, heated
5 eggs, separated

Yield: 4 servings

Place cheese, butter, flour, dry mustard, salt, hot milk and egg yolks into blender. Blend on high 15 seconds, until liquified. Pour into saucepan and cook over low heat, stirring constantly until sauce becomes thick and smooth. Beat egg whites to stiff peaks; fold into sauce carefully. Pour into greased 1½-quart souffle dish. Bake 30 minutes at 375°F until well browned. Serve immediately.

Hollis Cassidy (Mrs. Eugene)

SPICED PEACHES

A nice accompaniment especially for a luncheon entree.

**3 (29 oz.) cans cling peach halves
    in heavy syrup
1 tsp. cornstarch
1 tsp. whole cloves
1 tsp. lemon juice
½ tsp. salt
½ tsp. whole allspice
3 (3-inch long) cinnamon sticks**

Yield: 25-30 peach halves

Drain peaches, reserving 1 cup of syrup; place peaches in large bowl. Stir cornstarch into 1 tablespoon of the reserved syrup until smooth; set aside. In a large microproof bowl, combine remaining reserved syrup, cloves, lemon juice, salt, allspice and cinnamon sticks. Microcook on high 5 to 6 minutes until mixture boils. Stir in cornstarch mixture. Microcook on high 5 to 6 more minutes until mixture boils and thickens slightly. Pour hot mixture over peaches in bowl; gently toss peaches to coat. Cover and refrigerate at least 2 hours to blend flavors.

Maureen Lyons (Mrs. Ken)

TOMATOES PROVENCALE

**4 firm, ripe tomatoes
salt
pepper
2 cloves garlic, crushed
3 Tbsp. green onion, minced
4 Tbsp. parsley, minced
⅛ tsp. thyme
¼ tsp. salt
⅛ tsp. pepper
¼ cup olive oil
½ cup bread crumbs**

Yield: 8 servings

Cut tomatoes in half horizontally; remove pulp. Sprinkle salt and pepper on the inside of each tomato shell. Combine garlic, green onion, parsley, thyme, salt, pepper, olive oil and bread crumbs. Stuff each tomato shell with mixture. Place in shallow baking pan or cookie sheet. Bake 15 minutes at 375°F.

Susan Malloy (Mrs. Patrick)

STRAWBERRY-SPINACH SALAD
Much visual appeal in this salad.

1 cup vegetable oil
5 Tbsp. cider vinegar
⅓ cup lemon juice
1 tsp. dry mustard
1 tsp. salt
¼ tsp. paprika
½ cup sugar
1 small onion, chopped
1 lb. fresh spinach, washed, torn
1 pint fresh strawberries, hulled, sliced

Mix vegetable oil, vinegar, lemon juice, dry mustard, salt, paprika, sugar and onion. Let stand overnight. Immediately before serving, toss spinach leaves and strawberries in salad bowl. Pour dressing over and toss.

Nan Ryden (Mrs. Rex)

Yield: 6-8 servings

FROZEN DATE SALAD
A sweet salad—good for the holidays.

1 (8 oz.) pkg. cream cheese,
  softened
1 (8 oz.) can crushed pineapple,
  undrained
1 cup dates, chopped
1 (4 oz.) jar maraschino cherries,
  drained, halved
1 Tbsp. lemon juice
⅛ tsp. salt
1 cup heavy cream, whipped
2 Tbsp. nuts, chopped

Blend cream cheese and pineapple. Add dates, cherries, lemon juice and salt. Fold in whipped cream and nuts. Pour into 1-quart mold. Freeze until firm. Unmold and serve.

Linda Blum (Mrs. Daniel)

Yield: 12 servings

LAYERED VEGETABLE SALAD

Excellent winter salad when not as many fresh vegetables are available.

1 (10 oz.) pkg. frozen
    chopped spinach
1 (10 oz.) pkg. frozen broccoli
1 (10 oz.) pkg. frozen peas
1 head iceberg lettuce
4 green onions, sliced
8 oz. fresh mushrooms, sliced
6 hard-cooked eggs, sliced
2 cups mayonnaise
1 cup dairy sour cream
1 (1.1 oz.) pkg. ranch-style
    dressing mix
8 oz. bacon, cooked, crumbled

Thaw spinach, broccoli and peas. Squeeze spinach dry. Drain all on paper towels. Shred lettuce and place in a deep 9x13-inch dish. Arrange spinach, broccoli and peas on top. Sprinkle with green onions. Layer mushrooms over onions; add egg slices. Mix mayonnaise, sour cream and dressing mix; spread over top. Garnish with bacon. Cover and chill 8 hours or overnight.

Maureen Lyons (Mrs. Ken)

Yield: 10 servings

SCONES WITH STRAWBERRY ALMOND BUTTER

A delightful recipe from England.

Scones:
2 ¼ cups flour
2 ½ tsp. baking powder
⅛ tsp. salt
¼ cup butter
1 egg
½ cup milk
2 Tbsp. sugar
1 egg, beaten

Strawberry Almond Butter:
¼ cup butter, softened
1 ¼ cups confectioners sugar, sifted
1 cup fresh strawberries, hulled
¼ cup blanched almonds,
    finely ground

To make scones, sift flour, baking powder and salt. Cut in butter with a pastry blender until crumbly. Beat egg with milk and sugar; stir into crumb mixture. Pat dough on floured surface to ½-inch thick. Cut with 1½-inch biscuit cutter. Brush tops with beaten egg. Bake 7 minutes at 450°F. Split when cool and serve with strawberry almond butter. To make butter, cream butter and confectioners sugar. Puree strawberries in food processor. Strain into butter mixture; beat until smooth. Beat in ground almonds.

Jan Rathke (Mrs. Richard)

Yield: 12-14 scones, 2 cups butter

FRENCH CREME MOLD

2 ⅓ cups heavy cream
¾ cup sugar
2 (¼ oz.) envelopes and 1 ½ tsp.
    unflavored gelatin, divided
2 cups dairy sour cream
1 tsp. vanilla
1 (10 oz.) pkg. frozen raspberries,
    thawed, drained, reserving juice
2 Tbsp. orange flavor liqueur

Heat cream, sugar and 2 envelopes gelatin on top of double boiler until gelatin is dissolved. Cool; add sour cream and vanilla. Pour into 1-quart mold and chill. Heat remaining 1½ teaspoons gelatin in reserved raspberry juice until dissolved. Add raspberries and liqueur. Cool. Unmold creme and serve raspberry glaze over top.

Yield: 6-8 servings

Mid Lander (Mrs. Chuck)

TOFFEE STRAWBERRY CONTINENTAL
Toffee Sauce is also delicious over ice cream.

4 pints strawberries, hulled
1 ½ cups dairy sour cream

Toffee Sauce:
¾ cup sugar
½ cup heavy cream
¼ cup light corn syrup
2 Tbsp. butter
3 (1.4 oz.) chocolate-covered
    toffee candy bars, crushed

Yield: 6-8 servings

Clean and dry strawberries. Alternate layers of strawberries and sour cream in a large glass bowl or individual stem glasses. To make sauce, combine sugar, cream, syrup and butter in a saucepan. Bring to a boil and boil 1 minute. Remove from heat and stir in crushed candy bars. The candy bars may not all dissolve. Cool, stirring occasionally. Drizzle over prepared strawberries.

Susan Malloy (Mrs. Patrick)

STRAWBERRY MERINGUE DESSERT

10 egg whites, room temperature
½ tsp. cream of tartar
2 ¾ cups sugar, divided
1 quart strawberry ice cream,
    softened
2 cups heavy cream
3 Tbsp. confectioners sugar
1 quart fresh strawberries,
    hulled and sliced

Yield: 10-12 servings

Beat egg whites until frothy. Add cream of tartar; beat to soft peaks. Gradually add 2 cups sugar and continue beating to stiff peaks. Grease two 9-inch round pans. Line with greased waxed paper. Spread the egg white mixture in the pans. Bake 1 hour at 275°F. Cool thoroughly; remove meringues from pans and peel off paper. Place one meringue on a large freezer-proof dish. Spread with softened ice cream and top with the other meringue. Beat heavy cream and confectioners sugar to soft peaks and frost meringue layers. Freeze for 6 hours or more. Combine sliced strawberries and ¼ cup sugar. When ready to serve, garnish with strawberries.

LaDean Peterson (Mrs. Carl)

CHOCOLATE TRUFFLE LOAF
WITH RASPBERRY SAUCE

2 cups heavy cream, divided
3 egg yolks, lightly beaten
16 (1 oz.) squares
·   semi-sweet chocolate
½ cup light corn syrup
½ cup margarine
¼ cup confectioners sugar
1 tsp. vanilla

Raspberry Sauce:
1 (10 oz.) pkg. frozen raspberries,
    thawed
⅓ cup light corn syrup

Yield: 8-10 servings

Mix ½ cup of the cream with egg yolks; set aside. Stir chocolate, corn syrup and margarine in 3-quart saucepan over medium heat until chocolate melts. Add egg yolk mixture; cook 3 minutes, stirring constantly. Cool to lukewarm. Beat remaining 1½ cups cream until soft peaks form; add sugar and vanilla. Fold into chocolate mixture carefully until no white streaks remain. Pour into 8½x4½x2½-inch loaf pan that has been lined with plastic wrap. Chill overnight. To make sauce, puree raspberries in blender; strain. Stir in corn syrup. To serve, pour sauce on each plate, place a thin slice of truffle loaf on top.

Jan Rathke (Mrs. Richard)

CHOCOLATE RASPBERRY CHEESECAKE

18 chocolate sandwich cookies,
finely crushed
2 Tbsp. margarine, melted
4 (8 oz.) pkgs. cream cheese,
softened, divided
1 ¼ cups sugar
3 eggs
1 cup dairy sour cream
1 tsp. vanilla
1 (12 oz.) pkg. semi-sweet
chocolate morsels, divided
⅓ cup raspberry preserves
¼ cup heavy cream

Yield: 10-12 servings

Combine cookie crumbs and margarine; press into bottom of 9-inch springform pan. Combine 3 packages of cream cheese and sugar in large bowl with mixer. Add eggs, one at a time, mixing well after each. Blend in sour cream and vanilla; pour over crust. Melt one-half of chocolate morsels; combine with remaining package of cream cheese. Add preserves. Drop chocolate batter by rounded teaspoons over batter in pan. Bake 1 hour and 20 minutes at 325°F. Loosen cake from rim; cool. Remove rim. Melt remaining chocolate morsels with cream over low heat, stirring until smooth. Spread over cheesecake. Chill. May garnish with whipped cream, raspberries and fresh mint.

Betsy Macke (Mrs. Mark)

WHITE CHOCOLATE CHEESECAKE WITH GLAZED RASPBERRIES

A special occasion dessert.

Crust:
1 cup chocolate wafer crumbs
3 Tbsp. sugar
¼ cup butter, melted

Cheesecake:
3 (8 oz.) pkgs. cream cheese,
    softened
1 ½ cups sugar
2 Tbsp. cornstarch
4 eggs
2 Tbsp. lemon juice
2 tsp. vanilla
¼ tsp. salt
2 cups dairy sour cream

White Chocolate Frosting:
4 (3 oz.) pkgs. cream cheese,
    softened
9 oz. white chocolate,
    melted and cooled
¾ cup butter, softened
    (do not substitute)
1 ½ Tbsp. lemon juice

Glazed Raspberries:
¾ cup sugar
3 Tbsp. cornstarch
¾ cup water
2 Tbsp. light corn syrup
3 to 4 drops red food coloring
3 to 4 cups raspberries

Yield 12-16 servings

To make crust, combine wafer crumbs, sugar and butter. Pat into bottom of greased 10-inch springform pan. Chill 30 minutes. To make cheesecake, beat cream cheese and sugar until smooth; mix in cornstarch. Add eggs, one at a time, beating until smooth after each. Mix in lemon juice, vanilla and salt. Fold in sour cream. Pour into crust. Set springform pan into larger pan; pour boiling water into larger pan to depth of 1-inch. Bake 45 minutes at 350°F or until set. Turn off oven but leave cake in for 1 hour. Cool; cover and chill overnight. To make frosting, beat cream cheese until smooth; add white chocolate and beat until smooth and fluffy. Beat in butter and lemon juice. Set aside 1 cup frosting; spread remainder over top and sides of cake. Pipe reserved frosting along upper and lower edges. To make glaze, combine sugar and cornstarch in a saucepan. Add ¾ cup water and cook over medium-high heat, stirring until it is thick and clear. Remove from heat; add corn syrup and food coloring. Cool to lukewarm. Arrange raspberries on cake and pour glaze over. Chill at least 3 hours.

Variation: Use strawberries or cherries in place of raspberries.

Maureen Lyons (Mrs. Ken)

Entrees

SHERRY ORANGE CHICKEN

Fast and easy to prepare, yet elegant enough for company.

**4 chicken breast halves,
   skinned and boned
4 Tbsp. sherry
2 Tbsp. soy sauce
1 Tbsp. brown sugar
1 tsp. snipped fresh oregano or
   ¼ tsp. crushed dried oregano
2 cloves garlic, finely chopped
1 (11 oz.) can mandarin orange
   segments, drained, reserve juice
1 tsp. vegetable oil
2 tsp. cornstarch
2 Tbsp. raisins
2 cups hot cooked rice
1 Tbsp. snipped fresh chives**

Yield: 4 servings

Place chicken in a glass or plastic container. Mix sherry, soy sauce, brown sugar, oregano, garlic and ¼ cup of the reserved mandarin orange juice. Pour over the chicken. Cover and refrigerate for at least 1 hour, turning once. Heat oil in a 10-inch non-stick skillet. Cook chicken over medium heat until lightly browned on both sides. Add marinade mixture. Reduce heat; cover and cook until chicken is done, about 10 minutes. Remove chicken to a platter; keep warm. Mix cornstarch with remaining reserved mandarin orange juice and stir into hot liquid in the skillet, stirring constantly until thickened. Stir in the orange segments and raisins; heat through. Serve chicken and sauce over rice. Garnish with chives.

Cathy Frost (Mrs. Curt)

CHICKEN MARENGO

Unique flavor and attractive dish for entertaining.

8 chicken breast halves, boned
¼ cup Dijon-style mustard
⅛ tsp. dried parsley
⅛ tsp. dried basil
⅛ tsp. dried thyme
⅛ tsp. salt
⅛ tsp. pepper
8 slices Monterey Jack cheese
¼ cup flour
2 Tbsp. vegetable oil

Sauce:
1 medium onion, chopped
8 oz. fresh mushrooms, sliced
½ green pepper, cut into strips
2 cloves garlic, minced
¼ cup snipped parsley
1 tsp. dried basil
1 tsp. dried thyme
1 (28 oz.) can whole tomatoes,
**   undrained**
½ cup dry white wine
⅛ tsp. salt
⅛ tsp. pepper

Yield: 8 servings

Wash and pat chicken dry. Flatten with a rolling pin between waxed paper. Spread lightly with mustard and sprinkle with parsley, basil, thyme, salt and pepper. Place cheese slices on top of chicken and roll up. Secure with toothpicks. At this point the chicken can be refrigerated and preparation completed at a later time. To complete preparation roll chicken in flour. Brown on all sides in oil until done in a 10-inch skillet. Remove chicken to a platter; keep warm. Saute onion, mushrooms and pepper with garlic. Add parsley, basil, thyme and tomatoes. Bring to a boil to reduce liquid. Add wine, salt and pepper; simmer until sauce has thickened. Serve chicken with the sauce on the side. Rice makes a good accompaniment.

Mary Kenagy (Mrs. Dean)

CHICKEN BREASTS DIANE

4 chicken breast halves,
   skinned and boned
½ tsp. salt
½ tsp. pepper
2 Tbsp. vegetable oil, divided
2 Tbsp. margarine, divided
3 Tbsp. chopped fresh chives or
   chopped green onions
1 to 1 ½ Tbsp. lemon or lime juice
2 Tbsp. brandy or Cognac (optional)
3 Tbsp. fresh parsley, chopped
2 tsp. Dijon-style mustard
¼ cup chicken broth

Yield: 4 servings

Place chicken between two sheets of waxed paper and flatten with a mallet. Sprinkle with salt and pepper. Heat 1 tablespoon oil and 1 tablespoon margarine in a 10-inch skillet. Brown chicken on high heat for 2 minutes per side. Remove to a platter and keep warm. Reduce heat; add chives, lemon juice, brandy, parsley and mustard. Cook 15 seconds stirring constantly. Whisk in broth and stir until the sauce is smooth. Stir in remaining 1 tablespoon oil and 1 tablespoon margarine. Pour sauce over chicken and serve.

Deb Keefe (Mrs. Kevin)

QUIK-CHIX MONTEREY STYLE

4 chicken breast halves, boned
4 Tbsp. prepared spaghetti sauce
4 slices Monterey Jack cheese

Yield: 4 servings

Place chicken in broiler pan; broil 10 minutes per side. Spoon 1 tablespoon spaghetti sauce over each chicken piece and top with a cheese slice. Broil an additional 1 to 2 minutes until cheese melts and sauce is warm.

Lorraine Schultz (Mrs. Ed)

CHICKEN STUFFING CASSEROLE

A favorite casserole served by the YWCA.

1 (6 oz.) package cornbread stuffing
 with seasoning mix packet
½ cup margarine, melted
4 cups chicken, cooked and cubed
2 (10 ¼ oz.) cans cream of
 chicken soup, undiluted
1 (12 oz.) can evaporated milk
1 (7 oz.) can whole water chestnuts,
 drained and thinly sliced

Yield: 12 servings

Combine cornbread stuffing mix and seasoning mix packet with melted margarine. Place one-half of this mixture into a 9x13-inch baking pan. Refrigerate 15 minutes. Combine chicken, soup, milk and water chestnuts. Pour over the crust and top with remaining stuffing mixture. Bake 40 minutes at 325°F. Let stand 5 minutes before cutting and serving.

Variation: Substitute chicken flavored stuffing with seasoning packet mix for the cornbread stuffing.

Verda Stief (Mrs. Charles)

FANCY CHICKEN BAKE

8 chicken breast halves,
 skinned and boned
8 slices bacon
1 (10 ¼ oz.) can cream of
 chicken soup, undiluted
1 cup dairy sour cream
2 cups mozzarella cheese, shredded
⅛ cup Parmesan cheese, grated
¼ tsp. paprika

Yield: 8 servings

Individually wrap chicken breasts in a bacon slice and place in a greased 9x13-inch baking pan. Combine soup, sour cream and mozzarella cheese and pour over chicken. Bake 1 hour at 350°F. Sprinkle with Parmesan cheese and paprika before serving.

Eleanor Handorf (Mrs. Wilmer)

POPPY SEED CHICKEN

4 cups chicken, cooked and cubed
1 cup dairy sour cream
1 (10 ¾ oz.) can cream of
    mushroom soup, undiluted
2 green onions, chopped
10 fresh mushrooms, diced
⅛ tsp. garlic salt
⅛ tsp. pepper
30 round buttery crackers, crushed
1-2 Tbsp. poppy seed
6 Tbsp. margarine, melted

Yield: 6-8 servings

Mix chicken, sour cream, soup, onion, mushrooms, garlic salt and pepper. Pour into a greased 8x8-inch baking pan. Top casserole with crushed crackers; sprinkle with poppy seed and drizzle melted margarine over top. Bake 20 to 30 minutes at 350°F.

Marcie Harvey (Mrs. Elwood)

STUFFED CHICKEN BREAST FOR TWO

2 chicken breast halves, boned
2 pickled jalapeno chilies,
    stemmed and seeded
2 slices Monterey Jack cheese
¼ cup dry bread crumbs
2 Tbsp. Parmesan cheese, grated
1 tsp. chili powder
¼ tsp. ground cumin
⅛ tsp. salt
⅛ tsp. pepper
¼ cup margarine, melted

Yield: 2 servings

Place chicken between two sheets of waxed paper and flatten to ¼-inch thick. Stem and seed chilies. Cut into ¼-inch strips. Arrange chilies on top of each chicken breast; place a slice cheese over the chilies. Roll chicken jelly-roll style tucking in the ends of the roll. Combine bread crumbs, Parmesan cheese and spices. Roll chicken in margarine and generously coat with crumb mixture. Arrange in a greased 8x8-inch baking pan. Drizzle leftover margarine over the top. At this point the chicken rolls can be refrigerated until ready to bake. Bake 30 to 35 minutes at 375°F.

Glady Winter (Mrs. David)

PARMESAN CHICKEN BAKE

Easy and very tasty family dish.

⅔ **cup Parmesan cheese, grated**
⅔ **cup dry bread crumbs**
4 lb. chicken, cut into pieces
6 Tbsp. margarine, melted

Yield: 4 servings

Combine Parmesan cheese and bread crumbs. Dip chicken in margarine and coat chicken with the crumb mixture. Arrange in a greased 9x13-inch baking pan. Bake 1 hour at 375°F.

Eleanor Tjossem (Mrs. Paul)

EASY AND ELEGANT CHICKEN BREASTS

8 chicken breast halves,
   skinned and boned
8 thin slices Swiss or
   mozzarella cheese
1 (10 ¾ oz.) can cream of
   mushroom soup, undiluted
¼ **to** ⅓ **cup dry white wine**
1 cup crushed herb-seasoned
   stuffing mix
¼ **cup margarine, melted**

Yield: 8 servings

Arrange chicken in a 9x13-inch greased baking pan. Place a cheese slice on top of each chicken piece. Combine soup and wine; pour over chicken and cheese. Sprinkle with stuffing and drizzle margarine over the top. Bake covered 45 minutes and uncovered for 15 minutes at 350°F.

Jan Hugen (Mrs. Terry)
Kindera Severidt (Mrs. Dean)

CHICKEN BREASTS DIJON

Our testers said this was a wonderful dish for entertaining.

¼ cup flour
1 tsp. salt
¼ tsp. freshly ground pepper
6 chicken breast halves,
    skinned and boned
2 Tbsp. margarine
2 Tbsp. vegetable oil

Sauce:
3 Tbsp. margarine
3 Tbsp. flour
3 Tbsp. Dijon-style mustard
1 ½ cups milk
¾ cup dry white wine
1 tsp. salt (optional)
¼ tsp. dried tarragon leaves

Yield: 6 servings

Combine flour, salt and pepper in a medium size bowl. Dredge chicken pieces in flour mixture. Saute chicken in margarine and oil about 5 minutes per side, until golden. Arrange in single layer in a 9x13-inch baking pan. To prepare sauce, melt margarine over medium heat in a medium size saucepan. Add flour and mustard. Cook, whisking constantly until mixture bubbles. Add milk, wine, salt and tarragon. Cook, whisking constantly until mixture bubbles and thickens, about 1 minute. Pour sauce over chicken; bake covered 30 minutes and uncovered 15 minutes at 350°F. Arrange on a platter with sauce spooned over the top. Extra sauce can be served on the side. This recipe can be made one day ahead and refrigerated, but increase baking time by 15 to 20 minutes.

Barbara Headley (Mrs. Michael)

KATIE'S CHICKEN

This has a snappy, lip smacking sauce!

6 chicken breast halves,
    skinned and boned
2 Tbsp. margarine, melted
⅓ cup soy sauce
⅓ cup steak sauce
2 Tbsp. Worcestershire sauce

Yield: 6 servings

Wash and pat chicken dry. Place in an 8x8-inch baking pan. Mix remaining ingredients; pour over chicken and marinate 1 to 2 hours. Bake covered in marinade 1 hour at 350°F.

Linda Bloom (Mrs. Michael)

CHICKEN BREASTS WITH SHERRY BUTTER

4 chicken breast halves,
   skinned and boned
½ cup unseasoned bread crumbs
¼ cup Parmesan cheese, grated
¼ tsp. salt
1 egg
2 Tbsp. water

Sauce:
2 Tbsp. margarine
3 Tbsp. sherry
½ tsp. garlic, minced or
   ½ tsp. garlic salt
½ tsp. Worcestershire sauce
½ tsp. Dijon-style mustard

Yield: 4 servings

Preheat oven to 500°F. Lightly grease a 9x13-inch baking pan. Flatten chicken to ¼-inch thick. Mix bread crumbs, cheese and salt. Beat egg and water together. Dip chicken in egg and then dip in crumb mixture; place in pan. Stir sauce ingredients together over low heat until margarine is melted. Pour over chicken and bake 12 to 15 minutes or until browned.

Ann Collison (Mrs. Mark)

CROUTON CHICKEN

The kids will love it served alone; on a ham slice it's elegant.

4 chicken breast halves,
   skinned and boned
4 tsp. parsley flakes
garlic salt to taste
¼ cup margarine, melted
1 cup crushed seasoned croutons

Yield: 4 servings

Sprinkle chicken with parsley and garlic salt. Roll up and secure with a toothpick. Roll in margarine, then crouton crumbs. Place in a greased 8x8-inch baking pan. Sprinkle remaining crumbs over the chicken and moisten lightly with a few drops of water. Bake 45 minutes at 350°F .

Susan Chadderdon

MAKE AHEAD CHICKEN BAKE

8 chicken breast halves, skinned
2 eggs, lightly beaten
1 cup seasoned bread crumbs
2 Tbsp. margarine
1 Tbsp. vegetable oil
1 lb. fresh mushrooms, sliced
½ lb. Muenster cheese, sliced
1 (10 ¾ oz.) can condensed
    chicken broth, undiluted

Yield: 8 servings

Dip chicken in egg and coat with bread crumbs. Melt margarine and oil in a skillet and lightly brown chicken. Arrange in a 9x13-inch baking pan. Sprinkle with three-fourths of the mushrooms and top with cheese slices; arrange remaining mushrooms over cheese. At this point it can be refrigerated for one day. Before baking, pour the broth over the chicken and bake 40 minutes at 375°F.

Tommie Warrington (Mrs. R.D.)

CHICKEN MOZZARELLA

1 Tbsp. vegetable oil
2 Tbsp. Parmesan cheese, grated
⅔ cup buttermilk biscuit baking mix
2 tsp. Italian seasoning
1 tsp. paprika
¼ tsp. pepper
6 chicken breast halves
⅔ cup chili sauce
¾ cup (3 oz.) mozzarella cheese,
    grated

Yield: 6 servings

Brush bottom of a 9x13-inch baking pan with oil. Mix Parmesan cheese, baking mix, Italian seasoning, paprika and pepper in a large plastic bag. Coat chicken with this mixture; arrange pieces skin side down in the baking pan. Bake 45 minutes at 425°F. Turn chicken and brush with chili sauce; sprinkle with mozzarella cheese and bake 5 minutes longer or until cheese melts.

Marcia Ward (Mrs. Curtis)

CHICKEN IN A HAM BLANKET

⅓ cup flour
2 Tbsp. Parmesan cheese, grated
salt to taste
pepper to taste
4 chicken breast halves,
*   skinned and boned*
1 egg, beaten with 1 Tbsp. water
2 Tbsp. vegetable oil
6 Tbsp. margarine, divided
¾ lb. fresh mushrooms, sliced
4 slices cooked ham
1 ½ to 2 cups (6-8 oz.) mozzarella
*   cheese, shredded*

Yield: 4 servings

Preheat oven to 350°F. Combine flour, Parmesan cheese, salt and pepper. Dip chicken pieces in egg, then dip in coating mixture. Heat oil and 4 tablespoons margarine in a skillet and brown 2 minutes on each side. Arrange in a 9x13-inch baking pan. Add remaining 2 tablespoons margarine to the skillet and saute mushrooms 4 minutes. Place a ham slice over each chicken piece; top with mushrooms and mozzarella cheese. Bake 35 to 40 minutes.

Microcook Variation: Prepare as directed but do not top with mozzarella cheese. Cover with plastic wrap and microcook at full power 6 minutes. Sprinkle with mozzarella cheese; cover and cook at full power an additional 6 minutes.

Susan Chadderdon

RUBY CHICKEN
Attractive, make-ahead holiday entree.

10 chicken breast halves,
*   skinned and boned*
1 (16 oz.) can whole cranberry sauce
1 (1 oz.) envelope dried onion
*   soup mix*
1 (8 oz.) bottle Russian salad dressing

Yield: 10 servings

Arrange chicken breasts in a single layer in a 9x13-inch baking pan. Mix cranberry sauce, onion soup mix, and dressing together and pour over the chicken. Marinate overnight. Bake 1 hour at 350°F.

Nancy Wilson (Mrs. David)

FOIL BAKED CHICKEN AND CANADIAN BACON

1 (10 ¾ oz.) can cream of mushroom
    soup, undiluted, divided
6 chicken breast halves
1 large sweet onion, cut in 12 slices
8 fresh mushrooms, sliced
8 slices Canadian bacon
salt
pepper

Yield: 6 servings

Spread out six 12-inch pieces of aluminum foil. Divide one-half can of soup between the foil sheets. Place a chicken breast on top of the soup. Top with an onion slice and one-half of the mushroom slices. Place a Canadian bacon slice on top of this and then top with remaining mushrooms, onion slices and soup. Salt and pepper to taste. Seal foil packets, folding edges so the juices can't escape. Place packets on a 10x15-inch baking pan and bake 1 hour at 375°F.

Carrie Barr (Mrs. Paul)

CHICKEN TETRAZZINI

8 oz. thin spaghetti
⅓ cup butter, melted
2 (10 ¾ oz.) cans cream of
    chicken soup, undiluted
1 ½ cups dairy sour cream
1 cup chicken broth
6 chicken breast halves, skinned,
    boned, cooked
1 pint fresh mushrooms, sliced

Topping:
½ cup bread crumbs
4 Tbsp. butter, melted
¼ cup Parmesan cheese, grated

Yield: 8 servings

Break spaghetti into 1-inch pieces; cook and drain. Combine butter, soup, sour cream and chicken broth. Cut chicken into bite-sized pieces. Stir chicken, mushrooms and spaghetti into sauce; place in a greased 9x13-inch baking pan. Combine topping ingredients and sprinkle over the top. Bake 40 minutes at 350°F.

Ellen Block (Mrs. W.S.)

114

SPINACH-STUFFED CHICKEN BREASTS

8 chicken breast halves,
boned, skin left on
1 tsp. fresh or dried thyme
salt to taste
1 tsp. olive oil, divided

Stuffing:
1 small onion, finely chopped
1 Tbsp. butter
1 Tbsp. olive oil
1 lb. spinach, washed and stemmed
½ cup low-fat ricotta cheese
½ cup Parmesan cheese,
freshly grated
1 tsp. fresh basil, finely chopped
freshly ground pepper to taste

Sauce:
1 cup plain yogurt
1 Tbsp. red wine vinegar
¼ tsp. salt
1 ripe tomato, peeled and chopped

Yield: 8 servings

To prepare stuffing, saute onion in butter and 1 tablespoon oil in a skillet until translucent. Add spinach and cook until wilted and moisture has evaporated. Transfer to a bowl and cool. Stir in cheeses, basil and pepper. To make pockets for stuffing, loosen the skin of each breast half by running a finger between the flesh and skin on one long side leaving the skin attached on the other side. Rub thyme and salt into the flesh. Fill each pocket with one-eighth of the stuffing mixture. Place chicken, skin side up, in a greased 8x8-inch baking pan. Drizzle ⅛ teaspoon olive oil onto the skin of each stuffed breast. Bake 25 to 30 minutes at 375°F until skin is golden. To make sauce, combine yogurt, vinegar, and salt in a small bowl. Sprinkle tomato on top of sauce and serve on the side.

Maureen Lewis (Mrs. Philip)

ELEGANT CHICKEN BREAST ON RICE

¼ cup margarine
8 chicken breast halves,
    skinned and boned
½ cup flour
salt to taste
pepper to taste
1 green pepper, chopped
1 medium onion, chopped
½ cup green olives, sliced
1 (13 ½ oz.) can pineapple
    chunks, drained, reserve juice
1 lb. package frozen shrimp
1 (10 ¾ oz.) can tomato soup,
    undiluted
½ cup chili sauce
cooked rice

Yield: 8 servings

Melt margarine in a 9x13-inch baking pan. Roll chicken in flour, salt and pepper. Place in pan and bake 30 minutes at 375°F. Turn chicken and sprinkle shrimp over top. Combine green pepper, onion, olives, pineapple, soup, chili sauce and ½ cup reserved pineapple juice. Pour over chicken and shrimp. Cover with aluminum foil and bake an additional 30 minutes; uncover and bake 10 minutes. Serve over rice.

Eleanor Handorf (Mrs. Wilmer)

MICROWAVE CHICKEN AND RICE

2 Tbsp. margarine
¼ cup onion, chopped
1 small clove garlic, minced
1 ½ cups water
1 ½ tsp. chicken-flavor
    bouillon granules
1 (16 oz.) can stewed tomatoes,
    undrained
1 ¼ cups instant rice
½ tsp. salt
⅛ tsp. pepper
½ tsp. paprika
1 bay leaf
1 ½ lb. boneless chicken

Yield: 6 servings

Place margarine, onion, and garlic in a 3-quart casserole. Microcook on full power 2 minutes. Stir in remaining ingredients, except the chicken. Place chicken on top and cover. Microcook on full power 20 to 25 minutes. Let stand 5 minutes. Discard bay leaf before serving.

Betsy Macke (Mrs. Mark)

CHICKEN AND WILD RICE CASSEROLE

1 (6 oz.) package long grain
    and wild rice
¼ cup margarine
⅓ cup onion, chopped
⅓ cup flour
1 tsp. salt
pepper to taste
1 cup milk
1 cup chicken broth
2 cups chicken, cooked and cubed
⅓ cup pimento, diced (optional)
⅓ cup parsley, chopped
¼ cup slivered almonds, chopped

Prepare rice according to package directions. While rice is cooking, melt margarine in a large skillet. Add onion and cook until tender. Stir in flour, salt and pepper. Gradually stir in milk and broth. Cook stirring constantly, until thickened. Stir in chicken, pimento, parsley, almonds and cooked rice. Pour into a greased 2-quart casserole. Bake uncovered 30 minutes at 400°F.

Jan Hugen (Mrs. Terry)

Yield: 6 servings

HERB CHICKEN STIR-FRY

A great recipe for using fresh garden produce.

2 Tbsp. flour
1 tsp. salt-free chicken seasoning
1 tsp. chicken-flavor
    bouillon granules
¼ tsp. poultry seasoning
½ tsp. dried basil
¾ cup water
2 Tbsp. vegetable oil
1 small onion, chopped
1 clove garlic, minced
4 chicken breast halves, skinned,
    boned, cut into 1-inch pieces
3 medium zucchini, sliced
3 medium tomatoes, cut in eighths
cooked rice

Combine flour, seasonings, and water; mix well. Pour oil around the top of a preheated wok or skillet, coating evenly. Heat 1 minute at 525°F. Add onion and garlic; stir-fry until tender. Remove and set aside. Add chicken and stir-fry 4 to 5 minutes. Remove and set aside. Add zucchini and stir-fry 5 minutes. Add seasoned water and tomatoes; stir-fry until bubbly. Return chicken, onion and garlic to wok; stir-fry 1 to 2 minutes more. Serve over rice.

Barbara Headley (Mrs. Michael)

Yield: 6 servings

EASY CHICKEN WELLINGTON

¼ cup mayonnaise
1 tsp. rosemary leaves, crushed
2 tsp. onion or chives,
*   finely chopped*
4 chicken breast halves,
*   skinned and boned*
1 tsp. salt
½ tsp. pepper
1 (8 oz.) tube refrigerated
*   crescent rolls*
1 egg, lightly beaten

Sauce:
1 Tbsp. flour
1 ½ Tbsp. white wine
1 (4 oz.) can sliced mushrooms,
*   drained, reserve juice*
3 Tbsp. heavy cream

Yield: 4 servings

Place mayonnaise in a skillet and melt over very low heat. Add rosemary and onions. Sprinkle both sides of chicken with salt and pepper and brown 3 minutes on each side. Separate crescent rolls into 8 triangles. Place 4 triangles on a 12x15-inch cookie sheet. Place chicken breast on each triangle and cover with a second triangle, stretching the dough to cover. Seal pastry edges and trim away any excess dough. The extra dough can be used to decorate pastry tops. Brush generously with egg. Bake 15 minutes at 375°F or until golden. Prepare sauce by adding the flour to the pan drippings. Stir over medium heat until bubbly; reduce heat and add wine, reserved mushroom juice and cream. Whisk until smooth. Stir in mushrooms. Serve sauce on the side with chicken pastries.

Caroline Larson (Mrs. Ronald)

CHICKEN BREASTS IN PHYLLO

Great for entertaining because you can make ahead and freeze.

24 chicken breast halves,
   skinned and boned
salt to taste
pepper to taste
24 sheets phyllo dough
1 ⅓ cups butter, melted
⅓ cup Parmesan cheese, grated

Sauce:
1 ½ cups mayonnaise
1 cup green onion, chopped
⅓ cup lemon juice
2 cloves garlic, minced
2 tsp. dried tarragon

Yield: 12 servings

Combine sauce ingredients. Lightly sprinkle chicken pieces with salt and pepper. Place a sheet of dough on working surface; brush with butter. Spread 1½ tablespoon sauce on each side of chicken breast or 3 tablespoons per breast. Place a breast in one corner of dough sheet. Fold corner over chicken, then fold sides over and roll breast up in the dough to form a package. Place in an ungreased 9x13-inch baking pan. Repeat this process with remaining chicken breasts and dough. Brush pastry packages with remaining melted butter and sprinkle with Parmesan cheese. At this point the casserole can be covered and frozen. Thaw completely before baking. Bake 20 to 25 minutes at 375°F or until golden.

Mary Kenagy (Mrs. Dean)

LEMON-MARINATED CHICKEN

Our testers recommended adding the lemon peel in this stir fry.

4 chicken breast halves,
  skinned and boned
⅓ cup water
¼ cup lemon juice
½ tsp. lemon peel,
  finely shredded (optional)
2 Tbsp. honey
2 Tbsp. soy sauce
1 clove garlic, minced
¼ tsp. pepper
1 Tbsp. cornstarch
1 Tbsp. vegetable oil
3 medium carrots, roll-cut
5 green onions,
  bias sliced 1-inch pieces
1 cup cashews
cooked rice

Yield: 4 servings

Cut chicken into 1-inch pieces. Combine water, lemon juice, lemon peel, honey, soy sauce, garlic and pepper. Add chicken; cover and marinate at room temperature 30 minutes or in the refrigerator 2 hours stirring occasionally. Drain chicken; reserve marinade. Add water to the marinade to make 1 cup liquid. Stir in cornstarch; set aside. Precook carrots in a small amount of water 3½ minutes; drain and set aside. Preheat wok or skillet over high heat; add oil. Stir-fry carrots 1 ½ minutes; add green onions and stir-fry 1 ½ minutes or until crisp-tender. Remove vegetables from wok. Add half the chicken and stir-fry 3 minutes; remove. Stir-fry remaining chicken 3 minutes. Return all chicken to the wok; push to the edges. Stir marinade mixture; add to the center of the wok and stir until thickened and bubbly. Cook and stir 1 minute more. Add vegetables and stir; cook 1 more minute. Stir in cashews. Serve over rice.

Deb Keefe (Mrs. Kevin)

120

MEXICAN CHICKEN CASSEROLE

2 (10 ¾ oz.) cans cream of
chicken soup, undiluted
2 (10 ¾ oz.) cans cream of
mushroom soup, undiluted
1 cup milk
1 ½ cups (¾ lb.) Cheddar cheese,
grated
1 small onion, chopped
6 chicken breast halves, skinned,
boned, cooked,
cut into 1-inch pieces
1 or 2 (4 oz.) cans chopped
green chilies
8 (10-inch) flour tortillas,
cut into strips, divided

Yield: 6-8 servings

Combine soups, milk, cheese and onion to make a sauce. In a 9x13-inch baking pan, layer one-half of the chicken, one-half of the chilies and one-third of the sauce. Spread one-half of the tortilla strips over the top. Repeat layering. Pour the remaining one-third sauce over all. This can be refrigerated after assembling and baked later. Bake 1 hour at 350°F.

Caroline Larson (Mrs. Ronald)

CHICKEN ENCHILADAS SUPREME

2 cups chicken, cooked and cubed
1 (4 oz.) can chopped green chilies
1 (7 oz.) can green chili salsa
½ tsp. salt
2 cups heavy cream
cooking oil
12 (6-inch) corn tortillas
1 ½ cups (6 oz.) Monterey Jack
cheese, grated

Yield: 6 servings

Combine chicken, green chilies and salsa; mix well. Mix salt and cream in a pan. Heat ½-inch oil in a small skillet. Dip each tortilla into hot oil for about 5 seconds, just to soften. Drain on paper towels. Dip each fried tortilla into the cream coating each side. Fill with chicken mixture; roll up and place in an ungreased 9x13-inch baking pan. Pour remaining cream over the enchiladas; sprinkle with cheese. Bake uncovered 20 to 25 minutes at 350°F.

Marty Nordmann (Mrs. Brian)

CHALUPAS

2 (10 ¾ oz.) cans cream of
 mushroom soup, undiluted
1 (4 oz.) can chopped green chilies
4-5 green onions, chopped
2 cups dairy sour cream, divided
3 cups (¾ lb.) Cheddar cheese,
 grated, divided
3 cups (¾ lb.) Monterey Jack cheese,
 grated, divided
1 (3 ½ oz.) can black olives,
 drained and sliced
5 cups chicken, cooked and cubed
12 (8-inch) flour tortillas
½ cup milk
paprika
salsa

Yield: 6 servings

Combine 1 can soup, chilies, onions, 1 cup sour cream, 1½ cups of each cheese and olives. Mix well; stir in chicken. Divide this mixture evenly between the 12 tortillas; roll up and place seam side down in a greased 9x13-inch baking pan. Combine remaining can of soup, sour cream and cheeses with the milk and pour over the top. Sprinkle with paprika. Cover with plastic wrap and refrigerate overnight or freeze. Thaw frozen casserole before baking. Bake 45 minutes at 350°F. Serve with salsa.

Pat Latham

TURKEY LASAGNA

1 lb. ground turkey
1 medium onion, chopped
1 (14 ½ oz.) can stewed tomatoes
1 cup water
1 tsp. basil
2-3 tsp. parsley flakes
1 (6 oz.) can tomato paste
8 oz. lasagna noodles, uncooked
2 cups (8 oz.) mozzarella cheese,
 grated

Cheese Filling:
2 ⅔ cups lowfat cottage cheese
1 Tbsp. parsley flakes
½ cup Parmesan cheese, grated
1 Tbsp. oregano

Yield: 8 servings

Brown turkey and chopped onion together; drain. Add tomatoes, water, basil, parsley flakes and tomato paste. Mix and set aside. To make cheese filling, combine cottage cheese, parsley flakes, Parmesan cheese and oregano. Lightly grease a 9x13-inch baking pan. Layer one-half meat sauce, one-half uncooked noodles, entire cheese filling, remaining uncooked noodles, and remaining meat sauce. Top with mozzarella cheese. Cover with aluminum foil and bake 30 minutes at 350°F; uncover and continue baking an additional 30 minutes.

Pat Johnson (Mrs. Craig)

TEX-MEX TURKEY ENCHILADAS

1 ½ cups cooked turkey,
    shredded or cubed
1 cup picante sauce, divided
1 (3 oz.) pkg. cream cheese
½ cup green onions, sliced
¾ tsp. ground cumin
¼ tsp. oregano leaves, crushed
1 ½ cups (6 oz.) Monterey Jack
    cheese, grated, divided
8 (6-inch) flour tortillas
1 cup shredded lettuce
½ cup radish slices
¼ cup ripe olive slices

Yield: 4 servings

Combine turkey, ¼ cup picante sauce, cream cheese, green onion, cumin and oregano in a skillet. Cook over low heat until cheese melts; stirring constantly. Stir in ½ cup Monterey Jack cheese. Spoon ⅓ cup turkey mixture into each tortilla, roll up and place seam side down in a lightly greased 9x13-inch baking pan. Spoon remaining picante sauce over the enchiladas; sprinkle with remaining cheese. Bake 15 minutes at 350°F. Garnish with lettuce, radishes and olives. Serve with additional picante sauce.

Donna Roasa (Mrs. Darryn)

STIR-FRY TURKEY FAJITAS
A colorful, flavorful, and low-fat Mexican dish.

4 (10-inch) flour tortillas
¼ cup soy sauce
2 Tbsp. sugar
2 Tbsp. lemon juice
1 Tbsp. cornstarch
¼ tsp. crushed red pepper
1 medium onion, chopped
3 medium green, red, or sweet
    yellow peppers, cut into strips
3 cloves garlic, minced
2 Tbsp. vegetable oil
12 oz. turkey breast meat, skinned,
    boned, and cut into thin strips

Yield: 4 servings

Wrap tortillas in aluminum foil and warm for 5 minutes in a 300°F oven . Combine soy sauce, sugar, lemon juice, cornstarch and crushed red pepper; set aside. Spray wok or skillet with non-stick vegetable spray. Stir-fry onion, peppers and garlic over medium heat 3 to 4 minutes. Remove and set aside. Add oil to the wok; stir-fry turkey over medium to high heat 3 to 4 minutes. Add soy sauce mixture; cook and stir until bubbly. Return vegetables to wok; heat through. Spoon into tortillas; roll up and serve immediately.

Abby Kersbergen (Mrs. Dan)
123

MICROWAVE CHOP SUEY

1 ½ lb. 85% lean ground turkey
    or beef
1 cup onion, chopped
2 cups celery, chopped
1 cup boiling water
2 tsp. beef-flavored bouillon granules
2 Tbsp. soy sauce
3 Tbsp. molasses
4 Tbsp. flour
½ cup cold water
cooked rice or chow mein noodles

Yield: 4-6 servings

In a 2-quart casserole microcook turkey, onion and celery on high 5 to 6 minutes stirring 2 or 3 times to break up the meat; drain grease. Dissolve bouillon in boiling water. Add molasses and soy sauce; stir well. Pour into the meat mixture. Combine flour and cold water; stir into meat mixture. Microcook on high uncovered 3 to 5 minutes until thickened. Serve over rice or chow mein noodles.

Barbara Headley (Mrs. Michael)

EASY FIXIN' PHEASANT

6 pheasant or chicken breast
    and thigh fillets
bacon drippings from 1 lb. bacon
1 cup seasoned bread crumbs
⅔ cup parsley flakes
2 cups Parmesan cheese, grated
white wine, champagne or beer

Yield: 6 servings

Preheat oven to 350°F. Wash and pat fillets dry. Fry bacon over low heat; remove from pan and set aside. Bacon will not be used in this recipe. Combine bread crumbs, parsley flakes and cheese in a large bowl. Quick fry the fillets in the hot bacon drippings. Dredge each piece in the bread crumb mixture and place in a 9x13-inch baking pan. After all the pieces have been fried, combine remaining bacon drippings with remaining crumbs and spread over the fillets. Add about ½-inch wine to the baking pan—drink the extra! Cover and bake 45 to 60 minutes.

Carroll McInroy (Mrs. Daniel)

PHEASANT PARMIGIANA

A very moist and tender dish with a wonderful sauce.

4 Tbsp. olive oil
2 cloves garlic
6 pheasant or chicken breast fillets
4 eggs, lightly beaten
¾ cup seasoned bread crumbs
6 slices mozzarella cheese

Sauce:
2 cups heavy cream
⅓ cup Parmesan cheese, grated
¼ cup parsley flakes
cooked fettuccine or rice

Heat oil in a skillet over medium heat with garlic cloves. Dry fillets, then dip in eggs and dredge in bread crumbs. Fry over medium heat 3 to 4 minutes per side. Place in a 9x13-inch baking pan with a slice of cheese over each fillet. Heat cream slowly; add the Parmesan cheese and parsley flakes. Pour sauce over fillets and bake 35 to 45 minutes at 375°F or until golden brown. Serve over fettuccine noodles or rice.

Yield: 6 servings

Carroll McInroy (Mrs. Daniel)

BAKED PHEASANT UNDER GLASS

This is a recipe Paul remembers watching his father prepare after spending a day hunting in northern Iowa.

2 pheasant breast fillets
½ cup flour
1 ½ tsp. seasoned salt
2 Tbsp. butter or vegetable oil
½ cup half and half

Pat pheasant until dry. Combine flour and seasoned salt; dredge fillets. Brown lightly in butter. Pour half and half into a 2-quart casserole; place fillets on top. Bake covered 1 hour and 15 minutes at 375°F.

Yield: 4 servings

Carrie Barr (Mrs. Paul)

CREAMED PHEASANT

1 whole pheasant breast
2 Tbsp. green pepper, chopped
¼ cup onion, chopped
2 Tbsp. butter
1 (10 ¾ oz.) can cream of
    mushroom soup, undiluted
⅓ cup milk
3 Tbsp. pimento, diced
⅛ tsp. pepper
cooked rice

Yield: 4 servings

Gently boil pheasant in water about 2 hours. Set aside. In a 2 ½-quart Dutch oven saute green pepper and onion in butter until tender. Stir in soup and milk. Cube pheasant; add to the soup mixture. Add pimento and pepper. Bring to a light boil. Serve over rice.

Dotty Goodman

OLD SCOTSMAN'S PHEASANT

¼ cup butter
¼ cup dry shallots
2 cloves garlic, minced
2 tsp. paprika
6 pheasant or chicken breast
    or thigh fillets
1 tsp. salt
pepper to taste
1 ½ cups broccoli,
    coarsely chopped
2 medium carrots, shredded
2 (2 oz.) jars pimento strips,
    drained
8-10 fresh mushrooms, sliced
1 cup dairy sour cream
⅓ cup mayonnaise or
    cream of celery soup, undiluted
⅓ cup Parmesan cheese, grated
⅓ cup cashews

Yield: 6 servings

Melt butter in a large skillet, add shallots and garlic. Saute 3 minutes. Stir in paprika. Sprinkle fillets with salt and pepper and quick sear in the skillet. In a separate pan, steam broccoli and carrots. Place vegetables and pheasant in a 3-quart casserole. Sprinkle with pimento and mushrooms. Combine sour cream and mayonnaise; spoon over meat and vegetables. Sprinkle with cheese and cashews. Bake 45 to 60 minutes at 350°F.

Carroll McInroy (Mrs. Daniel)

93803

BROCCOLI-HAM CASSEROLE

1 (10 oz.) pkg. frozen chopped
   broccoli or equivalent
   fresh broccoli
1 cup baked ham, chopped
1 Tbsp. parsley, chopped
2 Tbsp. green pepper, chopped
2 hard-cooked eggs, chopped
4 tsp. lemon juice
1 Tbsp. onion, chopped
1/4 cup American cheese, grated
3 Tbsp. butter or margarine
3 Tbsp. flour
1/2 tsp. salt
1 1/2 cups milk
1/2 cup buttered bread crumbs

Yield: 6 servings

Cook broccoli until barely tender. Drain and place in buttered 1 1/2-quart casserole. Combine ham, parsley, green pepper, eggs, lemon juice, onion and cheese; spoon mixture over broccoli. Melt butter in saucepan; stir in flour and salt and heat to bubbling. Remove from heat and stir in milk. Heat again until bubbling and cook 1 minute; pour sauce over the broccoli-ham mixture. Sprinkle with buttered crumbs. Bake 15 to 20 minutes at 350°F until bubbly. May be prepared ahead and refrigerated or frozen. Thaw before baking.

Dorothy Apgar (Mrs. Patton)

APRICOT GLAZED HAM

4 lb. ham, fully cooked
4 Tbsp. butter or margarine
1/2 cup apricot preserves
1/2 cup mustard
4 Tbsp. brown sugar

Yield: 12-16 servings

Bake ham 1 hour at 350°F. Melt butter; stir in apricot preserves, mustard and brown sugar. Brush ham generously with apricot glaze; bake 30 minutes longer, basting occasionally with glaze. Slice ham. Heat remaining glaze and serve as a sauce.

Marilyn Downs (Mrs. Jim)

PARTY HAM CASEROLE

2 cups (4 oz.) noodles
1 (10 ¾ oz.) can cream of
    mushroom soup, undiluted
½ cup milk
1 tsp. instant minced onion
2 tsp. mustard
1 cup dairy sour cream
2 cups cooked ham,
    cut in 1 inch slivers
¼ cup dry bread crumbs
1 ½ Tbsp. butter or margarine,
    melted
1 Tbsp. Parmesan cheese, grated

Yield: 6 servings

Preheat oven to 325°F. Cook the noodles per package directions. Combine soup and milk in a small saucepan, stirring until smooth. Add onion, mustard and sour cream, stirring until blended. Layer one-half of the noodles, one-half of the ham and one-half of the sauce in a greased 1½-quart casserole. Repeat layers. Toss bread crumbs with butter; sprinkle over casserole. Top with Parmesan cheese. Bake uncovered 25 minutes or until golden brown.

Julie Schlesinger (Mrs. Michael)

PORK TENDERLOIN DIANE

1 lb. pork tenderloin
2 tsp. lemon pepper
2 Tbsp. butter
2 Tbsp. lemon juice
1 Tbsp. Worcestershire sauce
1 tsp. Dijon-style mustard
1 Tbsp. parsley or chives, minced

Yield: 4 servings

Slice pork tenderloin crosswise into 8 slices; press each to 1-inch thick. Sprinkle surfaces with lemon pepper. Heat butter in heavy skillet. Cook tenderloin medallions 3 to 4 minutes per side. Remove to serving platter and keep warm. Add lemon juice, Worcestershire and mustard to pan juices in skillet. Cook, stirring until heated through. Pour sauce over medallions; sprinkle with parsley or chives.

Jayne Hager Dee (Mrs. Eric)
Fran Hermanson (Mrs. Paul)

ORANGE-GLAZED PORK TENDERLOINS

8 (¼-inch thick) slices
    pork tenderloin cutlets
freshly ground pepper
¼ tsp. garlic powder
2 Tbsp. Worcestershire sauce
4 Tbsp. orange juice concentrate,
    thawed
4 green onions, sliced
fresh orange slices

Yield: 4 servings

Spray a heavy non-stick skillet with non-stick vegetable spray. Brown pork over medium heat; sprinkle with pepper and garlic powder. Cover and continue to cook over low heat 10 minutes. Combine Worcestershire and orange juice. Pour over meat; add green onions and cook over low heat 3 more minutes. Garnish with fresh orange slices.

Abby Kersbergen (Mrs. Dan)

PORK AND APPLE SAUTE

1 lb. pork tenderloin
    (can substitute pork cutlet)
¼ tsp. salt
¼ tsp. pepper
½ tsp. ground sage
½ tsp. thyme
½ tsp. ground cinnamon
½ tsp. ground ginger
3 Tbsp. shallot or onion, minced
2 medium cooking apples,
    cored and sliced
½ cup apple cider
non-stick vegetable spray
1 Tbsp. oil
cooked brown rice

Yield: 4 servings

Slice pork crosswise into 8 slices; flatten each with hand. Combine seasonings; coat both sides of each slice of meat with seasonings. Spray skillet with non-stick vegetable spray; saute pork on both sides until browned, 3 to 4 minutes. Remove meat from skillet. Pour oil in skillet; saute shallots and apple slices until golden, turning frequently. Add cider; boil, stirring frequently, until reduced to ¼ cup. Return pork to skillet. Simmer covered 5 to 7 minutes. Serve hot with brown rice.

Alicemary Borthwick (Mrs. Gordon)

129

MARINATED PORK LOIN

4 to 5 lb. pork loin, boneless
2 cups white wine
1 tsp. tarragon
½ cup onion, finely chopped
2 Tbsp. Dijon-style mustard
2 Tbsp. brown sugar
1 Tbsp. salt
1 clove garlic, minced

Yield: 10-12

Marinate pork loin in white wine, tarragon and onions overnight. Mix mustard, sugar and salt; rub on loin. Place loin in roasting pan with garlic. Cook uncovered 30 minutes at 350°F. Cover with foil and reduce temperature to 325°F. Bake 1 hour and 30 minutes to 1 hour and 45 mintes until internal temperature is 170°F.

Linda Bloom (Mrs. Michael)

TANGY GLAZED PORK LOIN

⅔ cup ketchup
½ cup orange marmalade
½ cup onion, chopped
¼ cup lemon juice
¼ cup soy sauce
½ tsp. marjoram
¼ tsp. pepper
3 ½ to 4 ½ lb. pork loin roast,
    boneless
salt
orange slices (optional)
green grapes (optional)

Yield: 8-10 servings

Combine ketchup, marmalade, onion, lemon juice, soy sauce, marjoram and pepper in saucepan; blend and heat through. Set aside. Place pork loin, fat side up, on rack in an open roasting pan. Rub with salt. Roast at 325°F until internal temperature reaches 170°F; about 30 to 40 minutes per pound. During the last 30 to 40 minutes of roasting time, brush with sauce at 10 to 15 minute intervals. Heat remaining sauce and serve with roast. Garnish with orange slices and green grapes for color.

Elaine Graeff (Mrs. Dan)

OLD FASHIONED PORK AND BEANS

2 to 3 lb. pork roast, boneless
1 (6 lb. 10 oz.) can pork and beans
1 (1 oz.) pkg. dry onion soup mix
1 (14 oz.) bottle ketchup
1 lb. brown sugar

Yield: 20 servings

Place pork roast in Dutch oven. Mix remaining ingredients and pour over roast. Cook uncovered 10 hours or overnight at 200°F. The next day, cut the pork into small pieces. This freezes well or half of the recipe works great in a slow cooker!

Julie Schlesinger (Mrs. Michael)

CREOLE PORK CHOPS

4 loin or center cut pork chops,
*   trimmed*
pepper
1 Tbsp. shortening or vegetable oil
⅓ cup ketchup
½ cup water
¼ tsp. salt
½ tsp. celery seed
3 Tbsp. cider vinegar
¼ tsp. ground ginger
1 tsp. sugar
1 tsp. flour

Yield: 4 servings

Sprinkle chops lightly with pepper. Brown chops on both sides in oil using a heavy skillet. Remove chops to 2-quart casserole. Combine remaining ingredients and pour over chops. Bake covered 1 hour and 30 minutes at 325°F. Turn chops after first hour of baking.

Barbara Headley (Mrs. Michael)

PORK CHOPS AND SOUR CREAM
Unique sauce makes these special!

4 loin pork chops
dried basil
1 chicken-flavor bouillon cube
½ cup boiling water
3 tsp. vinegar
salt to taste
1 ½ Tbsp. sugar
1 cup dairy sour cream
¼ cup water (optional)
1 T. flour (optional)

Yield: 4 servings

Brown chops and place in a 2-quart casserole. Sprinkle chops with basil. Dissolve bouillon cube in water in saucepan. Add vinegar, salt and sugar; then add sour cream. Pour sauce over chops. Bake uncovered 30 minutes at 350°F. Remove chops to platter. Skim fat from sauce. If sauce needs to be thickened, mix water and flour and blend into sauce. Pour sauce over meat when serving.

Ann Collison (Mrs. Mark)

PORK CHOP CASSEROLE

6 butterfly pork chops
vegetable oil
seasoned salt
pepper
1 medium onion, sliced
4-5 medium potatoes,
  pared and thinly sliced
1 (10 ¾ oz.) can cheddar cheese
  soup, undiluted

Yield: 6 servings

Brown chops in small amount of oil in skillet. Place chops in a 9x13-inch baking dish, and sprinkle with seasoned salt and pepper. Cover with sliced onion and potatoes; top with soup. Cover with foil. Bake 1 hour and 15 minutes at 350°F or until potatoes are tender.

Deb Keefe (Mrs. Kevin)

CHERRY GLAZE

A tangy addition to ham or pork roast!

1 cup cherry preserves
2 tsp. corn syrup
¼ cup red wine vinegar
¼ tsp. nutmeg
¼ tsp. cloves
¼ tsp. ginger

Combine ingredients and glaze roast for last 30 minutes of roasting.

Maureen Lyons (Mrs. Ken)

Yield: 1 ½ cups

BAKED CORNED BEEF WITH MUSTARD SAUCE

4 to 5 lb. packaged corned beef
1 or 2 cloves garlic
4 bay leaves

Sauce:
2 Tbsp. butter or margarine
⅓ cup brown sugar, firmly packed
1 Tbsp. mustard
⅓ cup ketchup
3 Tbsp. cider vinegar

Yield: 8-10 servings

Place corned beef in a large kettle; cover with cold water. Add garlic and bay leaves. Cover and bring to a boil. Reduce heat and let simmer 4 to 5 hours or until beef is tender. Drain meat; wrap and refrigerate. When ready to serve, slice meat and arrange in pan. Preheat oven to 350°F. Mix sauce ingredients in small saucepan; cook on medium heat only to blend. Pour over corned beef. Bake covered 30 minutes or until browned, basting occasionally.

Maureen Lewis (Mrs. Philip)

REUBEN CASSEROLE
A make ahead, 5 ingredient main dish!

10 slices rye bread, cubed
1 ½ lb. cooked corned beef
2 ½ cups (10 oz.) Swiss cheese,
  shredded
6 eggs, lightly beaten
3 cups milk
¼ tsp. pepper

Yield: 10 servings

Arrange bread cubes in greased 9x13-inch baking dish. Coarsely shred corned beef and layer over bread. Sprinkle with cheese. Combine eggs, milk and pepper. Pour over bread-beef mixture. Cover with foil; refrigerate overnight. Preheat oven to 350°F. Bake covered 45 minutes and uncovered 10 minutes until bubbly and puffed.

Barbara Beichley (Mrs. Duane)

MICROWAVE PIZZA CASSEROLE

1 lb. ground beef
½ cup onion, chopped
½ cup green pepper, chopped
1 (16 oz.) can pizza sauce
1 (4 oz.) can mushrooms, sliced
4 oz. pepperoni, sliced
2 cups uncooked noodles
1 ½ cups water
½ tsp dried oregano
½ tsp. garlic powder
½ tsp. crushed basil
¾ cup (3 oz.) mozzarella cheese,
  shredded

Yield: 6-8 servings

Microcook ground beef in 2-quart microproof casserole on high 3 minutes and 30 seconds. Stir and microcook 2 minutes and 30 seconds or until done. Drain thoroughly. Add remaining ingredients except cheese, mixing well. Microcook on high 17 minutes, stirring twice during cooking. Sprinkle cheese over casserole; microcook 1 minute on high until cheese melts.

Lorraine Schultz (Mrs. Ed)

134

DEEP DISH CHICAGO STYLE PIZZA

1 pkg. active dry yeast
1 cup warm water
3 to 3 ½ cups flour
⅓ cup olive oil
½ tsp. salt
1 lb. mozzarella cheese, sliced
½ lb. mild Italian sausage, cooked
1 (16 oz.) can peeled tomatoes,
*   crushed, undrained*
1 ½ tsp. dried oregano, crushed
1 tsp. dried basil, crushed
¼ cup onion, chopped
½ cup fresh mushrooms, sliced
*   (optional)*
16 slices pepperoni (optional)
black olives (optional)
Parmesan cheese, grated

Yield: 4-6 servings

In large mixer bowl, sprinkle yeast into warm water and stir until dissolved. Stir in 1½ cups flour, ⅓ cup olive oil and salt. Beat at low speed 30 seconds, scraping bowl constantly. Beat 2 minutes at high speed. Stir in as much of remaining flour as needed to form a soft dough. Cover and let rise in warm place until double. Punch down. Let rest 5 minutes. Generously brush 10x2-inch round deep dish pizza pan (or 12x2-inch) with olive oil. With oiled hands, turn dough into pizza pan and spread evenly over bottom and partially up sides of pan. Cover and let rise until nearly double, 30 minutes. Arrange cheese slices in ¼-inch thick layer on dough. Press crumbled Italian sausage onto cheese. Place crushed tomatoes over sausage, sprinkle with herbs, onion and other desired toppings. Sprinkle with Parmesan cheese. Preheat oven to 500°F and bake 25 to 30 minutes until edges of crust are crisp and golden brown. Let stand 5 to 10 minutes before cutting.

Sherry McCune (Mrs. Mike)

THREE CHEESE ENCHILADAS

1 ½ cups (6 oz.) Monterey Jack
   cheese, shredded, divided
1 ½ cups (6 oz.) Cheddar cheese,
   shredded, divided
1 (3 oz.) pkg. cream cheese, softened
1 cup picante sauce, divided
1 medium red or green pepper, diced
½ cup green onion, sliced
1 tsp. crushed cumin
8 (8-inch) flour tortillas
lettuce, shredded
tomato, chopped
black olives, sliced

Yield: 4 servings

Combine 1 cup Monterey Jack cheese, 1 cup Cheddar cheese, cream cheese, ¼ cup picante sauce, red pepper, onion and cumin; mix well. Spoon ¼ cup cheese mixture down the center of each tortilla. Roll and place seam side down in a lightly greased 9x13-inch baking dish. Spoon remaining ¾ cup picante sauce evenly over enchiladas. Cover with remaining ¾ cup Monterey Jack and ¾ cup Cheddar cheeses. Bake 20 minutes at 350°F. Top with lettuce, tomato and black olives. Serve with additional picante sauce.

Abby Kersbergen (Mrs. Dan)

SANTE FE ENCHILADAS

1 lb. ground beef
½ cup onion, diced
1 (10 oz.) can enchilada sauce
1 (15 oz.) can chili without beans
10 (8-inch) flour tortillas
1 to 1 ½ lb. Colby cheese, sliced

Yield: 5-6 servings

Crumble meat in a large mixing bowl and microcook on high 6 to 8 minutes or until meat loses pink color; drain. Add enchilada sauce and chili to meat and microcook on high 3 minutes. Wrap tortillas in paper towels and microcook on high 1 to 2 minutes or until soft. Spoon 2 tablespoons of meat mixture on each tortilla add 1 slice of cheese. Roll and place seam side down in greased 9x13-inch baking dish. Pour any remaining meat mixture over tortillas and top with remaining cheese slices. Microcook on high 5 minutes, turn. Cover with plastic wrap; microcook on high an additional 5 minutes. Let stand covered 5 minutes before serving.

Barbara Beichley (Mrs. Duane)

CHIMICHANGAS

2 lb. lean round steak or stew meat,
    small cubes
1 ½ cups water
2 cloves garlic, minced
2 Tbsp. chili powder
1 Tbsp. vinegar
2 tsp. dried oregano, crushed
1 tsp. salt
1 tsp. ground cumin
⅛ tsp. pepper
1 ½ Tbsp. cornstarch
1 (14 ½ oz.) can beef broth
8 (10-inch) flour tortillas
oil
taco sauce

Garnishes:
lettuce, shredded
dairy sour cream
Cheddar cheese, shredded
green onion, sliced
tomato, chopped
guacamole
black olives

Yield: 8 servings

Combine meat with water, garlic, chili powder, vinegar, oregano, salt, cumin and pepper in medium saucepan. Bring to boiling. Cover, reduce heat and simmer about 2 hours or until meat is very tender. Uncover and boil rapidly until about ½ cup of liquid remains. Remove from heat. Remove meat to platter and using two forks shred meat coarsely. Mix cornstarch and beef broth; add to liquid in saucepan. Heat until sauce thickens, stirring frequently. Keep warm. Wrap stack of tortillas in aluminum foil; heat 15 minutes at 350°F. Spoon about ¼ to ½ cup meat near one edge of each tortilla. Drizzle on a small amount of taco sauce. Fold edge nearest filling over until meat is just covered. Fold in two ends, then roll up rest of the way. Fasten with a toothpick, if needed. In heavy skillet, fry filled tortillas in ½-inch oil about 1 minute on each side or until golden brown. Drain on paper towels. Keep warm in 300°F oven while frying remaining chimichangas. Serve on a bed of shredded lettuce. Spoon on warmed gravy mixture. Garnish with desired condiments.

Deb Keefe (Mrs. Kevin)

TOSTADO CASSEROLE

1 lb. ground beef
1 (15 oz.) can tomato sauce, divided
1 (1.25 oz.) envelope taco seasoning
3 cups corn chips, divided
1 (15 ½ oz.) can refried beans
1 cup (4 oz.) Cheddar cheese,
   shredded

Yield: 6 servings

Brown ground beef; drain. Add 1 ½ cups of the tomato sauce and the taco seasoning; mix well. Line bottom of a 11x7-inch baking dish with 2 cups corn chips. Crush remaining corn chips, set aside. Spoon meat mixture over corn chips in baking dish. Combine remaining ½ cup tomato sauce with refried beans; spread evenly over meat mixture. Bake 25 minutes at 375°F. Sprinkle with Cheddar cheese and crushed corn chips. Bake additional 5 minutes or until cheese melts.

Mary Holmer (Mrs. Tom)

QUICK LASAGNA
"Working Mom's dream!"

1 lb. ground beef
1 (32 oz.) jar spaghetti sauce
1 (16 oz.) container cottage cheese
1 egg
½ tsp. dried parsley
½ tsp. salt
⅛ tsp. pepper
1 (8 oz.) pkg. lasagna noodles,
   divided
12 oz. mozzarella cheese, sliced,
   divided
½ cup water
½ cup Parmesan cheese, grated
dried parsley

Yield: 10 servings

Brown the ground beef; drain. Add spaghetti sauce and set aside. Combine cottage cheese, egg, ½ teaspoon parsley, salt and pepper. Layer one-half of uncooked noodles in a greased 9x13-inch baking dish, one-half of cottage cheese mixture, one-half of meat mixture, and one-half of mozzarella cheese slices. Repeat layers ending with mozzarella cheese. Pour ½ cup water over all and sprinkle with Parmesan cheese and parsley to taste. Bake 1 hour at 350°F.

Joan Boyce (Mrs. Steven)

LOBSTER-STUFFED TENDERLOIN OF BEEF

3 to 4 lb. whole beef tenderloin
2 (4 oz.) frozen lobster tails
1 Tbsp. margarine, melted
1 ½ tsp. lemon juice
6 slices bacon, partially cooked

Wine Sauce:
½ cup green onion, sliced
½ cup butter or margarine
½ cup dry white wine
⅛ tsp. garlic salt

Yield: 8 servings

Cut beef tenderloin lengthwise to within ½-inch of bottom to butterfly. Place frozen lobster tails in boiling salted water to cover. Return to boiling; reduce heat and simmer 5 to 6 minutes. Carefully remove lobster from shells. Cut in half lengthwise. Place lobster end-to-end inside beef. Combine butter and lemon juice; drizzle on lobster. Close meat around lobster; tie roast together securely with string at 1-inch intervals. Place on rack in shallow roasting pan. Roast 45 to 50 minutes at 425°F for rare. Lay bacon slice on top; roast additional 5 minutes. In saucepan, cook green onion in butter over low heat until tender, stirring frequently. Add wine and garlic salt; heat through. To serve, slice roast; spoon on wine sauce.

Cindy Mack (Mrs. Thomas)

PEPPERED BEEF TENDERLOIN
Serve tenderloin cold with a choice of two different sauces.

**1 ½ to 2 lb. beef tenderloin,
   trimmed and tied
1 Tbsp. pepper, coarsely ground
salt
3 Tbsp. vegetable oil**

**Tarragon Caper Sauce:
1 egg yolk
2 Tbsp. heavy cream
2 Tbsp. white-wine vinegar
1 tsp. Worcestershire sauce
1 ½ tsp. Dijon-style mustard
½ cup olive oil
1 ½ tsp. fresh tarragon, minced
1 Tbsp. capers, drained
2 Tbsp. scallions, minced
2 Tbsp. fresh parsley leaves, minced
salt**

**Jellied Horseradish Cream:
2 (¼ oz.) envelopes unflavored
   gelatin
¼ cup cold water
4 ½ cups dairy sour cream, divided
6-10 Tbsp. bottled horseradish
salt
6 Tbsp. fresh parsley, minced
watercress sprigs (optional)**

Yield: 4-6 servings

Pat tenderloin dry and coat with pepper. Sprinkle with salt. In a roasting pan just large enough to hold tenderloin, heat oil over high heat until hot, but not smoking. Brown tenderloin on all sides. Roast the tenderloin in the pan in preheated 500°F oven 15 to 20 minutes or until meat thermometer reads 130°F for medium rare. Let cool to room temperature. This may be roasted 2 days in advance, kept well wrapped and chilled.

Tarragon caper sauce: in a blender or food processor blend the yolk, cream, vinegar, Worcestershire and mustard. Let the blender run and add the oil in a stream; blend the mixture until it is emulsified. Transfer the mixture to a small bowl and stir in the tarragon, capers, scallion, parsley and salt to taste. The sauce may be made 1 day in advance and kept covered and chilled. Slice the tenderloin crosswise ⅓-inch thick, arrange it on a platter and spoon some of the sauce over the meat. Serve remaining sauce separately.

Jellied horseradish cream: line three empty 12 oz. juice cans with small plastic bags. Sprinkle gelatin over cold water in a small saucepan and let soften 10 minutes. In a bowl, stir sour cream, parsley, horseradish and salt to taste. Add 1 cup sour cream to gelatin mixture and heat over moderately low heat, stirring until gelatin is melted. Add mixture to remaining sour cream mixture. Stir well and spoon into the lined cans. Chill covered overnight. The horseradish cream may be made two days in advance and kept covered and chilled. To remove cream, pull plastic bags from cans; peel bags off gently and slice thin. Slice tenderloin crosswise about ⅓-inch thick. Arrange on a platter with alternating slices of horseradish cream. Garnish with watercress sprigs.

Carrie Barr (Mrs. Paul)
Diane McComber (Mrs. Larry)

BEEF AND SPINACH ROLL

1 lb. beef round steak,
**   cut ½-inch thick**
2 Tbsp. margarine, softened
1 small clove garlic, minced
1 egg, beaten
3 cups (4 oz.) spinach,
**   finely chopped**
⅓ cup herb-seasoned stuffing mix
salt to taste
pepper to taste
assorted mustards
French bread, thinly sliced

Yield: 12 servings

Trim meat. Pound meat to ¼-inch thick; about a 12x8-inch rectangle. Combine margarine and garlic; spread over meat. Combine egg, spinach, and stuffing mix. Spoon evenly over beef. Roll up jelly-roll style, beginning from long side. Tie roll in several places if necessary. Place meat roll, seam side down, on rack in shallow roasting pan. Rub salt and pepper into meat. Roast uncovered 25 minutes at 400° for medium. Cool. Wrap and refrigerate several hours or overnight. Cut into ½-inch slices. Serve with mustard and French bread.

Nancy Veldey (Mrs. John)

141

SLOW COOKER ITALIAN SAUSAGE

3 lb. mild Italian link sausage
1 large onion, sliced
1 large green pepper, sliced
1 (48 oz.) jar spaghetti sauce
cooked noodles or spaghetti

Yield: 4-6 servings

Pre-cook sausage in boiling water for 10 minutes. Drain. Place sausage in slow cooker; arrange onion and pepper slices on top. Pour spaghetti sauce over all. Cover; cook on low 6 to 8 hours. Serve over cooked noodles or spaghetti.

Barbara Beichley (Mrs. Duane)

TRADER'S PIE
Loaded with beef and broccoli!

pastry for 2 crust 9-inch pie pan
1 lb. ground beef
¼ cup onion, chopped
1 (10 oz.) pkg. frozen
    chopped broccoli
1 ¼ cups milk
1 (3 oz.) pkg. cream cheese
2 Tbsp. flour
¾ tsp. salt
¼ tsp. garlic salt
1 egg, beaten
4 oz. Monterey Jack cheese, sliced
1 Tbsp. milk

Yield: 6-8 servings

Prepare your favorite pie crust recipe and set aside. Brown beef and onion; drain and set aside. Cook broccoli according to package directions; drain and set aside. Combine milk, cream cheese, flour and salt and garlic salt in a saucepan. Cook and stir over medium heat until smooth. Add a little hot mixture to egg; stir; return egg to hot mixture. Let thicken. Add beef, onion and broccoli. Pour into 9-inch pie shell; top with cheese slices. Cover with crust; seal and flute. Prick top of pie with fork. Brush crust with milk. Cover edge of crust with 2 to 3-inch strip of aluminum foil to prevent browning; remove aluminum foil last 15 minutes of baking. Bake 40 minutes at 350°F. Cool 15 minutes.

Marty Nordmann (Mrs. Brian)

WAIKIKI MEATBALLS

Can make smaller balls for appetizers.

1 ½ lb. ground beef
⅔ cup cracker crumbs
⅓ cup onion, minced
1 egg
¼ cup milk
1 ½ tsp. salt
¼ tsp. ginger
1 Tbsp. shortening
2 Tbsp. cornstarch
½ cup brown sugar, firmly packed
1 (15 ¼ oz.) can pineapple tidbits
⅓ cup vinegar
1 Tbsp. soy sauce
⅓ cup green peppers, chopped
cooked rice

Yield: 6-8 servings

Mix beef, crumbs, onion, egg, milk, salt and ginger thoroughly. Shape mixture by tablespoons into balls. Melt shortening in large skillet; brown and cook meatballs. Transfer to platter and keep warm. Drain skillet. Combine cornstarch and brown sugar in separate bowl. Drain pineapple, reserving juice. Add reserved pineapple juice, vinegar and soy sauce to cornstarch mixture; stir until smooth. Pour into skillet; cook over medium heat, stirring constantly until mixture thickens and boils; stir and boil 1 minute. Add meatballs, pineapple tidbits and green peppers. Heat through. Serve with rice.

Noel Lund (Mrs. Ted)

SICILIAN MEAT ROLL

2 eggs, beaten
¾ cup soft bread crumbs
½ cup tomato or
    cocktail vegetable juice
2 Tbsp. parsley
½ tsp. dried crushed oregano
¼ tsp. salt
¼ tsp. pepper
1 clove garlic, minced
2 lb. ground beef
8 thin slices boiled ham
1 ½ cups (6 oz.) mozzarella cheese,
    shredded
3 slices mozzarella cheese,
    halved diagonally

Yield: 8 servings

Combine eggs, bread crumbs, juice, parsley, oregano, salt, pepper, garlic and beef. Pat mixture into 10x12-inch rectangle on waxed paper or aluminum foil. Arrange ham slices on top leaving margin around edges. Sprinkle shredded cheese over ham. Carefully roll meat and seal edges. Place roll in 9x13-inch baking pan, seam side down. Bake 1 hour at 350°F. Center will be pink due to ham. Place cheese slices on top and bake 5 additional minutes or until cheese melts.

Donna Roasa (Mrs. Darryn)

143

HEARTY CHILI CON CARNE

5 slices bacon, chopped
1 lb. ground beef
1 medium onion, chopped
1 small green pepper, chopped
2 cloves garlic, minced
1 (28 oz.) can tomatoes,
 undrained, chopped
1 (10 ¾ oz.) can tomato soup,
 undiluted
1 (6 oz.) can tomato paste
1 (4 oz.) can chopped green chilies,
 undrained
1 cup water
3 tsp. chili powder
1 tsp. salt
½ tsp. ground cumin
½ tsp. crushed red pepper
¼ tsp. pepper
¼ tsp dried oregano leaves
1 (15 ½ oz.) can chili or
 kidney beans, undrained

Yield: 6-8 servings

Brown bacon, beef and onion in a large Dutch oven; drain. Add remaining ingredients, except beans. Cover; simmer over low heat 2 hours. Add beans and heat through.

Jayne Hager Dee (Mrs. Eric)

HAWAIIAN MEAT LOAF WITH PINEAPPLE SAUCE

Meat Loaf:
1 (8 oz.) can unsweetened
   crushed pineapple, undrained
2 lb. ground chuck
1 ½ cups soft bread crumbs
⅔ cup onion, chopped
2 Tbsp. soy sauce
¼ tsp. salt
¼ tsp. pepper
1 clove garlic, minced

Pineapple Sauce:
1 (8 oz.) can unsweetened
   crushed pineapple, undrained
½ cup green onion, thinly sliced
¼ cup plus 2 Tbsp. salt-free
   tomato paste
¼ cup reserved pineapple juice
2 Tbsp. soy sauce
2 Tbsp. white wine vinegar
1 Tbsp. brown sugar
¼ tsp gingerroot, peeled and grated

Yield: 8 servings

Drain pineapple, reserving ¼ cup juice for pineapple sauce. Combine drained pineapple and remaining ingredients in a large bowl; stir well. Press mixture into a loaf pan. Bake 45 minutes at 350°F. Or put into microproof 2-quart ring mold; cover with waxed paper. Microcook on high 14 minutes or until meat is no longer pink, rotating ring mold a quarter turn every 3 minutes. Let meat stand for 5 minutes. Drain; invert onto a wire rack. Blot with paper towels. Place on platter and keep warm. To prepare sauce, combine all ingredients in a 2-cup glass measure; stir well. Microcook on high 2 minutes or until thoroughly heated, stirring once. Serve warm with meat loaf.

Linda Bloom (Mrs. Michael)

SALISBURY STEAK AND MUSHROOM SAUCE

¾ cup bread crumbs
¼ cup beef broth
¾ cup onion, chopped
¼ cup green pepper, chopped
5 Tbsp. butter or margarine, divided
2 lb. ground beef
2 Tbsp. parsley
½ tsp. garlic salt
¼ tsp. hot pepper sauce
2 tsp. Worcestershire sauce

Mushroom Sauce:
1 pt. fresh mushrooms or
   1 (4 oz.) can, drained
2 Tbsp. butter or margarine
2 (10 ¾ oz.) cans golden mushroom
   soup, undiluted
¼ cup beef broth
1 cup half and half or milk
¼ tsp. hot pepper sauce

Yield: 8 servings

Soak bread crumbs in beef broth for 5 minutes. Saute onions and peppers in 2 tablespoons butter. Combine meat, onion and peppers. Mix soaked crumbs, parsley, garlic, hot pepper sauce and Worcestershire into meat. Mix thoroughly. Shape into 8 patties. Melt remaining butter in skillet; brown patties. Place in buttered 9x13-inch baking dish. To prepare sauce, saute mushrooms in butter. In separate bowl, combine soup, beef broth, cream and hot pepper sauce. Add to mushrooms and bring to boil, stirring frequently. Pour sauce over patties and bake 45 minutes at 350°F.

Donna Roasa (Mrs. Darryn)

146

CAVATINI

1 lb. ground beef
1 clove garlic, minced
1 medium onion, chopped
1 medium green pepper, chopped
1 (8 oz.) pkg. pepperoni, sliced
1 (4 oz.) can mushrooms,
*   sliced and drained*
1 (32 oz.) jar spaghetti sauce
4 oz. curly noodles,
*   cooked and drained*
4 oz. large shell macaroni,
*   cooked and drained*
2 cups (8 oz.) mozzarella cheese,
*   grated, divided*
Parmesan cheese, grated,
*   or bread crumbs*

Yield: 8-10 servings

Brown ground beef until crumbly. Stir in garlic, onion and green pepper. Cook, stirring frequently, until onion is soft; drain. Place meat mixture in large bowl. Stir in pepperoni, mushrooms and spaghetti sauce. In buttered 9x13-inch baking dish, place one-half the noodles and macaroni. Cover with one-half mozzarella cheese and one-half meat sauce. Repeat layers. Sprinkle Parmesan cheese or bread crumbs on top. Bake 40 minutes at 375° F or until bubbly. Let stand 10 minutes before serving.

Joy Banyas (Mrs. Thomas)
Joan Boyce (Mrs. Steven)

PANTRY CASSEROLE

A great family casserole.

1 lb. ground beef
⅓ cup onion, chopped
4 oz. thin or wide egg noodles
½ to 1 tsp. garlic powder to taste
⅛ tsp. pepper
1 tsp. salt-free seasoning
1 cup whole kernel corn, drained
1 (10 ¾ oz.) can tomato soup,
*   undiluted*
1 (8 oz.) can tomato sauce, divided
¾ cup Parmesan cheese,
*   grated, divided*

Yield: 6 servings

Brown onion and ground beef in a microproof casserole on high for 5 to 8 minutes or until meat is no longer pink. Stir twice while cooking. Drain. Cook noodles per package directions. Drain and set aside. To meat mixture, add seasonings, corn, tomato soup, ½ cup tomato sauce, ½ cup Parmesan cheese and cooked noodles. On top of casserole, place remaining ¼ cup Parmesan cheese around outer 1½-inch edge of casserole. Place remaining ½ cup tomato sauce in center. Bake 35 to 40 minutes at 375°F.

Barbara Headley (Mrs. Michael)
147

WILD RICE BARON

2 cups wild rice
4 cups water
4 tsp. salt, divided
2 lb. lean ground beef
1 lb. fresh mushrooms
½ cup celery, chopped
1 cup onion, chopped
½ cup margarine or butter
¼ cup soy sauce
2 cups dairy sour cream
¼ tsp. pepper
½ cup slivered almonds, divided

Yield: 12-16 servings

Combine rice, water and 2 teaspoons salt in a saucepan. Bring to a boil; reduce heat, cover and simmer for 45 minutes. Drain if necessary. Brown ground beef; drain. Rinse mushrooms, cut off tips of stems and slice. Saute mushrooms, onions and celery in butter for 5 minutes; set aside. Combine soy sauce, sour cream, pepper and remaining 2 teaspoons salt. Add wild rice, beef, mushroom mixture and almonds, reserving some almonds for garnish. Toss lightly; place in lightly greased 3-quart casserole. Bake uncovered 1 hour at 350°F. Stir several times. Garnish with almonds.

Arla Stegall (Mrs. Robert)

CLASSIC ITALIAN SPAGHETTI SAUCE

1 lb. Italian sausage
2 lb. ground beef
½ lb. mushrooms, sliced
2 medium onions, chopped
2 cloves garlic, minced
1 small green pepper, chopped
olive oil
3 (28 oz.) cans tomatoes, undrained
2 (6 oz.) cans tomato paste
2 cups Parmesan cheese, grated
2 tsp. Italian herb seasoning
2 tsp. sugar
1 tsp. salt
¾ tsp. pepper
1 cup parsley, chopped

Yield: 8 pints

Two hours before serving, cook sausage and ground beef in a 8-quart Dutch oven over medium-high heat. With slotted spoon, remove beef to bowl. Cook mushrooms, onions, garlic and green pepper in drippings in Dutch oven over medium heat until tender. Add olive oil, if necessary. Return meat to Dutch oven; add tomatoes, tomato paste, Parmesan cheese, Italian seasoning, sugar, salt, pepper and parsley. Heat to boiling on high, stirring to break up tomatoes. Reduce heat and simmer 30 minutes. One pint of sauce will serve 8 ounces of pasta. Freeze remaining sauce in pint-size containers.

Abby Kersbergen (Mrs. Dan)

CHEESE MEATBALLS WITH SPAGHETTI SAUCE

Sauce:
2 tsp. olive oil
½ cup onion, chopped
¼ cup green pepper, chopped
1 clove garlic, minced
2 (6 oz.) cans tomato paste
3 cups water
1 Tbsp. salt
¼ tsp. pepper
2 tsp. chili powder
¼ tsp. oregano
1 (12 oz.) can tomato sauce

Meatballs:
1 lb. ground chuck
½ lb. ground pork
1 cup Parmesan cheese, grated
1 cup milk
1 egg, beaten
1 cup soft bread crumbs
½ cup parsley, chopped
1 clove garlic, minced
1 tsp. salt
¼ tsp. pepper
½ tsp. oregano
vegetable oil

Yield: 8 servings

Heat oil in large Dutch oven. Add onion, green pepper and garlic; cook slowly until transparent. Blend in remaining sauce ingredients. Cover and simmer 30 minutes. Combine meatball ingredients, except vegetable oil. Shape mixture into 24 meatballs. Brown slowly in vegetable oil in large skillet and then place in hot cooked sauce; cover and simmer an additional 30 minutes.

Avy Tank (Mrs. William)

TOMATO MEAT SAUCE

¼ cup olive oil
2 medium carrots, pared, sliced thinly
2 medium onions, sliced thinly
3 Tbsp. green pepper, chopped
2 cloves garlic, crushed
8 anchovy filets (optional)
1 Tbsp. oregano
1 ¾ lb. ground round steak
2 (8 oz.) cans tomato sauce or
   1 cup sauce and
   1 cup canned tomatoes
2 Tbsp. Parmesan cheese, grated
salt
pepper

Saute carrots in oil until brown. Add onion, green pepper and garlic; continue cooking until soft. Add anchovies and oregano. Stir in meat, tomatoes and Parmesan cheese. Salt and pepper to taste. Simmer for 2 to 3 hours.

Hollis Cassidy (Mrs. Eugene)

Yield: 4-6 servings

MUSHROOM SPAGHETTI SAUCE

2 Tbsp. olive oil
1 lb. ground beef
1 lb. Italian sausage
1 large onion, chopped
½ cup green pepper, chopped
4 cloves garlic, minced
olive oil
1 lb. fresh mushrooms, sliced
1 (28 oz.) can tomatoes, chopped
3 (6 oz.) cans tomato paste
1 cup dry red wine
1 Tbsp. sugar
1 Tbsp. Worcestershire sauce
1 tsp. celery salt
2 bay leaves
salt to taste
pepper to taste
cooked pasta

Brown meats, onion, green pepper and garlic in olive oil; drain. Add remaining ingredients and simmer covered about 3 hours, stirring occasionally. Discard bay leaves. Serve hot over pasta.

Suzanne Brown (Mrs. Gregory)

Yield: 8 servings

Catch of the Day

LOW-CAL GOURMET FISH

2 lb. fillets of sole, cod, or flounder
2 Tbsp. prepared horseradish,
  drained
2 Tbsp. Dijon-style mustard
2 Tbsp. lemon juice
4 Tbsp. Parmesan cheese,
  grated, divided
⅓ cup plain yogurt
2 Tbsp. margarine, melted

Yield: 6 servings

Preheat broiler. Arrange fillets in a single layer in a foil-lined broiler pan. Combine horseradish, mustard, lemon juice, 3 tablespoons Parmesan cheese and yogurt in a small bowl. Add margarine, stir until smooth. Spread mixture over fillets in a thin layer. Sprinkle 1 tablespoon Parmesan cheese over top. Broil about 5 to 6 minutes until fish is just cooked through and sauce is bubbly and slightly glazed.

Jinita Boyd (Mrs. Douglas)

MONKFISH WITH GRAPES AND CASHEWS

1 lb. white fish fillets
  or orange roughy
3 Tbsp. margarine
¾ cup seedless grapes, halved
½ cup cashews
½ tsp. orange peel,
  finely shredded
3 Tbsp. orange juice

Yield: 4 servings

Cut fillets in 1-inch pieces. Heat margarine in large skillet; add fillets and fry over medium heat 4 to 6 minutes. Turn carefully. Gently transfer to heated platter. Cover to keep warm. In same skillet, add grapes, cashews, orange peel and orange juice. Cook and stir until heated through. Spoon over fish.

Donnis Grier (Mrs. Jack)

152

ORANGE ROUGHY AND RICE
Colorful and Good.

1 Tbsp. margarine, melted
1 tsp. lemon juice
1/8 tsp. salt
1/8 tsp. pepper
1 cup instant rice
3/4 cup water
1/2 tsp. chicken-flavor
    bouillon granules
1/4 tsp. fine herbs
2 small green, red or yellow
    peppers (or combination), diced
1/3 cup green onion, sliced
2 Tbsp. Parmesan cheese, grated
1 to 1 1/2 lb. orange roughy fillets

Yield: 4 servings

Combine all ingredients except fillets in small bowl. Spread mixture in 8-inch square baking dish. Arrange fillets on top. Bake covered 20 minutes at 350°F. Uncover and bake an additional 5 to 10 minutes.

Marcie Harvey (Mrs.Elwood)

PARMESAN ORANGE ROUGHY
Very attractive for entertaining.

2 lb. orange roughy fillets
    or other skinless white fish
2 Tbsp. fresh lemon juice
1/2 cup Parmesan cheese,
    freshly grated
4 Tbsp. margarine, softened
3 Tbsp. mayonnaise
3 Tbsp. green onions, chopped
1/4 tsp. salt
pepper, freshly ground to taste
1/8 tsp. hot pepper sauce

Yield: 4 servings

Preheat broiler. In a buttered 9x13-inch baking dish, place fillets in a single layer. Brush with lemon juice; let stand for 10 minutes. Combine remaining ingredients in a small bowl. Broil fillets 3 to 4 inches from broiler 5 minutes. Spread with cheese mixture and broil an additional 2 to 3 minutes. Watch closely so fish does not over-brown.

Sue Miller (Mrs. Lewis)

PORTUGUESE SOLE

¼ cup sliced almonds
3 Tbsp. butter, divided
¼ cup flour
½ tsp. salt
½ tsp.pepper
½ tsp. paprika
2 Tbsp. butter
2 large fillets of sole
½ cup dry white wine
2 Tbsp. lemon juice
2 Tbsp. brown sugar
½ tsp. ground ginger
1 banana, cut in quarters

Yield: 2 servings

Toast almonds in 1 tablespoon butter in small skillet; set aside. Combine flour, salt, pepper and paprika in small bowl. In medium skillet, melt 2 tablespoons butter over medium heat until hot. Dip fillets into flour mixture, then cook in skillet 2 to 3 minutes per side. Do not overcook. Remove fillets to heated platter and let skillet cool slightly. Add remaining ingredients to skillet. Simmer 2 minutes. Pour sauce over fillets and sprinkle with toasted almonds.

Nan Ryden (Mrs. Rex)

SALMON CROQUETTES
Great to make ahead, refrigerate and fry when ready.

1 (16 oz.) can salmon
1 large egg, lightly beaten
1 ½ cups crushed cracker crumbs, divided
cooking oil

Yield: 4 servings

Drain salmon and reserve the liquid. Discard skin and bones. Combine salmon, a little salmon liquid, egg and enough cracker crumbs to make mixture hold together. This should be moist; use reserved liquid as needed. Divide into 10 portions and roll into cylinders about 3-inches long. Roll in remaining cracker crumbs and fry in hot oil in large skillet 4 to 5 minutes, turning as they cook. Drain on paper towels.

Marty Nordmann (Mrs. Brian)

MICROWAVE SALMON LOAF

1 (16 oz.) can red salmon,
*   drained and flaked*
1 ½ cups whole wheat fresh
*   bread crumbs*
½ cup plain yogurt or
*   dairy sour cream*
¼ cup celery, chopped
½ cup onion, chopped
¼ cup chicken broth
2 eggs
1 tsp. Worcestershire sauce

Yield: 4-6 servings

Combine all ingredients in a bowl; mix well. Spray 8½x4½-inch glass loaf pan with non-stick vegetable spray. Spoon mixture into pan. Cover. Microcook on high 5 minutes. Rotate dish one-quarter turn. Microcook on medium 7 to 8 minutes.

Barbara Headley (Mrs. Michael)

SALMON QUICHE

1 (9 or 10-inch) unbaked pie shell
1 (16 oz.) can salmon
1 small onion, finely chopped
¼ cup butter
¼ cup flour
1 tsp. salt
¼ tsp. pepper
1 (5.33 oz.) can evaporated milk
2 eggs, lightly beaten
½ tsp. dill weed
1 cup frozen peas
1 cup (4 oz.) Cheddar cheese,
*   shredded*

Yield: 6 servings

Prepare your favorite pie shell. Do not bake. Drain liquid from salmon into measuring cup; add enough water to make one cup. Set aside. Cook onion in butter in saucepan until just tender. Blend in flour, salt and pepper. Add water mixture and milk to sauce; stirring constantly, until thick. Flake salmon with fork; add salmon and remaining ingredients to sauce. Pour into pie shell. Bake 30 to 35 minutes at 400°F or until firm. Let stand 10 minutes before serving.

Jayne Hager Dee (Mrs. Eric)

TUNA BAKE

8 cups fresh bread crumbs
2 cups boiling milk
3 (6 oz.) cans tuna or salmon
2 eggs, lightly beaten
juice and peel of one lemon, grated
salt to taste
pepper to taste

Yield: 6 servings

Pour boiling milk over bread crumbs in a bowl. Drain tuna or salmon and flake with a fork; add to the crumb mixture. Add the eggs, lemon juice, grated lemon rind, salt and pepper; mix well. Pour into a buttered 1½ or 2-quart casserole. Bake 1 hour and 30 minutes at 350°F.

Patricia Marble (Mrs. Edwin)

TUNA ORIENTAL

¾ cup celery, chopped
¼ cup onion, chopped
1 Tbsp. margarine
1 (10 ¾ oz.) can mushroom soup, undiluted
1 (4 oz.) can sliced mushrooms, drained
1/2 cup milk
1 (6 ½ oz.) can tuna, drained, flaked
1 ½ cups chow mein noodles, divided
½ cup cashews (optional)
½ tsp. salt
⅛ tsp. pepper
2 cups cooked rice

Yield: 4-5 servings

In a 1½-quart casserole, microcook celery, onion and margarine for 3 minutes on full power until tender. Stir in 1 cup chow mein noodles and remaining ingredients except rice. Microcook on full power for 8 to 10 minutes. Before serving, top with remaining ½ cup chow mein noodles. Serve over hot rice.

Linda Blum (Mrs. Daniel)

STIR-FRIED ALMOND SHRIMP AND PEPPERS

3 Tbsp. lemon juice, divided
3 cloves garlic, finely chopped
⅛ tsp. red pepper flakes
½ tsp. pepper
1 Tbsp. olive oil
1 ½ lb. medium raw shrimp,
    peeled, deveined
¾ cup blanched slivered almonds
4 Tbsp. butter, divided
1 red pepper, cut in julienne strips
2 Tbsp. fresh chives, thinly sliced
salt to taste
pepper to taste
lemon wedges
hot cooked rice

Yield: 6 servings

Combine 2 tablespoons lemon juice, garlic, red pepper flakes, pepper and olive oil. Marinate shrimp in mixture 15 minutes at room temperature. Saute almonds in 2 tablespoons butter until golden. Add shrimp and red pepper; saute 2 to 3 minutes until shrimp are tender. Remove from heat and stir in chives, salt, pepper, remaining 1 tablespoon lemon juice and remaining 2 tablespoons butter. Garnish with lemon wedges and serve over hot cooked rice.

Nan Ryden (Mrs. Rex)

ISOLA'S SHRIMP CURRY

4 Tbsp. butter
1 small onion, minced
1 green pepper, diced
1 large apple, peeled and chopped
1 tsp. salt
½ tsp. sugar
1 tsp. curry powder
¼ tsp. dry mustard
2 ½ cups stewed tomatoes
1 (12 oz.) pkg. frozen
    deveined shrimp
2 Tbsp. cornstarch
3 Tbsp. water
hot cooked rice

Yield: 6 servings

Melt butter in skillet. Stir in onions, green pepper, apple, salt, sugar, curry powder and dry mustard; cook until onion is tender. Add tomatoes. Stir and cook until thickened. Add shrimp and cook 10 minutes. Mix cornstarch with water. Add to shrimp mixture. Cook 1 to 2 minutes more until slightly thickened. Serve over rice.

Maxine Britten (Mrs. Wayne)

BROILED SCAMPI

1 Tbsp. parsley, chopped
1 cup butter, melted
1 tsp. Dijon-style mustard
½ tsp. chili powder
1 lemon, sliced
1 tsp. Worcestershire sauce
4 cloves garlic, pressed
3 Tbsp. white wine
¼ tsp. salt
¼ tsp. pepper
¼ tsp. paprika
24 jumbo shrimp, peeled, deveined

Yield: 6 servings

Mix all ingredients except shrimp. Pour sauce over shrimp. Cover and refrigerate for at least 24 hours. Place shrimp and sauce in large broiler pan. Broil 5 minutes. Turn shrimp over and broil 5 more minutes.

Patty Bowman (Mrs. Jim)

SHRIMP MOSTACCIOLI

¼ cup butter
¼ cup flour
2 cups milk
½ cup Parmesan cheese, grated
½ tsp. garlic salt
⅛ tsp. thyme
⅛ tsp nutmeg
1 (4 ½ oz.) can tiny shrimp,
    drained
2 ½ cups mostaccioli,
    cooked, drained
1 (10 oz.) pkg. chopped broccoli,
    cooked, drained
½ cup (2 oz.) Swiss cheese,
    shredded

Yield: 6 servings

Melt butter in medium saucepan; stir in flour. Add milk; cook and stir until thick. Stir in Parmesan cheese, seasonings and shrimp. Remove from heat. Combine shrimp mixture, mostaccioli and broccoli in large bowl. Turn into 11x7-inch pan. Sprinkle Swiss cheese over top. Bake 15 to 20 minutes at 375°F.

Maureen Lyons (Mrs. Ken)

From the Grill

HONEY APPLE PORK CHOPS

A family favorite at Barbara's house.

**4 (8 oz.) pork loin chops,
    about 1-inch thick
1 ½ cups apple cider
¼ cup lemon juice
¼ cup soy sauce
2 Tbsp. honey
1 clove garlic, minced
¼ tsp. pepper**

Yield: 4 servings

Combine all ingredients except pork chops. Place chops in shallow dish and pour marinade over chops. Cover and refrigerate overnight, turning meat occasionally. Remove pork chops from marinade. Grill on low or medium for 40 to 50 minutes, turning and basting with marinade every 10 to 15 minutes.

Barbara Beichley (Mrs. Duane)

PORK CHOP TERIYAKI

**¼ cup lemon juice
1 Tbsp. chili sauce
¾ cup soy sauce
1 Tbsp. brown sugar
1 clove garlic, minced
6 rib or Iowa chops,
    about 1 ½-inch thick**

Yield: 6 servings

Combine first five ingredients for marinade. Place chops in 9x13-inch glass pan. Add marinade and marinate covered at least 3 hours or overnight, turning once. Broil in oven or grill 15 to 20 minutes per side, basting with marinade occasionally.

Carole Weber (Mrs. Delano)

BARBECUED RIBS

3 to 4 lb. baby back ribs
¼ cup margarine
½ cup brown sugar, firmly packed
1 Tbsp. onion, minced
½ tsp. chili powder
1 Tbsp. Worcestershire sauce
1 cup ketchup
⅛ tsp. hot pepper sauce
1 tsp. salt
¼ cup vinegar
1 tsp. dry mustard

Yield: 6-8 servings

Place ribs in shallow roasting pan, meaty side up. Cover with aluminum foil and bake 1 hour and 30 minutes at 325°F. Prepare sauce by combining remaining ingredients in saucepan. Bring to a boil and simmer 30 minutes. Remove aluminum foil from ribs in oven, pour off liquid and cover with sauce. Bake uncovered an additional 1 hour at 325°F. May also dip the partially baked ribs in the sauce and grill about 40 to 50 minutes, turning and basting with the sauce after 20 minutes.

Linda McGregor (Mrs. Robert)

MARINATED FLANK STEAK
Try this marinade with other cuts of beef.

2 medium flank steaks
1 ½ cups vegetable oil
¾ cup soy sauce
¼ cup Worcestershire sauce
2 Tbsp. dry mustard
2 tsp. salt
1 tsp. pepper
½ cup cider vinegar
1 ½ tsp. dry parsley
¼ tsp. garlic powder
⅓ cup lemon juice

Yield: 6-8 servings

Score flank steaks diagonally on both sides. Combine remaining ingredients to make marinade. Marinate steaks in a shallow covered container overnight. Grill to desired doneness.

Ann Junker (Mrs. Waldo)

MOCK FILETS

2 lb. ground beef
2 tsp. salt
1 Tbsp. Worcestershire sauce
¼ tsp. pepper
2 eggs
1 cup (4 oz.) sharp Cheddar cheese,
    shredded
6 slices bacon
vinegar

Yield: 6 servings

Mix ground beef, salt, Worcestershire, pepper and eggs thoroughly; form into 12 patties about 3-inches in diameter. Put 2 tablespoons Cheddar cheese on 6 of the patties; place another patty on top. Pinch sides together to seal. Wrap sides with a slice of bacon, securing with toothpicks. Brush with vinegar. Grill approximately 10 minutes per side; brush other side with vinegar after turning.

Ann Junker (Mrs. Waldo)

HAMBURGER PINWHEELS

Freeze extra uncooked pinwheels for a quick meal.

3 lb. lean ground beef
½ tsp. lemon pepper
¼ cup Parmesan cheese, grated
1 cup green olives
1 (4 oz.) can mushrooms, drained
2 medium green peppers
1 small onion
1 (16 oz.) pkg. bacon

Yield: 12-18 servings

Lay an 18-inch sheet of wide freezer paper on counter, waxed side up. Pat uncooked ground beef onto it. Place waxed paper over top (may need 2 sheets). With a rolling pin, roll to ¼-inch thick. Remove top layer of waxed paper. Sprinkle with lemon pepper and Parmesan cheese. Finely chop olives, mushrooms, green peppers and onion. Sprinkle over Parmesan cheese. Starting from 18-inch side, roll up jelly-roll fashion, removing freezer paper from bottom as you roll. Freeze 30 to 45 minutes for easier slicing. Slice into 1 to 1½- inch slices. Wrap each pinwheel with a slice of bacon, securing with toothpicks. Broil or grill to desired doneness, turning once.

Sherry McCune (Mrs. Mike)

GRILLED TURKEY BREAST

1 cup vegetable oil
2 Tbsp. soy sauce
¼ cup wine or sherry
2 Tbsp. lemon juice
⅛ tsp. pepper
⅛ tsp. garlic salt
2 Tbsp. instant minced onion
1 whole turkey breast or
    2 lb. turkey breast fillets

Yield: 8 servings

Blend oil, soy sauce, wine, lemon juice, pepper, garlic salt and onion. Place turkey in shallow pan; pour marinade over; turn breast to cover. Marinate several hours. Grill to desired doneness.

Marcie Harvey (Mrs. Elwood)

GRILLED CHICKEN BUNDLES
Can be prepared ahead and refrigerated until ready to grill.

¼ lb. American cheese
8 chicken breast halves,
    skinned and boned
12 slices bacon
¼ cup barbecue sauce (optional)

Yield: 8 servings

Pound chicken breasts to ¼-inch thick. Cut cheese into 8 equal pieces. Place a piece of cheese at one end of each chicken breast. Roll up chicken, tucking sides in. Cut 4 bacon slices in half. Wrap a half-slice of bacon around center of each chicken roll. Wrap a full slice of bacon around the length of the chicken roll, securing with toothpicks. Using heavy-duty foil, make a tray with edges to grill chicken. This prevents flare-ups from the bacon. Grill over medium high heat 30 to 40 minutes, turning after 15 minutes. Remove bundles from tray during last 10 minutes and grill over direct heat, turning 2 to 3 times to crisp bacon. Brush with barbecue sauce, if desired.

Deb Keefe (Mrs. Kevin)

163

JODY'S CHICKEN BREAST

¼ cup vegetable oil
¼ cup white wine
2 Tbsp. lemon juice
1 tsp. salt
½ tsp. dry mustard
½ tsp. dried whole rosemary
½ tsp. dry parsley flakes
⅛ tsp. garlic powder
8 chicken breast halves, skinned

Yield: 8 servings

Mix oil, wine, lemon juice, salt, mustard, rosemary, parsley and garlic for marinade. Place chicken breasts in 9x13-inch pan and pour marinade over. Marinate 2 to 3 hours. Grill 30 minutes, basting with marinade.

Nan Ryden (Mrs. Rex)

CHICKEN FAJITAS
Also good in pita bread instead of tortillas.

½ cup fresh lime juice
¾ tsp. pepper
¾ tsp. garlic salt
8 chicken breast halves,
    skinned and boned
1 large onion, sliced into rings
1 Tbsp. margarine
1 large green pepper,
    sliced into strips
6 to 8 (10-inch) flour tortillas,
    warmed
guacamole
diced tomatoes
shredded Cheddar cheese
dairy sour cream

Yield: 4-6 servings

Combine lime juice, pepper and garlic salt. Marinate chicken breasts covered overnight in refrigerator. Turn chicken once or twice. In large skillet, saute onion in margarine for 2 minutes. Add green pepper and cook 2 more minutes or until vegetable are crisp-tender. Set aside. Grill chicken breasts for 2 minutes per side. Slice chicken diagonally into strips. Add chicken to vegetables in skillet and cook only until heated through. Fill warmed tortillas with chicken mixture. Garnish with guacamole, tomatoes, Cheddar cheese and sour cream as desired. Roll up and serve immediately.

Suzanne Brown (Mrs. Gregory)

FAJITAS

Good for a large, casual group because everyone can fix their own!

½ tsp. lime peel, finely grated
½ cup lime juice
2 cloves garlic, minced
½ tsp. salt (optional)
½ tsp. oregano
½ tsp. ground cumin
7 dashes hot pepper sauce
8 chicken breast halves,
    skinned and boned
3 red, yellow or green peppers,
    cut into thin strips
1 medium onion, sliced
8 (10-inch) flour tortillas
lettuce, shredded
tomatoes, diced
plain yogurt or dairy sour cream
Cheddar cheese, shredded

Yield: 4-6 servings

To make marinade, combine lime peel, lime juice, garlic, salt, oregano, cumin, and hot pepper sauce. Add chicken breasts, peppers and onion. Cover and chill at least 2 hours or overnight, turning once or twice. Remove chicken, reserving marinade. With slotted spoon, remove peppers and onion; wrap them in an 18-inch square of heavy-duty aluminum foil. Stack tortillas and wrap in another 18-inch square of aluminum foil. Grill pepper-onion packet and chicken over medium coals for 6 minutes. Add tortilla packet to grill. Turn chicken, continue to grill 4 to 6 minutes or until chicken is tender, brushing chicken occasionally with reserved marinade. Remove chicken, cover to keep warm. Continue grilling foil packets 4 to 6 minutes until vegetables are tender and tortillas are heated through. Thinly slice chicken. Place tortilla on plate; add chicken, peppers, onions, lettuce, tomatoes, yogurt and Cheddar cheese. Fold. Vegetables can be stir-fried and tortillas warmed in the oven for 20 minutes at 200°F, if not enough grill space.

Cathy Frost (Mrs. Curt)

MARINATED SALMON

½ cup vegetable oil
½ cup sherry
½ cup soy sauce
⅓ cup lemon juice
2 Tbsp. sugar
1 tsp. salt
¼ cup onion, chopped
1 Tbsp. liquid smoke
½ tsp. ground ginger
6 salmon steaks

Mix oil, sherry, soy sauce, lemon juice, sugar, salt, onion, liquid smoke and ginger. Pour over salmon steaks. Marinate at least 3 hours. Place steaks in buttered aluminum foil pan. Grill 5 to 7 minutes on each side over low heat.

Kathy Briggs (Mrs. Terrence)

Yield: 6 servings

SAUCE FOR MARINATING
Use for chops, steaks, roasts, stews or fondue meat.

2 cloves garlic, minced
½ cup soy sauce
2 to 4 Tbsp. vegetable oil
¼ cup brown sugar
¼ tsp. ginger
¼ tsp. pepper

Mix all ingredients. Rub on meat at least one hour before cooking.

Patty Bowman (Mrs. Jim)

Yield: 3/4 cup

WESTERN LITE MARINADE
Low in calories as it has no oil.

1 cup soy sauce
½ cup water
¼ cup lemon juice
¼ cup honey or brown sugar
½ tsp. garlic powder
2 green onion tops, chopped or
    2 Tbsp. instant minced onion

Combine all ingredients. Use to marinate meat 12 to 48 hours in the refrigerator. Enough for 3 to 4 lb. of beef (steaks, cubes or strips).

Barbara Beichley (Mrs. Duane)

Yield: 2 ¼ cups
166

TERIYAKI MARINADE

¼ *cup soy sauce*
2 *Tbsp. sugar*
1 *Tbsp. freshly grated ginger or*
   1 ½ *tsp. ground ginger*
2 *cloves garlic, crushed*
½ *cup white wine or vermouth*
¼ *cup vegetable oil*
1 *or 2 green onions, finely chopped*

Yield: 1 cup

Mix all ingredients. Use to marinate steaks and beef or pork kabobs. Marinate 24 hours in refrigerator before grilling.

Pat Shobe (Mrs. Richard)

JIMMY'S MARINADE FOR BEEF
Has a somewhat exotic, mysterious flavor.

1 *clove garlic*
2 *cups soy sauce*
1 *(12 oz.) can beer*
1 *papaya*
2 ¼ *cups dark brown sugar,*
   firmly packed
1 *fresh ginger root*
1 *(4 oz.) can crushed pineapple*

Yield: 4 cups

Place garlic, soy sauce, beer, papaya, brown sugar and ginger root in blender; blend until smooth. Add pineapple. Marinate your favorite beef for 24 hours in refrigerator. Baste with marinade as you grill. This makes a large quantity of marinade. Recipe may be halved.

Variation: Omit beer if marinating chicken.

Cathy Frost (Mrs. Curt)

167

SPICY BAR-B-QUE SAUCE
This is an old family recipe.

2 Tbsp. butter
1 onion, chopped
½ cup brown sugar, firmly packed
1 clove garlic, crushed
1 Tbsp. dry mustard
¼ cup soy sauce
½ cup wine vinegar
1 cup beef bouillon
½ cup celery, chopped
1 Tbsp. pepper
6 Tbsp. liquid smoke
5 Tbsp. steak sauce
3 cups tomato sauce
1 cup ketchup
3 Tbsp. Worcestershire sauce
1 Tbsp. hot pepper sauce

Yield: 4 cups

Mix all ingredients and simmer one hour. Use on loin back ribs, chicken, etc.

Jean Brennecke (Mrs. Allen)

THOMPSON'S TANGY RIB SAUCE
Don developed and refined this recipe over the last 20 years—he's finally happy with it!

2 ½ cups ketchup
1 (6 oz.) can frozen orange
   juice concentrate, thawed
½ cup lemon juice
3 cups brown sugar, firmly packed
1 tsp. dry mustard
2 Tbsp. chili powder
2 tsp. red pepper
1 medium onion, finely chopped

Yield: 4 cups

Mix ingredients in saucepan and simmer for 20 minutes. Excellent on loin back ribs.

Sanny Thompson (Mrs. Donald)

On the Side

PERFECT BAKED ASPARAGUS

1 to 1 ½ lbs. fresh asparagus,
    trimmed
salt
pepper
3 Tbsp. butter

Yield: 4 servings

Arrange asparagus in shallow 1-quart casserole. Sprinkle with salt and pepper to taste. Dot with butter. Cover and bake 30 minutes at 300°F.

Valois Brintnall (Mrs. Lee)

ASPARAGUS AND PEA CASSEROLE

1 (15 oz.) can asparagus
1 (15 oz.) can very young
    small sweet peas
1 (4 oz.) can mushrooms
¼ cup margarine
3 Tbsp. flour
1 ½ cups milk
1 (5 oz.) jar sharp pasteurized
    process cheese spread
42 round butter crackers
½ cup margarine, melted

Yield: 6 servings

Drain asparagus, peas and mushrooms. Melt ¼ cup margarine in saucepan; blend in flour. Gradually add milk, stirring constantly until mixture is smooth. Add cheese, stirring until well blended; set aside. Make crumbs by rolling crackers until fine; mix with remaining melted margarine. In greased 2-quart casserole layer asparagus, peas, three-fourths of the crumb mixture, mushrooms, cheese sauce and remaining crumb mixture. Bake uncovered 40 minutes at 375°F.

Marge Solley (Mrs. Larry)

BEETS WITH MANDARIN ORANGES

2 (1 lb.) cans small whole beets
2 (11 oz.) cans mandarin oranges
½ cup sugar
1 ½ tsp. cornstarch
2 Tbsp. lemon juice
½ cup dry wine, white or red
2 Tbsp. butter

Yield: 6 servings

Drain beets and mandarin oranges. Combine sugar, cornstarch, lemon juice, wine and butter in saucepan. Cook over medium heat, stirring constantly until sauce is clear. Add beets and oranges. Pour ingredients into 2-quart casserole. Bake 15 minutes at 325°F or until heated through.

Barbara Harkness (Mrs. Jack)

SWEET AND SOUR RED CABBAGE

"Skeptical spouse liked this very much!" says our tester.

1 large head red cabbage
½ cup butter
¼ cup white vinegar
1 tsp. caraway seed
½ cup water
½ cup brown sugar, firmly packed

Yield: 6 servings

Wash cabbage and shred. In heavy 10-inch skillet melt butter; stir in cabbage. Add vinegar, water and caraway. Cover. Reduce heat and simmer 1 to 1 ½ hours, tossing frequently. Add brown sugar and cook for 15 minutes longer or until sugar is dissolved and cabbage is coated.

Hollis Cassidy (Mrs. Eugene)

ORANGE CARROTS

1 lb. carrots, cut in julienne strips
½ tsp. cinnamon
1 Tbsp. brown sugar
1 Tbsp. butter
3 Tbsp. fresh orange juice

Yield: 4-6 servings

In saucepan cook sliced carrots in small amount of water for 10 minutes or until tender crisp. Drain. Combine remaining ingredients and pour over carrots. Simmer until only a small amount of liquid remains.

Nan Ryden (Mrs. Rex)

NAPA CABBAGE, CARROT AND SNOW PEA SAUTE

2 medium carrots
¼ lb. snow peas
½ lb. Napa cabbage
1 Tbsp. vegetable oil
1 Tbsp. Oriental sesame oil
salt
pepper

Yield: 4 servings

Coarsely grate carrots. Remove ends and strings of snow peas and cut on a sharp diagonal into strips. Cut cabbage crosswise into ¼-inch shreds, about four loosely packed cups. Heat oils over medium high heat in large skillet. Do not let oils smoke. Saute carrots with salt and pepper to taste, stirring constantly for 1 minute. Add snow peas and continue cooking for 30 seconds. Add cabbage. Stir-fry 1 minute or until cabbage is wilted.

Diane McComber (Mrs. Larry)

COMPANY CARROTS

1 lb. carrots
2 Tbsp. horseradish
1 Tbsp. instant minced onion
salt to taste
pepper to taste
½ cup mayonnaise
¼ cup fine, dry bread crumbs
2 Tbsp. butter or margarine, melted

Yield: 4 servings

Slice carrots ¼-inch thick. Place carrots in saucepan with enough water to cover. Simmer until tender crisp. Drain well; reserve ¼ cup cooking liquid. Mix cooking liquid with horseradish, onion, salt, pepper and mayonnaise. Arrange carrots evenly over bottom of greased 1½ to 2-quart casserole. Pour horseradish mixture over carrots. Mix bread crumbs with butter and sprinkle over top. Bake 20 minutes at 375°F or until crumbs are nicely browned.

Ann Meiners (Mrs. Gerald)

CARROTS VICCHY
Pretty, quick and easy!

5 cups carrots
¾ cup boiling water
¼ cup butter
2 tsp. salt
¼ tsp. nutmeg
⅛ tsp. pepper
1 Tbsp. sugar
1 Tbsp. lemon juice
½ tsp. monosodium glutamate
    (optional)
¼ cup parsley, snipped

Yield: 6 servings

Slice carrots diagonally ¼-inch thick. Combine water, butter, salt, nutmeg, pepper, sugar and carrots in a saucepan. Simmer covered 8 to 10 minutes or until tender crisp. Before serving, stir in lemon juice, monosodium glutamate and parsley.

Jinita Boyd (Mrs. Douglas)

LAYERED CAULIFLOWER CASSEROLE

1 medium head cauliflower
5 carrots, sliced
1 lb. fresh mushrooms, sliced
⅓ cup butter
½ cup flour
¼ cup white wine
2 cups chicken stock
salt to taste
pepper to taste
½ tsp. tarragon
½ tsp. basil
½ tsp. garlic powder
1 tsp. onion powder
¾ lb. pasteurized process
    cheese spread, grated

Yield: 6-8 servings

Cook cauliflower until tender crisp. Cook carrots until tender crisp. Saute mushrooms. Set vegetables aside. Melt butter in saucepan and blend in flour. Gradually add remaining ingredients stirring until mixture is smooth. In a 2-quart casserole, layer one-half cauliflower, one-fourth sauce, one-half mushrooms, one-half carrots and one-fourth sauce. Repeat. Bake 45 minutes at 350°F until hot and bubbly.

Nancy Hull (Mrs. Joseph)

CORN BACON CURRY BAKE

A new twist on a midwest favorite.

4 eggs
1 ½ cups milk
1 ½ cups (6 oz.) Swiss cheese,
    shredded
¼ tsp. salt
¼ tsp. pepper
2 cups whole kernel corn, drained
2 ½ Tbsp. green onion, minced
1 Tbsp. pimento, chopped
¼ tsp. curry powder
1 ½ cups bacon,
    cooked and crumbled

Beat eggs, milk, cheese, salt and pepper. Stir in corn, onion, pimento and curry powder. Pour half of the mixture into a greased 2-quart baking dish. Sprinkle with bacon; pour remaining mixture over top. Bake 45 to 60 minutes at 350°F or until knife inserted into center comes out clean.

Barbara Beichley (Mrs. Duane)

Yield: 6-8 servings

PEARL ONIONS AND PEAS IN MUSTARD SAUCE

An onion lovers delight!

4 lbs. white pearl onions
2 (10 oz.) pkgs. frozen peas
½ cup butter
½ cup flour
3 cups heavy cream
1 ½ tsp. salt
¼ tsp. white pepper
3 Tbsp. white vinegar
3 Tbsp. lemon juice
½ tsp. dry mustard
⅛ tsp. powdered saffron (optional)

Pour boiling water over onions. Let stand awhile, then peel. Cook onions in boiling salted water until tender. Cook peas according to package directions. Melt butter in double boiler and blend in flour. Gradually add cream stirring until mixture is smooth. Add remaining ingredients to sauce. Drain onions and peas and place in a serving bowl. Pour sauce over vegetables.

Yield: 8-12 servings

Gayle Boyd (Mrs. James)

174

MIKE'S POTATOES

3 medium baking potatoes, unpeeled
3 Tbsp. butter
1 ¼ cups (5 oz.) Monterey Jack
    cheese, grated
1 ¼ cups (5 oz.) Cheddar cheese,
    grated
⅔ cup tomatoes, diced
2 Tbsp. minced onion
salt
2 Tbsp. green onion, chopped
½ cup avocado, diced
dairy sour cream

Yield: 4-6 servings

Boil potatoes; cool and dice. Melt butter in large heavy skillet over medium high heat. Add potatoes and cook until brown and a little crisp, stirring frequently. Add cheeses, tomatoes and onions, stirring until cheese melts. Season with salt. Gently mix in avocado. Spoon onto large serving platter and top with sour cream. Best when served immediately.

Maureen Lewis (Mrs. Philip)

BAKED POTATO SALAD

8 medium potatoes
½ lb. bacon
½ lb. Cheddar cheese, cubed
¼ cup stuffed olives, sliced
1 cup mayonnaise (do not substitute)

Yield: 8 servings

Cook, peel and dice potatoes. Dice, fry and drain bacon. Combine all ingredients and place in a 9x13-inch baking dish. Bake 50 minutes at 325°F.

Deb Keefe (Mrs. Kevin)

SPINACH SPOON BREAD

1 (10 oz.) pkg. frozen
   chopped spinach
¼ cup onion, chopped
½ cup butter or margarine,
   melted, divided
2 eggs, lightly beaten
1 cup dairy sour cream
¼ tsp. salt
1 (8 ½ oz.) pkg. corn muffin mix
½ cup (2 oz.) Swiss cheese,
   shredded

Yield: 8 servings

Cook spinach according to package directions; drain well. Saute onion in 1 tablespoon butter. In large mixing bowl combine sauted onion, spinach, eggs, sour cream, remaining butter and salt; stir in corn muffin mix. Pour mixture into greased 1½-quart casserole. Bake 30 to 35 minutes at 350°F until toothpick inserted in center comes out clean. Sprinkle top of bread with Swiss cheese; bake about two minutes longer or until cheese is melted. Serve spoon bread warm.

Barbara Beichley (Mrs. Duane)

"VOILA" SPINACH PUDDING

2 (10 oz.) pkgs. frozen
   chopped spinach
2 cups low-fat cottage cheese, drained
1 tsp. salt or salt substitute
⅓ cup Parmesan cheese, grated
2 eggs

Yield: 8-10 servings

Cook spinach according to package directions; drain well. Add remaining ingredients and stir until well blended. Pour into buttered 1-quart casserole and bake 30 minutes at 350°F. Garnish with additional Parmesan cheese if desired.

Lorraine Schultz (Mrs. Ed)

QUICK SPINACH

1 (10 oz.) pkg. frozen
   chopped spinach
⅓ cup light cream cheese
½ cup cottage cheese
½ cup (2 oz.) Swiss cheese, grated
garlic salt to taste
nutmeg to taste

Yield: 4-6 servings

Cook spinach according to package directions; drain well. Add remaining ingredients and place in a greased 8-inch square baking dish. Bake 15 to 20 minutes at 325°F.

Nan Ryden (Mrs. Rex)

SQUASH CASSEROLE

4 to 5 (2 cups) summer squash
6 Tbsp. margarine, melted
2 cups cracker crumbs,
   buttery round-type
1 cup evaporated milk
2 eggs, beaten
1 cup onion, chopped
1 cup (4 oz.) Cheddar cheese, grated
1 tsp. salt
½ tsp. pepper

Yield: 8 servings

Slice squash. Mix remaining ingredients in a small bowl. Add squash and mix well. Place in a greased 2-quart casserole and bake uncovered 40 minutes at 375°F.

Marge Solley (Mrs. Larry)

MUSHROOM-SPINACH FLORENTINE
May prepare ahead.

2 (10 oz.) pkgs. frozen
   chopped spinach
1 tsp. salt
¼ cup onion, chopped
¼ cup butter, melted
1 lb. fresh mushrooms
3-4 Tbsp. butter
1 tsp. garlic salt
1 cup (4 oz.) sharp Cheddar cheese,
   grated, divided

Yield: 8 servings

Thaw spinach and drain well. Add salt, onion and ¼ cup melted butter and set aside. Wash and dry mushrooms removing stems. In remaining butter, saute stems and caps (cap side down first) until brown; add garlic salt. Place spinach mixture in shallow 10-inch casserole; sprinkle with half of the cheese. Arrange the sauted mushrooms; sprinkle with remaining cheese. Bake 20 minutes at 350°F until cheese is melted and browned.

Nan Ryden (Mrs. Rex)

ORANGE-GLAZED SWEET POTATOES
Great with your holiday turkey!

*1 (1 lb.) can whole sweet potatoes,
  drained
⅛ tsp. salt
½ cup brown sugar, firmly packed
1 Tbsp. cornstarch
¼ tsp. salt
1 cup fresh orange juice
2 Tbsp. dry sherry
⅓ cup raisins
½ tsp. orange peel, shredded
walnut halves (optional)*

Yield: 4-6 servings

Arrange potatoes in shallow 8-inch square baking dish; sprinkle with ⅛ teaspoon salt. Combine sugar, cornstarch and ¼ teaspoon salt in a saucepan; blend in orange juice and sherry; add raisins. Cook and stir over high heat to boiling. Add orange peel and walnuts; pour over potatoes. Bake uncovered 25 to 30 minutes at 350°F until well glazed.

Margaret Gervich (Mrs.Douglas)

PECAN SWEET POTATOES

*3 lbs. sweet potatoes,
  cooked and peeled
2 eggs
¾ cup light brown sugar,
  firmly packed, divided
½ cup margarine, melted, divided
1 tsp. salt
1 tsp. cinnamon
¾ cup (3 oranges) fresh
  orange juice
1 cup whole pecans*

Yield: 6-8 servings

Mash potatoes, about six cups. Beat in eggs, ½ cup brown sugar, ¼ cup margarine, salt and cinnamon. Beat in enough orange juice to make potatoes moist and fluffy. Place in a 2-quart casserole. Potato mixture may be refrigerated, if preparing ahead. Just before baking, arrange pecans on top of potatoes. Sprinkle with remaining brown sugar and drizzle with remaining melted margarine. Bake 20 minutes at 375°F.

Tanya Davison (Mrs. Dennis)

VEGETABLE MEDLEY
Easy company dish!

1 ½ cups onions
2 cups celery
1 ½ cups carrots
2-3 cups green pepper
1 (16 oz.) can tomatoes
1 (10 oz.) pkg. frozen green beans
1 Tbsp. sugar
4 Tbsp. butter or margarine, melted
½ tsp. pepper
2 tsp. salt
3 Tbsp. quick cooking tapioca

Yield: 8 servings

Slice onions. Cut celery and carrots diagonally into ½-inch pieces. Slice green pepper into strips. Drain and chop tomatoes. Combine all ingredients in a large bowl. Place in large casserole and bake covered 1 hour and 15 minutes at 350°F, uncover and bake an additional 15 minutes.

Catherine Shipton (Mrs. William)

ZUCCHINI PARMESAN
Wonderful! Great eye appeal! Great taste!

4 cups zucchini, sliced
2 cups boiling water
2 eggs
1 cup mayonnaise
1 small onion, chopped
¼ cup green pepper, chopped
1 cup Parmesan cheese, grated
salt to taste
pepper to taste
1 Tbsp. butter or margarine
2 Tbsp. bread crumbs, buttered

Yield: 6 servings

Cook zucchini in water until tender crisp; drain. In large bowl, beat eggs and stir in mayonnaise, onion, green pepper, Parmesan cheese, salt and pepper. Add zucchini; turn into a greased 1½- quart casserole. Dot with butter and sprinkle with bread crumbs. Bake 30 minutes at 350°F until bubbly.

Joan Boyce (Mrs. Steven)

LAYERED VEGETABLE AND CHEESE CASSEROLE

1 (16 oz.) can whole tomatoes
1 (10 oz.) pkg. frozen broccoli spears
1 (10 oz.) pkg. frozen lima beans
1 cup (4 oz.) Cheddar cheese,
  shredded
1 large onion, finely chopped
4 Tbsp. butter or margarine, divided
2 Tbsp. flour
salt
pepper
marjoram leaves, dried and crushed
1 cup soft bread crumbs
3 Tbsp. Romano or Parmesan cheese,
  grated

Yield: 6-8 servings

Drain tomatoes, reserving liquid, chop coarsely and set aside. Cook broccoli according to package directions. Remove with a slotted spoon and put in greased shallow 2-quart casserole. Cook lima beans in same liquid until tender. Drain lima beans, reserving liquid, and layer beans on top of broccoli. Sprinkle Cheddar cheese over vegetables. Saute onion in 2 tablespoons margarine in a saucepan until soft and transparent. Stir in flour and cook for two minutes. Gradually add reserved tomato and vegetable liquid, stirring until thick and smooth; add tomatoes. Add salt, pepper and marjoram to taste. Pour sauce over cheese and vegetables. Saute bread crumbs in remaining margarine until golden brown. Mix with Romano cheese and sprinkle over casserole. Bake 15 minutes at 425°F until topping is browned.

Mid Lander (Mrs. Chuck)

180

ZUCCHINI CASSEROLE

3 medium zucchini
2 cups boiling water with 1 tsp. salt
1/4 cup dairy sour cream
1 1/2 Tbsp. lemon juice
2 Tbsp. butter
2 Tbsp. Parmesan cheese, grated
1/2 tsp. salt
1/8 tsp. paprika
1 egg yolk, beaten
2 Tbsp. chives, chopped
1 tsp. basil
1/3 cup bread crumbs, buttered
Parmesan cheese

Wash zucchini and cut crosswise in 1/4-inch slices. Cook in boiling salt water 6 to 8 minutes. In saucepan over low heat combine sour cream, lemon juice, butter, cheese, 1/2 teaspoon salt and paprika. When cheese has melted, remove from heat and stir in egg yolk, chives and basil. Drain zucchini and place in a 1-quart casserole. Spread sauce evenly over zucchini. Top with bread crumbs and additional Parmesan cheese. Bake at 375°F until browned.

Yield: 4-6 servings

Ann Collison (Mrs. Mark)

BAKED BEANS WITH FRUIT
Vary the flavor with different fruits.

3 or 4 pork and bacon links
2 (16 oz.) cans pork and beans, drained
3/4 cup barbecue sauce
1/2 cup brown sugar, firmly packed
1/2 small onion, chopped
1 tart apple, peeled, cored and chopped
3/4 cup pineapple chunks, well drained
1/4 cup golden raisins

Cook and thinly slice pork and bacon links. Combine all ingredients in a 1 1/2-quart casserole. Bake uncovered 45 to 60 minutes at 350°F until bubbly.

Mary Holmer (Mrs. Tom)

Yield: 6 servings

EM'S GNOCCI

Emily Cartright's potato substitute for dinner or brunch.

3 cups milk
1 tsp. salt
¼ cup butter
¾ cup farina
2 eggs, lightly beaten
½ cup Parmesan cheese, grated
Canadian bacon (optional)

Yield: 6-8 servings

In saucepan heat milk, salt and butter to scalding; do not boil. Slowly add farina, stirring constantly. Cook and stir 5 minutes until very thick. Combine small amount of farina with beaten eggs; return to hot farina, stirring well. Pour farina into a greased loaf or cake pan and cover with waxed paper. Chill until firm. Slice into serving pieces and place on buttered 10x15-inch jelly roll pan. Dot with butter and sprinkle with Parmesan cheese and Canadian bacon. Bake 15 minutes at 400°F.

Nan Ryden (Mrs. Rex)

HAM-FLAVORED CORNBREAD DRESSING

1 (8 ½ oz.) box corn muffin mix
2 Tbsp. butter or margarine
2 large ribs celery, diced
1 large onion, diced
1 ½ cups dinner rolls, crumpled
2 tsp. sage
½ tsp. black pepper
salt to taste
1 ½ to 2 ½ cups ham hock broth
    or chicken broth
4 eggs, hard-cooked, chopped

Yield: 6 servings

Prepare cornbread according to package directions. Cool and crumble to make 3 cups. Melt butter in large skillet over medium heat. Add celery and onion; saute about 5 minutes. Stir cornbread, rolls, sage, pepper and salt into skillet. Pour in 1½ cups broth, adding up to 1 cup more broth for desired moistness. Spread mixture in 2-quart casserole and bake 35 minutes at 325°F. Stir in eggs and continue baking 5 more minutes or until browned. Cover for very moist dressing, uncover for crisp dressing.

Dorothy Cagwin (Mrs. K. L.)

HERB SEASONING MIX

1 tsp. oregano
1 Tbsp. parsley flakes
1 tsp. dill weed
½ tsp. garlic salt
2 Tbsp. Parmesan cheese (optional)

Yield: 2 tablespoons

Combine seasonings and add Parmesan cheese, if desired. Sprinkle on cooked vegetables. This is especially good with green beans.

Nan Ryden (Mrs. Rex)

HERB BUTTER

1 cup butter or margarine
2 tsp. dried parsley
½ tsp. oregano
1 tsp. dill weed
½ tsp. garlic powder
Parmesan cheese, grated
French bread

Yield: 1 cup/1 loaf

Combine butter, parsley, oregano, dill weed, and garlic powder. Slice a medium size loaf of French bread and spread herb butter between slices. Wrap in a foil boat leaving top open. Spread additional herb butter on top and sprinkle with Parmesan cheese and parsley as desired. Bake 10 to 15 minutes at 350°F.

Lucy Grossman, (Mrs. Richard)

RED TOMATO CHUTNEY

4 lbs. ripe tomatoes
1 lb. cooking apples
1 lb. onions
1 ½ cups golden raisins
1 ½ cups dark raisins
1 tsp. dry mustard
2 tsp. ground allspice
1 Tbsp. salt
1 Tbsp. cayenne pepper
3 cups brown sugar, firmly packed
3 ¾ cups vinegar

Yield: 6-7 pints

Peel, seed and chop tomatoes; peel, core and chop apples; peel and chop onions. In large preserving kettle, combine all ingredients and bring to a boil, stirring. Reduce heat and simmer, stirring frequently until chutney is thick, 3 to 4 hours. Ladle into hot jars; adjust lids at once. Process in boiling water bath 5 minutes.

Dorothy King (Mrs. C. F.)

183

ASPARAGUS WITH PASTA
Only 92 calories per 1 cup serving!

1 cup mostaccioli, uncooked
¾ lb. fresh asparagus
non-stick vegetable spray
2 tsp. olive oil
1 medium yellow pepper,
    cut into julienne strips
1 clove garlic, minced
1 Tbsp. fresh basil, chopped
⅛ tsp. salt
⅛ tsp. white pepper
1 cup tomatoes,
    seeded and chopped
¼ cup Parmesan cheese, grated

Yield: 6 servings

Cook mostaccioli in boiling water without salt or oil. Wash and snap off ends of asparagus; cut into 1-inch pieces. Cover and cook in a small amount of boiling water for 30 seconds. Drain asparagus and pasta well; set aside. Coat large skillet with non-stick vegetable spray; add oil and place over medium-high heat until hot. Add peppers and garlic; saute 2 minutes. Add asparagus; saute 1 minute. Add basil, salt, pepper and pasta; toss gently. Spoon mixture onto a large platter. Sprinkle with tomatoes and Parmesan cheese.

Linda Bloom (Mrs. Michael)

CHEESE MANICOTTI

1 (8 oz.) pkg. manicotti shells
2 cups (8 oz.) mozzarella cheese,
    shredded
2 cups ricotta cheese
¼ cup Parmesan cheese, grated
2 Tbsp. parsley, chopped
½ tsp. salt
¼ tsp. pepper
4-5 cups spaghetti sauce

Yield: 6-8 servings

Cook manicotti according to package directions, drain. Combine cheeses, parsley, salt and pepper. Spoon into manicotti shells. Spread a thin layer of sauce on bottom of 9x13-inch baking dish. Arrange manicotti in single layer. Cover with remaining sauce. Bake covered with aluminum foil 40 minutes at 350°F. Remove foil and bake an additional 15 minutes.

Ann Collison (Mrs. Mark)

STUFFED PASTA SHELLS

1 (10 oz.) pkg. frozen
    chopped spinach
1 (8 oz.) pkg. manicotti shells
1 Tbsp. vegetable oil
2 cups low fat cottage cheese,
    drained
2 egg whites or 1 whole egg
1 cup (4 oz.) mozzarella cheese,
    shredded
¼ tsp. garlic powder
pepper to taste
2 cups spaghetti sauce

Yield: 6-8 servings

Cook spinach according to package directions; drain thoroughly. Cook manicotti according to package directions, including 1 tablespoon oil. Drain and cover with cold water. Combine spinach, cottage cheese, egg whites, mozzarella cheese, garlic powder and pepper. Drain shells and stuff cheese mixture into shells. Place in 11x7-inch baking dish. Cover with spaghetti sauce. Bake covered 45 minutes at 350°F until bubbling.

Linda McGregor (Mrs. Robert)

SPINACH LASAGNA
Colorful and Delicious!

1 (8 oz.) pkg. lasagna noodles
6 Tbsp. butter
8 Tbsp. flour
4 cups milk
3 cups spinach, cooked
⅔ cup onion, minced
2 (4 oz.) jars pimento strips,
    divided
2 cups ricotta cheese, divided
3 cups Parmesan cheese, grated,
    divided

Yield: 8 servings

Cook lasagna according to package directions. Drain and cover with cold water. In saucepan, melt butter and blend in flour. Gradually add milk stirring until mixture is smooth; set aside. Drain lasagna. In oiled 9x13-inch baking dish layer one-half lasagna, one-half spinach, one-half pimento strips, one-half ricotta cheese, 1 cup Parmesan cheese and one-half sauce. Repeat layers. Top with remaining Parmesan cheese. Bake 45 to 60 minutes at 350°F until lightly browned. Cool 20 minutes before cutting.

Jan Rathke (Mrs. Richard)

PERFECT PASTA PRIMAVERA

1 cup broccolli flowerets
1 cup asparagus, cut in 1-inch pieces
1 cup snow peas
1 small zucchini or summer squash,
.   unpeeled, cut in 1-inch pieces
1 cup corn kernels, fresh or frozen
3 cloves garlic, finely minced
1 Tbsp. olive oil
1 large or 2 small tomatoes, diced
½ cup mushrooms, sliced
½ cup carrots, pared, shredded
¼ cup parsley, finely minced
½ tsp. pepper, freshly ground
12 oz. spaghetti or linguine,
    cooked al dente

Sauce:
2 tsp. butter or margarine
1 Tbsp. flour
1 cup skim or 1% milk
½ cup chicken broth
½ cup Parmesan cheese, grated
¼ cup finely minced fresh basil
    or 1 tsp. dried basil

Yield: 4-5 servings

Steam broccoli and asparagus 5 minutes. Blanch snow peas, zucchini and corn 1 minute. Combine vegetables and keep warm. Saute garlic in oil 1 minute in a large skillet, do not brown. Add tomatoes, mushrooms, carrrots, parsley and pepper; cook 4 minutes. Add this to reserved vegetables; toss to combine. Set aside. Melt butter in a small heavy saucepan. Add flour, whisking over medium-low heat for 1 minute. Gradually add milk and chicken broth stirring constantly until sauce thickens slightly. Add Parmesan cheese and basil; continue stirring until cheese melts. Pour sauce over vegetables; toss gently to coat. Place pasta in a large heated serving bowl or platter. Spread vegetables and sauce over the pasta; toss gently and serve.

Sue Miller (Mrs. Lewis)

RICE CASSEROLE

2 cups instant rice
3 Tbsp. margarine
1 (10 oz.) can beef consomme,
    undiluted
1 (10 ¾ oz.) can chicken and
    rice soup, undiluted
10-12 fresh mushrooms, sliced
½ cup almonds, toasted
1 to 2 ribs celery, sliced

Yield: 6 servings

Melt margarine and brown rice in a large skillet. Add remaining ingredients and heat through. Pour into 2-quart casserole and bake covered 1 hour at 350°F.

Sally Robertson (Mrs. James)

BAKED BROWN RICE

1 to 1 ¼ cups regular rice
2 (10 ¾ oz.) cans beef consomme
    or 1 can beef consomme and
    1 can French onion soup,
    undiluted
4 Tbsp. margarine
1 (4 oz.) can mushrooms (optional)
1 Tbsp. parsley (optional)

Yield: 6-8 servings

Combine all ingredients and pour into a greased 2-quart casserole. Bake covered one hour at 350°F.

Joan Heddens (Mrs. J.D.)
Fran Hermanson (Mrs. Paul)

QUICK STOVE TOP RICE PILAF

1/4 cup margarine
1 (10 ¾ oz.) can beef consomme,
    undiluted
2 cups instant rice

Yield: 4 servings

Melt margarine in medium saucepan over medium heat. Add consomme and rice; stir to mix. Cover and reduce heat to low. Cook about 5 minutes or until most of consomme is absorbed and rice is tender.

Deb Keefe (Mrs. Kevin)

SUPERB WILD RICE

"This is great! Worth the effort!" says our tester.

1 cup wild rice
5 slices bacon
½ cup onion, chopped
¼ cup green pepper, chopped
1 (4 oz.) can mushrooms, undrained
2 Tbsp. butter
**1 (10 ¾ oz.) can cream of
    mushroom soup, undiluted**
1 cup canned tomatoes, crushed
1 tsp. seasoned salt
½ cup sherry

Yield: 10-12 servings

Soak wild rice in water overnight. Fry bacon in large skillet until crisp; drain. Add onion, green pepper and mushrooms with liquid to the bacon drippings and saute for about 5 minutes. Add butter, soup, tomatoes and seasoning; heat until well blended. Wash and drain wild rice; add to the soup mixture. Stir in the sherry. Pour into a well buttered 2-quart casserole. Top with crumbled bacon. Bake covered 2 hours at 325°F.

Caroline Larson (Mrs. Ronald)

CELEBRATION CASSEROLE

A potluck favorite!

1 cup wild rice
1 (14 ½ oz.) can chicken broth
1 cup fresh mushrooms, sliced
**½ cup (2 oz.) Cheddar cheese,
    shredded**
½ cup slivered almonds, toasted
¼ cup onion, chopped
¼ cup celery, chopped
¼ cup green pepper, chopped
1 clove garlic, minced
¼ cup margarine or butter, melted
⅛ tsp. pepper

Yield: 8 servings

Run cold water over the wild rice in a strainer for 1 minute while lifting the wild rice to rinse well. Transfer rinsed and drained wild rice to a 2-quart casserole. Stir in chicken broth, sliced mushrooms, Cheddar cheese, almonds, onion, celery, green pepper, garlic, margarine and pepper. Cover and bake 1 hour and 15 minutes at 325°F. Stir the mixture. Bake uncovered for 20 to 30 minutes more or until most of the liquid is absorbed, stirring once. May combine ingredients ahead, then cover and refrigerate before baking.

Barbara Beichley (Mrs. Duane)

The Cookie Tray

BRANDY ALEXANDER BROWNIES

6 Tbsp. margarine, softened
¾ cup sugar
2 eggs
1 (1 oz.) square unsweetened
    chocolate, melted
2 Tbsp. creme de cacao
2 Tbsp. brandy
⅔ cup flour
½ tsp. baking powder
¼ tsp. salt
⅓ cup walnuts, chopped

Sweet brandy frosting:
2 Tbsp. margarine, softened
1 cup confectioners sugar
1 Tbsp. creme de cacao
1 Tbsp. brandy

Yield: 24 small bars

Cream margarine and sugar until fluffy; add eggs; beat well. Blend in chocolate, creme de cacao and brandy. Mix dry ingredients. Stir into chocolate mixture; fold in nuts. Spread in greased 9x9-inch pan. Bake 20 to 25 minutes at 350°F; cool. Combine margarine, confectioners sugar, creme de cacoa and brandy. Frost brownies.

Maureen Lyons (Mrs. Ken)

SALTED NUT ROLL

1 (18.25 oz) yellow cake mix
1 cup margarine, divided
1 egg
3 to 4 cups miniature marshmallows
1 (12 oz.) pkg. peanut butter morsels
2 Tbsp. vanilla
⅔ cup light corn syrup
2 cups (12 oz.) salted cocktail peanuts

Yield: 24 bars

Combine cake mix, ⅔ cup margarine and egg; spread in a greased 9x13-inch baking pan. Bake 10 minutes at 325°F. Sprinkle marshmallows over cake and bake 5 minutes. Melt peanut butter morsels, vanilla, and remaining ⅓ cup margarine in a saucepan; pour over marshmallows. Press peanuts into syrup. Cool; cut into squares.

Kathryn Blaha (Mrs. David)

CHOCO-CARAMEL COOKIE BARS

1 (8 oz.) box rectangular
    butter crackers
½ cup margarine, melted
⅓ cup milk
½ cup sugar
¾ cup brown sugar, firmly packed
1 cup graham cracker crumbs
⅔ cup creamy peanut butter
1 cup semi-sweet chocolate morsels

Yield: 60 small bars

Line a 9x13-inch pan with crackers; set aside. Combine margarine, milk, sugars, and graham cracker crumbs in saucepan; boil gently 5 minutes stirring constantly. Pour over crackers. Immediately top with another layer of crackers. Melt peanut butter and chocolate morsels in top of double boiler. Spread over cracker mixture. Refrigerate until firm.

Verda Stief (Mrs. Charles)

DOUBLE CHOCOLATE BROWNIES
A favorite after-school snack.

4 (1 oz.) squares
    unsweetened chocolate
1 cup butter or margarine
2 cups sugar
4 eggs
2 tsp. vanilla
1 cup flour
⅛ tsp. salt
1 (12 oz.) pkg. semi-sweet
    chocolate morsels
2 cups miniature marshmallows
confectioners sugar

Yield: 24 bars

Melt unsweetened chocolate and butter; add sugar; cool. Add eggs, one at a time, beating after each. Add vanilla, flour and salt; mix until well-blended. Fold in chocolate morsels and marshmallows. Pour into a greased 9x13-inch pan. Bake 30 to 35 minutes at 350°F. Do not test with toothpick as top may look bubbly. Dust with confectioners sugar.

Marty Nordmann (Mrs. Brian)

CHUNKY BROWNIES

Brownie base:
1 ¼ cups flour, divided
¼ cup sugar
½ cup margarine

Filling:
**1 (14 oz.) can sweetened
    condensed milk**
¼ cup cocoa
1 egg
1 tsp. vanilla
½ tsp. baking powder
**1 (8 oz.) milk chocolate bar,
    broken in small chunks**
¼ cup nuts, chopped
confectioners sugar

Yield: 36 bars

Combining 1 cup flour and sugar; cut in margarine until crumbly. Press into a 9x13-inch pan. Bake 10 to 15 minutes at 350°F. While brownie base is baking, beat milk, cocoa, egg, baking powder, vanilla and remaining flour. Stir in chocolate chunks and nuts. Spread over prepared crust. Bake additional 20 minutes or until center is set. Sprinkle with confectioners sugar when cool.

Arla Stegall (Mrs. Robert)

QUICK SUPER BROWNIES

1 (22.9 oz.) pkg. regular brownie mix
1 cup dairy sour cream
**1 (6 oz.) pkg. semi-sweet
chocolate morsels**
**confectioners sugar
    or candy sprinkles**

Yield: 24 bars

Mix brownies according to package directions adding sour cream and chocolate morsels. Spread into a greased and floured 9x13-inch pan. Bake 20 to 25 minutes at 350°F; do not over bake. While hot top with confectioners sugar or candy sprinkles.

Mary Wessels (Mrs.William)

ROCKY ROAD FUDGE BARS

Brownie base:
½ cup margarine, melted
1 (1 oz.) square
   unsweetened chocolate, melted
1 cup sugar
1 cup flour
½ to 1 cup nuts, chopped
1 tsp. baking powder
1 tsp. vanilla
2 eggs

Cream cheese layer:
2 (3 oz.) pkgs. cream cheese,
   softened
½ cup sugar
2 Tbsp. flour
¼ cup margarine
1 egg
½ tsp. vanilla
¼ cup nuts, chopped
1 cup semi-sweet chocolate morsels
2 cups miniature marshmallows

Frosting:
¼ cup margarine
1 (1 oz.) square unsweetened chocolate
2 oz. cream cheese
¼ cup milk
3 cups confectioners sugar
1 tsp. vanilla

Yield: 36 bars

Combine brownie base ingredients; blend well. Spread in greased 9x13-inch baking pan; set aside. Beat cream cheese, sugar, flour, margarine, egg and vanilla until fluffy. Spread over chocolate layer. Sprinkle nuts and chocolate morsels over cream cheese layer. Bake 25 to 30 minutes at 350°F or until toothpick inserted in center comes out clean. Sprinkle with marshmallows and bake 2 minutes. Melt margarine, chocolate, cream cheese and milk in large saucepan over low heat. Add confectioners sugar and vanilla; stir until smooth. Pour immediately over marshmallows and swirl together. Store in refrigerator.

Julie Schlesinger (Mrs. Michael)

BUTTERSCOTCH BARS

1 (18.25 oz.) box yellow cake mix
½ cup margarine, melted
3 eggs, divided
1 cup pecans, chopped
1 (8 oz.) pkg. cream cheese, softened
1 (16 oz.) box confectioners sugar
1 tsp. vanilla

Yield: 30 bars

Combine cake mix, margarine, 1 egg and pecans at low speed until blended. Pat evenly in lightly greased 9x13-inch baking pan; set aside. Combine remaining 2 eggs, cream cheese, sugar and vanilla; beat at medium speed until soft and creamy. Pour over top of cake mixture. Bake 40 to 50 minutes at 350°F until middle is set and lightly browned.

Hollis Cassidy (Mrs. Eugene)

NO BAKE BUTTERSCOTCH BARS

1 cup sugar
2 eggs, beaten
¾ cup butter or margarine
2 ½ cups graham cracker crumbs
2 cups miniature marshmallows
1 cup coconut
1 cup creamy peanut butter
1 (12 oz.) pkg. butterscotch morsels

Yield: 36 bars

Combine sugar, eggs and butter in a sauce pan; cook 5 minutes over low heat, stirring constantly. Stir in graham cracker crumbs, marshmallows and coconut. Press into greased 9x13-inch pan. Place peanut butter and butterscotch morsels in microproof bowl; microcook on high 1 to 2 minutes until melted; stir. Spread over first layer; refrigerate.

Mary Kenagy (Mrs. Dean)

CARAMEL PECAN DREAM BARS

1 (18.25 oz.) box yellow cake mix
⅓ cup margarine, softened
1 egg

Filling:
1 (14 oz.) can sweetened
    condensed milk
1 egg
1 tsp. vanilla
1 cup pecans, chopped
1 (6 oz.) pkg. almond brickle
    baking morsels

Yield: 24 bars

Combine cake mix, margarine and egg in large bowl; mix at high speed until crumbly. Press into a greased 9x13-inch baking pan; set aside. Beat milk, egg and vanilla until blended; stir in pecans and almond brickle morsels. Pour over crust; spread to cover. Bake 25 to 35 minutes at 350°F until light brown. Center may appear liquid, but will set upon cooling. Cool completely before cutting.

Marty Nordmann (Mrs. Brian)

ENERGY BARS
Excellent for hiking and bicycling trips.

½ cup margarine
½ cup chunky or creamy
    peanut butter
1 (10 oz.) pkg. miniature
    marshmallows
2 cups quick cooking rolled oats
2 ½ cups crispy rice cereal
1 ½ cups raisins or dried fruit bits
1 cup salted cocktail peanuts
sesame seed (optional)

Yield: 24 bars

Melt margarine, peanut butter and marshmallows in heavy saucepan. Combine oats, rice cereal, raisins and peanuts in large bowl. Pour peanut butter mixture over dry ingredients; stir. Spread mixture with greased hands into a greased 9x13-inch pan. Sprinkle top with sesame seed and press down lightly. Cool; cut into bars. Wrap individually with plastic wrap and refrigerate.

Alicemary Borthwick (Mrs. Gordon)

LEMON CHEESE BARS

1 (18.25 oz) box lemon cake mix
   with pudding
2 eggs, divided
⅓ cup vegetable oil
1 (8 oz.) pkg. cream cheese,
   softened
⅓ cup sugar
1 tsp. lemon juice

Yield: 24 bars

Combine cake mix, 1 egg and oil until crumbly; reserve 1 cup. Press crumb mixture lightly into an ungreased 9x13-inch pan. Bake 15 minutes at 350°F. Beat cream cheese, sugar, lemon juice and 1 egg until light and smooth. Spread over baked layer; sprinkle with remaining crumb mixture. Bake 15 minutes. Cool; cut into bars; refrigerate.

Caroline Larson (Mrs. Ronald)

MOM'S CHEWY CEREAL BARS
A Christmas tradition in Maureen's family.

3 cups crispy rice cereal
3 cups corn flakes, lightly crushed
1 cup coconut
1 cup salted peanuts
1 cup sugar
1 cup corn syrup
1 cup half and half or heavy cream
1 tsp. vanilla

Yield: 24 bars

Mix cereals, coconut and peanuts in large bowl; set aside. Combine sugar, corn syrup and cream in saucepan; cook until thick, between soft and hard-ball stage. Add vanilla. Pour syrup over cereal mixture; stir to blend. Pour into greased 9x13-inch pan. Cool; cut into bars.

Maureen Lyons (Mrs. Ken)

MIXED NUT BARS

First layer:
1 ½ cups brown sugar,
    firmly packed
1 cup butter, softened
3 cups flour
1 tsp. salt
2 cups mixed fancy nuts

Second layer:
½ cup light corn syrup
2 Tbsp. butter
1 Tbsp. water
1 cup butterscotch morsels

Yield: 40 bars

Cream sugar and butter; add flour and salt. Spread into ungreased 10x15-inch baking pan. Bake 10 to 12 minutes at 350°F. Sprinkle nuts over crust. Combine corn syrup, butter, water and butterscotch morsels in saucepan; boil, stirring constantly for 2 minutes. Pour over crust, covering all nuts. Bake 10 to 12 minutes. Cool; cut into bars.

Marilyn Dodd (Mrs. Charles)

OATMEAL BARS

1 ¼ cups boiling water
1 cup rolled oats
½ cup margarine
2 eggs
1 cup sugar
1 cup brown sugar, firmly packed
1 ½ cups flour
1 tsp. baking soda
1 tsp. cinnamon
1 tsp. salt

Frosting:
1 cup brown sugar, firmly packed
¾ cup margarine
½ cup pecans, chopped
½ cup milk
2 Tbsp. flour
1 cup coconut
2 tsp. vanilla
1 cup confectioners sugar

Yield: 24 bars

Pour boiling water over oats and margarine, let stand 20 minutes. Add eggs, sugars, flour, baking soda, cinnamon and salt; mix well. Pour into greased 10x15-inch baking pan. Bake 15 to 18 minutes at 350°F; cool. Melt brown sugar, margarine, pecans, milk, flour and coconut in a saucepan. Boil 3 minutes; remove from heat. Add vanilla; cool slightly. Add confectioners sugar; mix well. Spread over bars.

Jan Hugen (Mrs.Terry)

OATMEAL FUDGIES

A potluck favorite.

1 cup plus 3 Tbsp. margarine, divided
1 (14 oz.) can sweetened
   condensed milk
1 (12 oz.) pkg. semi-sweet
   chocolate morsels
2 tsp. vanilla
1 cup brown sugar, firmly packed
2 eggs
2 ¼ cups flour
1 tsp. baking soda
½ tsp. salt (optional)
3 cups quick cooking rolled oats

Melt 3 tablespoons margarine, milk, morsels and vanilla in a saucepan over low heat; set aside. Cream 1 cup margarine and sugar; add eggs. Add flour, soda and salt; stir. Stir in oats. Pat two-thirds of dough into a lightly greased 10x15-inch baking pan. Pour fudge mixture over the top. Drop remaining batter by tablespoons over the fudge mixture. Bake 20 to 25 minutes at 350°F; do not over bake. Cool before cutting.

Yield: 36 bars

Barbara Beichley (Mrs. Duane)

RAISIN CREAM BARS

Crust:
1 cup brown sugar, firmly packed
1 cup butter
1 ¾ cups flour
1 ¾ cups rolled oats
1 tsp. baking soda

Filling:
1 ½ cups raisins
3 egg yolks
2 ½ tsp. corn starch
2 cups half and half
1 cup sugar
⅛ tsp. salt

Yield: 24 bars

Mix sugar, butter, flour, rolled oats and soda; press one-half of crumb mixture in a 9x13-inch pan; set aside. Cook raisins in a small amount of water in saucepan; drain and set aside. Beat egg yolks in a saucepan; add cornstarch, half and half, sugar and salt. Mix well; add raisins. Cook over medium heat, stirring constantly until very thick. Pour over crust; top with remaining crumb mixture. Bake 15 to 20 minutes at 350°F.

Mary Baker (Mrs. Dean)

RHUBARB BARS

Filling:
2 Tbsp. cornstarch
¼ cup water
3 cups rhubarb, sliced
1 cup sugar
1 tsp. vanilla

Base:
1 ½ cups rolled oats
1 ½ cups flour
1 cup brown sugar, firmly packed
½ tsp. baking soda
1 cup shortening
½ cup nuts, chopped

Yield: 24 bars

Dissolve cornstarch in water in a saucepan; add rhubarb, sugar and vanilla. Cook until thick; rhubarb will not be tender. Mix oats, flour, sugar, soda and shortening until crumbly. Pat three-fourths of crumbs in ungreased 9x13-inch baking pan. Pour rhubarb mixture over crust. Sprinkle with nuts and remaining crumbs. Bake 30 to 35 minutes at 375°F.

Valois Brintnall (Mrs. Lee)

PEANUT BUTTER CUP BARS

1 cup butter or margarine, softened
1 ⅔ cups graham cracker crumbs
1 cup creamy peanut butter
3 to 3 ½ cups confectioners sugar
*1 (6 oz.) pkg. semi-sweet
    chocolate morsels*

Yield: 24 bars

Mix butter, graham cracker crumbs, peanut butter and sugar until well-blended. Press evenly into greased 9x13-inch pan; refrigerate one hour. Melt chocolate morsels and spread over peanut butter mixture. Cut immediately into squares. Store at room temperature.

Barbara Headley (Mrs. Michael)

BROWNIE BITES

½ cup margarine
4 (1 oz.) squares
   unsweetened chocolate
1 ½ cups sugar
1 tsp. vanilla
3 eggs
1 cup flour
40 walnut halves (optional)

Yield: 40 mini-muffins

Melt margarine and chocolate in saucepan over low heat; remove from heat. Stir in sugar and vanilla; add eggs, one at a time, beating well after each. Stir in flour. Spoon batter into paper-lined mini-muffin cups filling three-fourths full. Place walnut on top. Bake 18 to 20 minutes at 325°F or until top looks dry. Let cool in pans for 10 minutes; transfer to cooling rack.

Ann Meiners (Mrs. Gerald)

CAROUSEL COOKIES

1 cup margarine
½ cup sugar
1 egg, separated
1 tsp. vanilla
¼ tsp. salt
2 cups flour
1 cup crispy rice cereal, crushed
fruit preserves

Yield: 3 dozen

Cream margarine and sugar; blend in egg yolk, vanilla and salt. Add flour; mix well. Beat egg white until frothy. Shape level tablespoons of dough into balls. Dip balls into egg white; roll in crushed cereal. Place on ungreased cookie sheet. Flatten slightly; indent centers; fill centers with scant ¼ teaspoon of preserves. Bake 10 to 12 minutes at 375°F or until lightly browned.

Maxine Eckles (Mrs. Kenneth)

CHOCOLATE MERINGUE DROPS
Low calorie and chocolate!

2 egg whites, room temperature
¼ tsp. cream of tartar
⅛ tsp. salt
⅔ cup sugar
2 Tbsp. cocoa
¾ tsp. almond extract
2 Tbsp. miniature chocolate morsels

Yield: 3 dozen

Line two large cookie sheets with aluminum foil. Beat egg whites, cream of tartar and salt in mixing bowl on high until soft peaks form. Gradually beat in sugar, 2 tablespoons at a time, beating well after each. Add cocoa and almond extract; continue beating until meringue stands in stiff, glossy peaks. Drop level tablespoons of dough on cookie sheets. Sprinkle chocolate morsels on top of each cookie. Bake 1 hour and 15 minutes at 200°F or until set. Place cookie sheets on wire racks for 10 minutes. Carefully loosen and remove cookies; cool completely. Store in tightly covered containers.

Ann Meiners (Mrs. Gerald)

DOUBLE CHOCOLATE CHIP COOKIES

1 cup butter or margarine
1 cup sugar
½ cup brown sugar, firmly packed
1 tsp. vanilla
1 egg
⅓ cup cocoa
2 Tbsp. milk
1 ¾ cup flour
¼ tsp. baking soda
1 cup pecans, chopped
1 cup semi-sweet chocolate morsels

Yield: 3 dozen

Cream butter, sugars and vanilla until light and fluffy. Add egg, cocoa, and milk; mix well. Combine flour and baking soda; add to creamed mixture. Stir in pecans and chocolate morsels. Drop teaspoons of dough onto ungreased cookie sheets. Bake 10 to 12 minutes at 350°F. Cool slightly before removing cookies from cookie sheets.

Marilyn Downs (Mrs. Jim)

GOOD 'N SOFT COOKIES

2 ½ cups flour
1 tsp. baking soda
1 cup butter or margarine
¼ cup sugar
¾ cup brown sugar, firmly packed
1 (3.4 oz.) pkg. instant chocolate
    or vanilla pudding
1 tsp. vanilla
2 eggs
1 (6 oz.) pkg. semi-sweet chocolate
    or peanut butter morsels
1 cup pecans, chopped (optional)

Yield: 4 ½ dozen

Mix flour and baking soda; set aside. Cream butter and sugars; add dry pudding; beat until smooth and creamy. Add eggs and vanilla; blend. Gradually add flour mixture into batter; stir in morsels and nuts. Drop walnut sized balls onto ungreased cookie sheets about 2-inches apart. Bake 8 to 10 minutes at 375°F.

Carole Weber (Mrs. Delano)

THE BEST EVER CHOCOLATE CHIP COOKIE

2 cups butter, softened
2 cups brown sugar, firmly packed
2 cups sugar
4 eggs
2 tsp. vanilla
5 cups rolled oats
4 cups flour
1 tsp. salt
2 tsp. baking soda
2 tsp. baking powder
2 (12 oz.) pkgs. semi-sweet
    chocolate morsels
1 (8 oz.) milk chocolate bar,
    melted
3 cups nuts, chopped

Yield: 10 dozen

Cream butter and sugars in a large bowl; add eggs and vanilla. Process rolled oats in food processor until fine powder forms. In a separate bowl, mix flour, pulverized oats, salt, baking powder and baking soda. Combine creamed mixture and flour mixture; add chocolate morsels, melted chocolate and nuts; stir. Roll into balls and place 2-inches apart on ungreased cookie sheet. Bake 6 to 8 minutes at 375°F. Do not over bake.

Betsy Macke (Mrs. Mark)

SUPER COOKIES

The secret is chopping the candy before adding to batter.

1 (16 oz.) pkg. "M&M's" ®
    plain chocolate candies
1 cup margarine, softened
¾ cup brown sugar, firmly packed
¾ cup sugar
2 eggs
1 tsp. vanilla
2 ½ cups flour
½ tsp. baking soda
½ tsp. salt

Coarsely chop 1½ cups of candy; set aside. Cream margarine and sugars; add eggs and vanilla; beat well. Combine dry ingredients; add to creamed mixture and beat well. Stir in chopped candy. Drop tablespoons of dough onto greased cookie sheet. Bake 9 to 11 minutes at 350°F. Immediately after baking press 3 whole candies into each cookie.

Yield: 3 ½ dozen

Maureen Lyons (Mrs. Ken)

CHOCOLATE BITTERSWEETS

1 cup butter
1 cup confectioners sugar
1 tsp. vanilla
½ tsp. salt
2 cups flour

Filling:
2 (3 oz.) pkgs. cream cheese, softened
2 cups confectioners sugar
2 Tbsp. flour
½ tsp. vanilla
grated coconut (optional)

Frosting:
⅔ cup semi-sweet chocolate morsels
3 Tbsp. margarine
2 to 3 Tbsp. water
¾ cup confectioners sugar

Cream butter and confectioners sugar; add vanilla. Gradually add flour and salt. Shape dough into small balls; place on ungreased cookie sheets. With thumb, press an indentation into center of each cookie. Bake 10 to 12 minutes at 350°F . Combine filling ingredients. Place a generous amount of filling in center of cookie while still warm; let cookies set. To prepare frosting, melt chocolate morsels, margarine and water in a saucepan; add confectioners sugar. Beat until smooth; cool. Frost the filled-cookies.

Ann Meiners (Mrs. Gerald)

Yield: 5 dozen

GEBACKENS

This is made by Marilyn's mother, Eleanor Stegmann, not only for Christmas, but all occasions.

4 ½ *cups flour*
1 *tsp. baking powder*
½ *tsp. cinnamon*
1 *cup butter or margarine*
1 ¾ *cup sugar*
½ *cup heavy cream*
2 *eggs, lightly beaten*
½ *tsp. vanilla*

Yield: 6 dozen

Sift flour, baking powder and cinnamon; set aside. Cream butter, sugar, cream, eggs and vanilla. Add flour mixture; mix well. Chill overnight. On lightly floured surface roll dough, one-half at a time, to ⅛-inch thick. Cut with small cookie cutters. Place on greased cookie sheet ½-inch apart. Bake 10 to 12 minutes at 375°F. Cool; frost and decorate.

Marilyn Downs (Mrs. Jim)

GIANT SUGAR COOKIES

4 *cups flour*
½ *tsp. cream of tartar*
½ *tsp. baking soda*
¼ *tsp. salt*
1 ¾ *cups sugar*
1 *cup butter or margarine*
2 *eggs*
2 *tsp. vanilla*
2 *Tbsp. milk*
sugar

Yield: 20 cookies

Combine flour, cream of tartar, baking soda and salt; set aside. Cream sugar and butter until fluffy; add eggs and vanilla; beat well. Add milk; beat again. Add dry ingredients; beat until well blended. Using a ¼ cup ice cream scoop, place scoops of dough 2-inches apart on ungreased cookie sheet. Dip bottom of glass in sugar; flatten cookie to a 3-inch diameter. Bake 12 to 15 minutes at 375°F or until golden.

Barbara Headley (Mrs. Michael)

GRANDMA'S CARAMEL CREAM SANDWICH COOKIE

1 cup butter or margarine
¾ cup brown sugar, firmly packed
1 egg, lightly beaten
2 ¼ cups flour, sifted
sugar

Frosting:
2 Tbsp. butter, do not substitute
1 ¼ cups confectioners sugar, sifted
½ tsp. vanilla
2 Tbsp. heavy cream

Yield: 2-3 dozen

Cream butter and brown sugar; beat in egg. Add flour; stir until mixture forms a ball. Chill slightly for handling ease. Shape into balls about ½-inch round. Place on ungreased cookie sheet and flatten to ⅛-inch thick with cookie stamp or bottom of glass dipped in sugar. Bake 8 minutes at 325°F or until lightly browned. For frosting, heat butter in saucepan until lightly browned; remove from heat. Add confectioners sugar and vanilla gradually. Add cream until frosting meets desired consistency. Sandwich two cookies with frosting as filling.

Suzanne Brown (Mrs. Gregory)

HONOLULU COOKIES

1 cup shortening
1 cup sugar
1 cup brown sugar, firmly packed
2 eggs
¼ tsp. orange flavoring
¼ tsp. butter flavoring
2 tsp. vanilla
½ tsp. coconut flavoring
1 ¾ cups flour
1 tsp. baking soda
1 tsp. baking powder
¾ tsp. salt
2 cups crispy rice cereal
2 cups rolled oats
1 cup nuts, chopped (optional)
1 cup coconut

Yield: 4 dozen

Cream shortening and sugar; add eggs one at a time; stir in flavorings. Add dry ingredients; mix well. Fold in cereals, nuts and coconut. Batter will be stiff. Drop teaspoonfuls of dough onto a greased cookie sheet; flatten slightly. Bake 10 minutes at 350°F or until golden.

Jinx Hill (Mrs. Michael)

ICED NUT ROLL COOKIES

5 cups flour
1 cup sugar
4 tsp. baking powder
1 tsp. salt
3 eggs, lightly beaten
1 cup milk
1 tsp. vanilla
1 cup butter

Filling:
¾ cup butter
1 ½ cup sugar
1 tsp. vanilla
7 cups walnuts, chopped
milk (optional)

Icing:
4 cups confectioners sugar
½ cup butter
1 tsp. vanilla
4 to 5 Tbsp. milk
1 cup nuts, chopped

Yield: 10 dozen

Mix flour, sugar, baking powder and salt; set aside. Cream eggs, milk and vanilla; pour liquid mixture into dry ingredients; mix lightly. Cut butter into mixture. Cover; chill 3 hours or overnight. For filling, cream butter, sugar, and vanilla; add nuts. Thin with milk if filling is too stiff. Divide dough into 10 sections. Roll each section into a rectangle shape. Sprinkle filling on top; roll jelly-roll style starting from long side; refrigerate. After chilling, cut rolls into 1-inch slices. Bake 10 to 15 minutes at 350°F on greased cookie sheet. Cream confectioners sugar, butter, vanilla and milk. Frost cookies and sprinkle with nuts.

Laura Allen

PEANUT BUTTER CHIP COOKIES

1 cup sugar
1 cup brown sugar, firmly packed
1 cup margarine
1 cup vegetable oil
1 egg
1 tsp. salt
1 tsp. baking soda
1 tsp. vanilla
2 cups flour
2 cups whole wheat flour
1 (12 oz.) pkg. peanut butter morsels

Yield: 4 dozen

Cream sugars, margarine, oil, egg, salt, baking soda and vanilla. Add flours; mix well; stir in peanut butter morsels. Form into 1½-inch balls or drop rounded tablespoons of dough onto ungreased cookie sheet. Press lightly with a fork. Bake 8 to 10 minutes at 350°F.

Variation: Substitute chocolate or butterscotch morsels or nuts in combination for the peanut butter morsels.

Deb Keefe (Mrs. Kevin)

REFRIGERATOR CRISP OATMEAL COOKIES

3 cups quick cooking rolled oats
1 cup brown sugar, firmly packed
1 cup flour
½ tsp. salt
1 cup margarine
1 tsp. baking soda
¼ cup boiling water

Yield: 4 ½ dozen

Mix oats, sugar, flour and salt; add margarine; mix well. Dissolve baking soda in boiling water and add to flour mixture. Form dough into a roll; wrap in waxed paper; chill overnight. Slice very thin; bake 10 to 12 minutes at 350°F.

Isola Harris (Mrs. G.W.)

WHOLE WHEAT OATMEAL COOKIES

1 cup butter or margarine
¾ cup brown sugar, firmly packed
¾ cup sugar
2 eggs
1 Tbsp. molasses
1 ½ cup whole wheat flour
1 tsp. baking soda
½ tsp. nutmeg
½ tsp. cinnamon
2 ½ cups quick cooking rolled oats
¾ cup walnuts, chopped
½ cup raisins

Yield: 5 dozen

Cream butter and sugars until light; beat in eggs and molasses. Add flour, baking soda and spices; mix well. Stir in rolled oats, nuts and raisins. Drop rounded teaspoons of dough onto greased cookie sheet. Bake 10 to 12 minutes at 350°F . Cool 1 minute on cookie sheet; remove cookies to wire rack.

Mary Holmer (Mrs. Tom)

SOUR CREAM COOKIES
WITH BROWN BUTTER FROSTING

A favorite recipe of Ann's grandmother which Ann now enjoys baking for her.

½ cup butter or margarine
1 ½ cups brown sugar,
    firmly packed
2 eggs
2 ½ cups flour
½ tsp. baking powder
1 tsp. baking soda
½ tsp. salt
1 cup dairy sour cream
1 tsp. vanilla

Brown Butter Frosting:
6 Tbsp. butter, do not substitute
2 cups confectioners sugar
½ tsp. vanilla
2 Tbsp. hot water

Yield: 5 dozen

Cream butter and sugar. Add eggs, one at a time, beating well after each; set aside. Combine flour, baking powder, baking soda and salt. Add the dry ingredients to the creamed mixture, alternating with the sour cream until well blended. Add vanilla. Chill dough until firm. Drop rounded teaspoonfuls of dough onto ungreased cookie sheets. Bake 10 to 12 minutes at 400°F; cool. Melt butter in saucepan 5 minutes or more until brown. It is important the butter browns; do not microcook. Keep hot; blend in sugar. Add vanilla and hot water; stir until it is the consistency for frosting. Frost cookies.

Ann Meiners (Mrs. Gerald)

THUMBPRINT COOKIE
A delicious and pretty cookie for that holiday cookie tray.

½ cup brown sugar, firmly packed
1 cup margarine
2 eggs, separated
1 tsp. vanilla
2 cups flour
½ tsp. salt
¾ cup pecans, finely chopped

Icing:
1 cup confectioners sugar
1 Tbsp. margarine, melted
1 to 2 Tbsp. milk
food coloring

Yield: 2-1/2 dozen cookies

Cream sugar, margarine, egg yolks and vanilla; add flour and salt; mix well. Roll a teaspoon of dough into a ball. Dip balls into lightly beaten egg whites. Roll in nuts. Bake 5 minutes at 350°F. Remove from oven; indent center with thumb. Return to oven and continue baking 8 minutes; cool. Combine sugar, margarine, milk and a few drops of food coloring. Blend until smooth; fill cookies with icing.

Variation: Substitute jelly for icing.

Joan Ballard (Mrs. Dale)

APPLETS

½ cup cold applesauce
2 (¼ oz.) envelopes
    unflavored gelatin
¾ cup applesauce
2 cups sugar
2 tsp. vanilla
1 cup pecans, chopped
confectioners sugar

Yield: 36 pieces

Combine ½ cup cold applesauce and gelatin; let stand 10 minutes. Place ¼ cup applesauce and sugar in a saucepan; heat to boiling. Add gelatin mixture and continue boiling gently for 15 minutes. Remove from heat; stir in vanilla and pecans. Pour into 8x8-inch baking pan; refrigerate overnight. Cut into squares and roll in confectioners sugar. Store in cool place.

Betty Twedt (Mrs. David)

CANDY IN A PAN

1 (6 oz.) pkg. semi-sweet
   chocolate morsels
1 (6 oz.) pkg. butterscotch morsels
¾ cup chunky or creamy
   peanut butter
½ cup margarine
2 cups miniature marshmallows
1 cup salted peanuts, divided

Yield: 48 pieces

Melt chocolate morsels, butterscotch morsels, peanut butter and margarine; cool slightly. Add marshmallows. Cover the bottom of a 9x13-inch pan with ½ cup salted peanuts. Pour chocolate mixture over peanuts; sprinkle top with remaining peanuts. Cool completely. Cut into squares.

Barbara Beichley (Mrs. Duane)

CHOCOLATE COVERED CHERRIES

3 Tbsp. margarine
3 Tbsp. light corn syrup
2 cups confectioners sugar
2 (10 oz.) jars stemmed
   maraschino cherries
1 (12 oz.) pkg. semi-sweet
   chocolate morsels
⅛ lb. (½ bar) of paraffin

Yield: 50 cherries

Combine margarine and corn syrup; add confectioners sugar. Keep mixing with hands. It will look like dry dough. Refrigerate. Drain cherries on paper towels. Melt chocolate morsels and paraffin on top of a double boiler. Take marble-size ball of sugar mixture and wrap around cherry. Dip in chocolate and place in a paper liner. Repeat steps with remaining cherries. Refrigerate 10 minutes to set chocolate. Set out at room temperature for one week. This allows sugar mixture to become liquid.

Linda McGregor (Mrs. Robert)

COCONUT CANDY

1 (2 lb.) box of confectioners sugar
1 ½ cups coconut
1 (14 oz.) can sweetened
    condensed milk
½ cup margarine, softened
1 cup nuts, chopped
1 (6 oz.) pkg. semi-sweet
    chocolate morsels
⅛ to ¼ lb. (½ to 1 bar) of paraffin

Yield: 2 dozen

Mix sugar, coconut, sweetened condensed milk and margarine; chill overnight. Melt the chocolate morsels and paraffin in a saucepan slowly. Form coconut mixture into small balls and pierce with a toothpick. Dip into warm chocolate to coat. Place on waxed paper to dry.

Kindera Severidt (Mrs. Dean)

CREAMY NUT CARAMELS

1 cup pecans, chopped (optional)
2 cups sugar
2 cups light corn syrup
½ cup butter
¼ tsp. salt
2 cups evaporated milk
1 tsp. vanilla

Yield: 30-40 squares

Grease a 11x15-inch baking pan. Pour pecans evenly over surface, if desired. Place sugar, corn syrup, butter and salt in a large saucepan. Bring slowly to a boil, stirring frequently. Slowly add milk; so as not to stop the boiling. Stir constantly and cook to the firm-ball stage, 240°F. Add vanilla and quickly pour into prepared pan. Mark into 2-inch squares, cool, cut and wrap each caramel in plastic wrap. Store in an airtight container and keep in a cool, dry place.

Heidi Krabbe (Mrs. Stephen)

211

CRUNCH-COATED PECANS

A holiday gift from the kitchen.

2 egg whites
1 cup brown sugar, firmly packed
¼ tsp. salt
1 tsp. vanilla
¼ cup margarine
1 lb. shelled pecans

Yield: 1 ½ quarts

Beat egg whites in a large mixing bowl until stiff peaks form. Beat in brown sugar gradually until meringue forms. Add salt and vanilla; beat well. Stir nuts into meringue until all are coated. Melt margarine in a 11x15-inch baking pan. Spread nut mixture in pan. Bake 1 hour at 250°F; stir every 10 minutes. Cool before removing from pan. Store in sealed container.

Tanya Davison (Mrs. Dennis)

FRENCH CHOCOLATES

2 Tbsp. flour
1 egg yolk
¼ cup sugar
1 cup milk, scalded
3 (8 oz.) sweet chocolate candy bars
chocolate sprinkles or pecans,
    chopped

Yield: 55 balls

Mix flour and egg yolk in top of double boiler. Add sugar gradually, continue stirring. Add milk very slowly. Cook stirring constantly until thick; cool. Melt chocolate in top of double boiler; add custard mixture gradually. Beat thoroughly with electric mixer until shiny. Cover and place in refrigerator 24 hours to chill. Make small balls and roll in chocolate sprinkles or chopped pecans. Refrigerate to store for a long time.

Joan Boyce (Mrs. Steven)

NEVER FAIL FUDGE

4 ½ cups sugar
1 (12 oz.) can evaporated milk
1 (12 oz.) pkg. semi-sweet
    chocolate morsels
1 (10 oz.) pkg. miniature
    marshmallows
½ cup butter
1 tsp. vanilla
2 cups nuts, chopped

Yield: 117 pieces

Mix sugar and milk in a large heavy saucepan. Slowly bring to a rolling boil; boil 8 minutes. Remove from heat. Add chocolate morsels, marshmallows and butter. When morsels, marshmallows and butter are melted; add vanilla and nuts. Blend; spread mixture in ungreased 9x13-inch pan. Cut into 1-inch squares.

Catherine McGregor (Mrs. Charles)
Charter Member

TIGER BUTTER

1 lb. white chocolate or
    vanilla flavored almond bark
½ cup creamy peanut butter
1 (6 oz.) pkg. semi-sweet
    chocolate morsels

Yield: 15-20 pieces

Place chocolate or almond bark in 2-quart microproof casserole and microcook at 50% power for 5 to 8 minutes until chocolate melts. Stir halfway through cooking time. Stir in peanut butter. Spread this on waxed paper coated cookie sheet. Immediately microcook chocolate morsels at 50% power for 3 to 5 minutes until melted. Drizzle chocolate over first mixture and swirl slightly. Refrigerate until firm; break into pieces. Place in airtight container and refrigerate.

Barbara Headley (Mrs. Michael)

TRUFFLES

1 ½ lb. milk chocolate morsels
⅓ cup heavy cream
⅓ cup light cream
1 ½ tsp. vanilla
cocoa

Yield: 3 dozen

Combine chocolate morsels and creams in 2-quart microproof casserole dish. Cook 2 minutes at full power; stir. Continue to cook until chocolate is melted; cool. Add vanilla. Beat until mixture is light and fluffy; refrigerate until firm. Roll into 1-inch balls and roll in cocoa. Store in cool place.

Jinita Boyd (Mrs. Douglas)

EASY CANDY

1 lb. vanilla flavored almond bark
½ cup creamy peanut butter
1 (8 oz.) jar dry roasted peanuts
2 cups miniature marshmallows
1 ½ cups crispy rice cereal

Yield: 45 pieces

Melt almond bark and peanut butter in large saucepan. Remove from heat; add peanuts, marshmallows and cereal. Drop by spoonfuls onto waxed paper. Allow 20 to 30 minutes to cool and set. Store in cool place.

Marilyn Downs (Mrs. Jim)

The Dessert Cart

HARVEST APPLE CAKE

Cake:
2 eggs
2 cups sugar
½ cup vegetable oil
1 tsp. vanilla
2 cups flour
½ tsp. salt
1 tsp. baking soda
2 tsp. cinnamon
¼ tsp. nutmeg
1 cup walnuts, chopped
4 cups apples, peeled and chopped

Preheat oven to 350°F. Beat eggs until light and fluffy. Gradually add sugar, vegetable oil and vanilla. Sift dry ingredients. Add to first mixture. Stir in apples and nuts. Grease a 9x13-inch baking pan. Pour batter into baking pan and bake about 45 minutes. Let cool in pan on rack for 15 minutes. Blend cream cheese, margarine, salt, vanilla and confectioners sugar until smooth. Spread over cooled cake.

Frosting:
1 (3 oz.) pkg. cream cheese, softened
3 Tbsp. margarine, softened
⅛ tsp. salt
½ tsp. vanilla
1 ½ cups confectioners sugar

Catherine Lester (Mrs. Carl)

Yield: 15-16 servings

CHOCOLATE CREAM CAKE
Makes its own frosting while it bakes!

1 (18.25 oz) German chocolate
    cake mix
½ cup margarine, melted
4 eggs, divided
1 (8 oz.) pkg. cream cheese, softened
1 (1 lb.) box confectioners sugar

Yield: 12-15 servings

Preheat oven to 350°F. Combine cake mix, margarine and two beaten eggs. Grease and flour a 9x13-inch baking pan. Pour cake batter into pan. Mix cream cheese, two beaten eggs and confectioners sugar. Pour evenly over chocolate batter. Bake 35 to 40 minutes or until top is lightly browned.

Verda Stief (Mrs. Charles)

BANANA CAKE SUPREME

Cake:
2 ½ cups flour, sifted
1 ⅔ cups sugar
1 ¼ tsp. baking powder
1 ¼ tsp. baking soda
1 tsp. salt (optional)
⅔ cup shortening
⅔ cup buttermilk, divided
1 ¼ cup bananas, mashed
2 large eggs, unbeaten
⅔ cup pecans or walnuts, chopped

Frosting:
1 cup milk
6 Tbsp. flour
1 cup butter or margarine, softened
1 cup sugar
1 tsp. maple extract

Yield: 16-20 servings

Preheat oven to 350°F. Grease and flour a 9x13-inch baking pan. Sift flour, sugar, baking powder, baking soda and salt in large mixing bowl. Add shortening, the first ⅓ cup buttermilk and bananas. Beat vigorously for 2 minutes. Add remaining buttermilk and eggs. Repeat beating for 2 minutes. Fold in chopped nuts and pour into prepared pan. Bake 30 to 35 minutes or until toothpick inserted in center comes out clean. Cool completely on wire rack. In medium-size sauce pan, combine milk and flour and stir until flour is dissolved. Cook over medium heat, stirring constantly until mixture is thickened and begins to pull away from the side of the pan. Remove from heat and cool completely. Cream butter and sugar until fluffy. Add vanilla and flour mixture. Beat 10 minutes on high speed. Frost cake and refrigerate. Frosting will harden somewhat. This makes a generous amount of frosting.

Variation: Substitute vanilla for maple extract for a vanilla frosting which can be used with any cake.

Barbara Headley (Mrs. Michael)

COCA-COLA® CAKE

*Margaret's father sold Coca-Cola® for over thirty years.
This was a special treat at her home.*

Cake:
1 cup butter, softened
1 ¾ cup sugar
2 eggs, lightly beaten
½ cup buttermilk
2 cups flour
3 Tbsp. cocoa
1 tsp. baking soda
1 tsp. vanilla
1 ½ cups miniature marshmallows
1 cup Coca-Cola®
½ cup nuts, chopped

Frosting:
¼ cup butter
2 Tbsp. plus 2 tsp. Coca-Cola®
2 cups confectioners sugar
1 ½ Tbsp. cocoa
½ cup nuts, chopped

Yield: 15-18 servings

Preheat oven to 350°F. Grease and flour a 9x13-inch baking pan. In small bowl, sift flour, cocoa and baking soda. Set aside. In large mixing bowl, cream butter and sugar. Add eggs. Beat well. Add flour mixture alternately with buttermilk. Beat well for 1 minute. Add vanilla. Beat again. Stir in marshmallows, Coca-Cola® and chopped nuts. Pour batter into prepared pan. Bake 45 minutes. Cool cake. Blend butter, Coca-Cola®, confectioners sugar and cocoa until creamy. Stir in nuts. Spread over cooled cake.

Margaret Gervich (Mrs. Douglas)

HUMMINGBIRD CAKE

Cake:
3 cups flour
1 tsp. baking soda
½ tsp. salt
2 cups sugar
1 tsp. cinnamon
3 eggs, beaten
¾ cup vegetable oil
1 ½ tsp. vanilla
1 (8 oz.) can crushed pineapple,
    undrained
1 ½ cup pecans, chopped, divided
1 ¾ cups bananas, mashed

Frosting:
½ cup butter or margarine,
    softened
1 (8 oz.) pkg. cream cheese, softened
1 (1 lb.) box confectioners sugar,
    sifted
1 tsp. vanilla

Yield: 14-16 servings

Preheat oven to 350°F. Grease and flour three 9-inch round cake pans. Combine flour, baking soda, salt, sugar and cinnamon in a large bowl. Add eggs and vegetable oil, stirring until dry ingredients are moistened. Do not beat. Stir in vanilla, pineapple, 1 cup pecans and bananas. Pour batter into three prepared cake pans. Bake 23 to 28 minutes or until a toothpick inserted in center comes out clean. Cool in pans 10 minutes. Remove from pans and let cool completely on wire racks. Cream butter and cream cheese. Gradually add confectioners sugar, beat until light and fluffy. Stir in vanilla. Stir remaining pecans into frosting, if desired, or reserve them to sprinkle over top of frosted cake. Spread frosting between layers and on top and sides of cake.

Pat Shobe (Mrs. Richard)

ITALIAN CREAM CAKE

This is a very rich and elegant dessert.

Cake:
½ cup butter, softened
½ cup shortening
2 cups sugar
5 egg yolks
2 cups flour
½ tsp. baking soda
1 cup buttermilk
1 tsp. vanilla
5 egg whites, room temperature

Frosting:
1 (8 oz.) pkg. cream cheese, softened
¼ cup butter, softened
3-4 cups confectioners sugar
1 tsp. vanilla
coconut

Yield: 14-16 servings

Preheat oven to 350°F. Cream butter, shortening, sugar and egg yolks until fluffy. Sift flour with baking soda and add alternately with buttermilk. Blend well. Add vanilla. Beat again. In separate bowl whip egg whites with clean beaters. Fold egg whites into batter. Line three 9-inch round cake pans with brown paper. Pour 2¼ cups batter into each pan. Bake for 25 to 30 minutes. Cool and remove from pans. Cool completely. Mix cream cheese, butter, confectioners sugar and vanilla until creamy. Spread between layers and on sides and top of cake. Sprinkle generously with coconut on top and sides of cake. In hot weather, refrigerate.

Maureen Lewis (Mrs. Philip)

TURTLE CAKE
A chocolate lovers dream!

Cake:
1 (18.25 oz.) box German
    chocolate cake mix
½ cup margarine, softened
1 ½ cups water
½ cup vegetable oil
1 (14 oz.) can sweetened
    condensed milk, divided
1 (1 lb.) bag of caramels
¾ cup pecans, chopped

Frosting:
½ cup margarine
3 Tbsp. cocoa
2-3 Tbsp. milk
1 (1 lb.) box confectioners sugar
1 tsp. vanilla

Yield: 18-21 servings

Preheat oven to 350°F. Grease a 9x13-inch baking pan. Combine cake mix, margarine, water, vegetable oil and one-half of the can of sweetened condensed milk. Beat well. Pour one-half of batter into prepared pan. Bake 20 to 25 minutes. While baking, melt and mix caramels and remaining one-half of sweetened condensed milk in saucepan over low heat. Spread over baked layer. Sprinkle with pecans. Cover with remaining half of batter. Bake 25 to 35 minutes longer. In saucepan, melt margarine and cocoa. Remove from heat and add milk, confectioners sugar and vanilla. Stir with a spoon until mixed. Beat with an electric mixer until smooth. Spread over cake. Makes a generous amount of frosting.

Marty Nordmann (Mrs. Brian)

WHOLE WHEAT CARROT CAKE

Cake:
2 cups whole wheat flour
1 Tbsp. toasted wheat germ
1 tsp. baking powder
1 tsp. baking soda
1 tsp. salt
1 tsp. cinnamon
1 1/4 cups honey
1/2 cup margarine or butter, melted
1 tsp. molasses
1 tsp. vanilla
4 eggs
3 cups carrots, finely shredded
1 cup pecans, chopped

Frosting:
1 (8 oz.) pkg. cream cheese
1/2 cup margarine or butter, softened
2 cups confectioners sugar
1 tsp. vanilla
1/2 tsp. molasses or honey
1/4 cup pecans, chopped

Yield: 12 servings

Preheat oven to 350°F. Grease and flour two 8-inch round baking pans. In a mixing bowl, combine flour, wheat germ, baking powder, soda, salt and cinnamon. Add honey, margarine, molasses and vanilla. Beat with electric mixer on low speed until combined. Add eggs, one at a time, beating well after each addition. Stir in carrots and pecans. Pour into prepared pans. Bake 30 to 35 minutes. Cool on wire racks 10 minutes. Remove from pans. Cool completely. Beat softened cream cheese and margarine with electric mixer on high speed until fluffy. Beat in 2 cups sifted confectioners sugar, vanilla and molasses. Stir in pecans. Frost between layers and top cake with frosting. Store covered in refrigerator.

Abby Kersbergen (Mrs. Dan)

CHOCOLATE CHIP CHEESECAKE

1 (6 oz.) ready-made chocolate
    pie crust
1 (8 oz.) pkg. cream cheese, softened
2 (3 oz.) pkgs. cream cheese, softened
1 cup sugar
1/2 cup dairy sour cream
1 Tbsp. flour
1 egg
1 (6 oz.) pkg. miniature
    chocolate morsels

Yield: 8 servings

Preheat oven to 325°F. Beat cream cheese and sugar until fluffy. Add sour cream, flour and egg. Blend well. Fold in chocolate morsels. Pour into crust. Bake 1 hour and 30 minutes. Cool on a wire rack. Refrigerate.

Variation: To make a homemade chocolate crumb crust, crush 24 chocolate wafer cookies. Add 1/4 cup sugar and 3 tablespoons melted margarine. Pat into a 9-inch pie pan.

Sally Walberg (Mrs. Ron)

STRAWBERRY CHEESECAKE

1 ¾ cups graham cracker crumbs
¼ cup walnuts, finely chopped
½ tsp. cinnamon
½ cup butter, melted
3 eggs
2 (8 oz.) pkgs. cream cheese,
  softened
1 cup sugar
¼ tsp. salt
2 tsp. vanilla
½ tsp. almond extract
3 cups dairy sour cream

Glaze:
3 cups fresh strawberries
1 cup water
1 ½ Tbsp. cornstarch
½ - ¾ cup sugar
2-3 drops red food coloring
  (optional)

Yield: 12-15 servings

Preheat oven to 375°F. Mix graham cracker crumbs, walnuts, cinnamon and butter. Press on bottom and sides of a 9-inch springform pan. Combine eggs, cream cheese, sugar, salt, vanilla and almond extract; beat until smooth. Blend in sour cream. Pour into crumb crust. Bake 35 to 45 minutes or just until set. Cool on a wire rack. Chill well, 4 to 5 hours. The filling will be soft. Crush 1 cup of the strawberries and place in a saucepan with water. Cook over medium heat for 2 minutes. Sieve strawberry mixture and return liquid to saucepan. Mix cornstarch with sugar. The amount of sugar used will depend on sweetness of berries. Stir sugar mixture into hot berry mixture and bring to a boil, stirring constantly. Cook and stir until it is thick and clear. Two to three drops of red food coloring may be added. Cool to room temperature. Place the remaining 2 cups of strawberries on the cheesecake. Pour the glaze over the top.

Noel Lund (Mrs. Ted)

223

ROYAL RASPBERRY CAKE

Cake:
2 cups flour
½ tsp. salt
1 Tbsp. baking powder
⅓ cup butter, softened
1 cup sugar
1 egg, room temperature
1 cup milk, room temperature
1 tsp. vanilla
3 ½ cups fresh or frozen (unthawed)
* unsweetened, whole raspberries*

Glaze:
1 ½ cups confectioners sugar
2 Tbsp. heavy cream or milk
1 Tbsp. margarine, melted
1 tsp. vanilla

Yield: 16-20 servings

Preheat oven to 350°F. Grease and flour a 9x13-inch baking pan. Stir flour, salt and baking powder in a bowl with wire whisk and set aside. Cream butter with mixer; add sugar gradually, beating well until mixture is fluffy and light. Stir in egg; beat 1 minute. Combine milk and vanilla. Add dry ingredients alternately with milk/vanilla mixture, beating well after each addition. Spread cake batter into prepared pan. Spread the berries evenly over the top of batter. Bake 35 to 45 minutes or until center of cake springs back when lightly pressed. Cool 5 minutes. Combine glaze ingredients; spread over cake, leaving berries exposed. Serve warm with vanilla ice cream, if desired.

Barbara Beichley (Mrs. Duane)

LEMONADE CAKE

Cake:
¾ cup water
1 (3 oz.) pkg. lemon gelatin
1 (18.25 oz.) box yellow cake mix
4 eggs
¾ cup vegetable oil

Glaze:
1 (6 oz.) can frozen lemonade
    concentrate, thawed, undiluted
½ cup sugar

Yield: 12-14 servings

Preheat oven to 350°F. Bring water to boiling; remove from heat and add gelatin. Stir until dissolved. In large mixing bowl, combine cake mix, eggs, vegetable oil and gelatin. Beat at low speed until combined, then at medium speed for 2 minutes. Grease and sugar an 8-cup bundt pan. Pour batter into pan and bake 50 minutes or until toothpick inserted comes out clean. Cool 10 minutes. Invert cake onto a cake plate approximately 11-inches in diameter with a raised edge. Combine lemonade and sugar and spoon slowly over cake while still hot. Lemonade will absorb into the cake making it tangy.

Cindy Mack (Mrs. Thomas)

BAKED BROWNIE PUDDING

1 cup flour
¼ tsp. salt
1 ¼ cup sugar, divided
2 tsp. baking powder
4 Tbsp. cocoa, divided
½ cup milk
2 Tbsp butter, melted
1 tsp. vanilla
½ cup nuts, chopped
½ cup brown sugar, firmly packed
1 cup water

Yield: 8-10 servings

Preheat oven to 350°F. Grease a 7x9-inch baking pan. Sift flour, salt, ¾ cup sugar, baking powder and 1½ tablespoons cocoa. Mix dry ingredients with milk, butter and vanilla. Fold in nuts and pour into prepared baking pan. Mix remaining ½ cup sugar, 2½ tablespoons cocoa and brown sugar. Sprinkle dry ingredients over brownie batter and then pour water over the top. Do not stir! Bake uncovered 30 to 35 minutes. Serve warm.

Beattie Noonan (Mrs. J.J.)
Charter Member

APRICOT BREAD PUDDING

1 large loaf day-old French bread
4 cups milk
½ cup amaretto
1 cup chopped dried apricots
1 cup sugar
6 large eggs, lightly beaten
1 Tbsp. vanilla

Sauce:
½ cup unsalted butter or margarine
1 cup confectioners sugar
1 egg, beaten

Yield: 8-10 servings

Tear bread into pieces and place in a large bowl. Pour milk over and let soak for 1 hour. Heat amaretto in a saucepan until bubbles form around the edges and then pour over the apricots. Let this set for 30 minutes. Preheat oven to 350°F. Remove apricots with a slotted spoon. Reserve amaretto. Add apricots to bread. Stir sugar, vanilla and eggs into bread. Stir to lightly mix. Pour into greased 9x13-inch baking pan (or a 2 ½-quart casserole). Bake 30 to 45 minutes (bake 1 hour if using 2 ½-quart casserole). Melt butter and confectioners sugar together in a double boiler over simmering water. Stir constantly until creamy. Stir in reserved amaretto. Place 3 tablespoons of hot liquid into beaten egg and combine, then return all to the saucepan. Heat, stirring constantly 3 to 4 minutes to cook egg. Serve pudding warm with sauce spooned over.

Mid Lander (Mrs. Chuck)

226

CHOCOLATE STEAM PUDDING
This may be made ahead and frozen!

**3 (1 oz.) squares unsweetened
  chocolate
1 cup sugar, divided
1 cup milk, divided
½ cup margarine, softened
2 eggs
2 cups flour
1 tsp. salt
1 tsp. vanilla
1 tsp. baking soda
1 Tbsp. water**

**Sauce:
¾ cup sugar
1 pasteurized egg or egg substitute
⅓ cup vegetable oil
1 tsp. vanilla
⅛ tsp. salt
1 cup heavy cream**

Yield: 10-12 servings

Combine chocolate, ½ cup sugar and ½ cup milk on top of a double boiler and melt chocolate. Stir to blend. Set aside and cool. Combine in a large bowl remaining ½ cup sugar and margarine. Add eggs and beat well. In a separate bowl, mix milk and vanilla. In another bowl, combine flour and salt. Add liquid ingredients alternately with dry ingredients to the batter. Add cooled chocolate and mix well. Combine baking soda and water in separate bowl. Add to batter and blend. Spray an 8-cup souffle dish with non-stick vegetable spray. Pour batter into souffle dish. Cover lightly with a round of waxed paper. Place in top rack of a steamer and cover. Steam on top of stove for 1 hour and 10 minutes. Do not overcook. At this point, the pudding may be served after cooling somewhat. To freeze, cool pudding completely. The center will fall. Remove gently from dish onto aluminum foil and wrap well. Freeze. Before serving, remove from freezer and place wrapped pudding into oven. Bake 45 minutes at 200°F. Unwrap carefully to serve. To prepare sauce, beat sugar and pasteurized egg well. Add oil, vanilla and salt. Beat well again. Beat cream until peaks form. Fold into sauce. Serve pudding slightly warmer than room temperature with sauce.

Dorothy Fisher (Mrs. J.W.)

GREAT GRANDMOTHER'S CHOCOLATE SOUFFLE

This recipe has been served on Christmas Eve
in the McKay family since Karen's great grandmother
was a new homemaker in the early 1900's.

1 cup sugar
3 Tbsp. cocoa
5 egg whites, room temperature
⅛ tsp. salt
1 tsp. vanilla

Hard Sauce:
1 cup confectioners sugar
5 Tbsp. butter, softened
⅛ tsp. salt
1 tsp. vanilla

Yield: 8 servings

Preheat oven to 325°F. Sift sugar, cocoa and salt together three times. Beat egg whites until stiff peaks form. Fold dry ingredients into egg whites 1 tablespoon at a time with a whisk. Fold in vanilla. Pour into ungreased glass souffle dish. This may be refrigerated up to 30 minutes before baking. Bake 30 minutes. Serve souffle immediately. While souffle is baking, sift confectioners sugar. Set aside. Beat butter; add confectioners sugar gradually. Beat until well blended. Add salt and vanilla. Continue beating. When sauce is very smooth, chill slightly. Serve sauce over souffle.

Variation: Coffee, rum, whiskey or brandy may be substituted for vanilla in the hard sauce.

Karen Neuroth (Mrs. Loras)

BROWNIE PIE

½ cup margarine, softened
1 cup sugar
2 eggs
1 tsp. vanilla
½ cup flour
3 Tbsp. cocoa
¼ tsp. salt
½ cup nuts, chopped

Yield: 8 servings

Preheat oven to 350°F. Mix margarine and sugar until well blended. Add eggs and vanilla; beat again. In separate bowl, combine flour, cocoa and salt. Combine with first mixture until well blended. Stir in nuts. Place in a 10-inch pie plate. Bake 30 minutes. Serve warm with a scoop of ice cream on top.

Kathy Storck (Mrs. Robert)

HERSHEY PENNSYLVANIA CHOCOLATE CREAM PIE

1 (10-inch) baked pie shell
3 (1 oz.) squares
*   semi-sweet chocolate*
3 cups milk, divided
1 cup sugar
3 Tbsp. flour
3 Tbsp. corn starch
3 egg yolks, beaten
½ tsp. salt
1 Tbsp. butter or margarine
1 ½ tsp. vanilla
1 cup heavy cream, whipped
shaved chocolate curls

Yield: 8 servings

Heat 2 cups milk and chocolate to boiling. Set aside. Mix sugar, flour and corn starch. Set aside. Combine remaining 1 cup milk and egg yolks. Mix dry ingredients with milk and blend well. Add ⅓ cup of hot mixture to batter to combine, then pour batter into saucepan. Return to boil and boil for 1 minute. Add butter and vanilla; blend. Pour into baked pie shell. Cover with waxed paper and chill. Before serving, spread top with whipped cream and shaved chocolate curls.

Nancy Hartliep (Mrs. Gill)

SUMMER HEAVEN-FRESH FRUIT PIE

Our tester's son thought this pie was "awesome!"

1 (9-inch) baked pie shell
½ to 1 cup sugar, to taste
1 Tbsp. quick cooking tapioca
2 Tbsp. cornstarch
2 cups warm water
1 (3 oz.) pkg. gelatin
4 to 6 cups fresh fruit, chilled
1 cup heavy cream, whipped

Yield: 8 servings

Mix sugar, tapioca and cornstarch in a small bowl. Add to warm water in large sauce pan and bring to a boil. Allow to boil for 1 minute. Remove from heat and add package of gelatin. Select strawberry gelatin with sliced strawberries, raspberry gelatin with whole raspberries, peach gelatin with sliced peaches, etc. Although it is not totally set up, let glaze cool completely. Fold in generous amount of cooled, prepared fruit. Pour into pie shell and refrigerate until serving. Garnish with dollops of whipped cream.

Lorraine Schultz (Mrs. Ed)

DOUBLE CRUST LEMON PIE

pastry for 2-crust 9-inch pie pan
¼ cup cornstarch
¼ cup water
1 ½ cups boiling water
1 ½ cups sugar
1 Tbsp. butter or margarine
2 eggs, lightly beaten
¼ cup lemon juice, freshly squeezed

Yield: 8 servings

Preheat oven to 350°F. Blend cornstarch with ¼ cup water in a saucepan. Add boiling water. Cook and stir over medium heat until mixture comes to a boil and is thick and clear. Add sugar and butter. Cool. Stir in eggs and lemon juice. Turn into pastry-lined 9-inch pie pan. Add top crust. Bake 1 hour until pie is golden.

Joynell Raymon (Mrs. Larry)

230

SOUR CREAM LIME PIE

1 (9-inch) baked pie shell
1 (¼ oz.) envelope unflavored gelatin
1 cup sugar, divided
¼ tsp. salt
3 eggs, separated
2 tsp. grated lime rind
⅓ cup fresh lime juice
⅓ cup water
½ cup dairy sour cream
green food coloring (optional)
dairy sour cream or
  whipped cream (optional)

Yield: 8 pieces

Combine gelatin, ¾ cup sugar and salt in top of a double boiler. Blend in egg yolks, lime juice and water. Cook over simmering water stirring constantly, about 20 minutes until it is thick enough to coat a spoon. Stir in lime rind and 2 to 3 drops of green food coloring. Chill until mixture mounds when spread, check in 15 to 20 minutes. Blend into this ½ cup sour cream. In a separate bowl, beat egg whites until stiff peaks form and add ¼ cup sugar while beating. Fold this into gelatin mixture and fill a 9-inch baked pie shell. May top pie with sour cream or whipped cream. Chill until serving.

Hollis Cassidy (Mrs. Eugene)

PINEAPPLE CREAM PIE

1 (9-inch) baked pie shell
2 Tbsp. cornstarch
⅔ cup sugar
1 cup milk
2 egg yolks, beaten
1 (8 oz.) can crushed pineapple

Meringue:
2 egg whites
¼ tsp. cream of tartar
¼ cup sugar
¼ tsp. vanilla

Yield: 6 servings

Mix cornstarch and sugar. Gradually add milk and egg yolks. Mix and cook until thick, stirring constantly. Add crushed pineapple and juice. Pour into crust. Preheat oven to 400°F. In another bowl, beat egg whites and cream of tartar until foamy. Beat in sugar 1 tablespoon at a time and continue beating until stiff and glossy. Beat in vanilla. Spread over top of pie. Bake about 10 minutes or until light brown. Chill before serving.

Margaret Gervich (Mrs. Douglas)

RHUBARB CUSTARD PIE

1 (9-inch) unbaked pastry shell
1 cup sugar
3 Tbsp. flour
¼ tsp. salt
3 egg yolks
3 Tbsp. frozen orange juice
    concentrate, thawed
2 Tbsp. margarine, softened
3 cups fresh rhubarb,
    cut in ½-inch pieces
3 egg whites
⅓ cup sugar
⅓ cup pecans, chopped
whipped cream (optional)

Yield: 8 servings

Preheat oven to 325°F. Combine sugar, flour and salt. Add egg yolks, orange juice concentrate and margarine; beat smooth with electric mixer. Stir in rhubarb. In separate bowl, beat egg whites to soft peaks while adding sugar. Gently fold whites into rhubarb mixture. Pour into pastry shell. Sprinkle with nuts. Bake 55 minutes. Cool completely. Garnish with whipped cream, if desired.

Joan Boyce (Mrs. Steven)

APRICOT BURRITOS

1 (8 oz.) pkg. dried apricots, snipped
1 cup water
¼ cup sugar
¼ cup brown sugar
¼ tsp. cinnamon
¼ tsp. nutmeg
20 to 25 (6-inch) flour tortillas
cooking oil

Yield: 20 to 25 burritos

In a small saucepan, combine apricots, water, sugar, brown sugar, cinnamon and nutmeg. Bring to boiling; reduce heat. Simmer uncovered 10 minutes or until mixture is tender and thickened, stirring occasionally. Cool. To assemble, spoon about 1 tablespoon of apricot mixture along one edge of each tortilla; roll up. In a 12-inch skillet heat about ¾-inch of cooking oil to 350°F. Place five tortillas, seam side down, in hot oil. Cook 2 minutes until golden, turning once. Drain tortillas on paper toweling. Repeat with remaining tortillas. Serve warm.

Joan Boyce (Mrs. Steven)

APPLE DUMPLINGS

This is a simplified version of an old-fashioned favorite.

1 (15 oz.) pkg. refrigerated
    ready-made pie crust
4 Jonathan, Winesap or other
    small baking apples
    (2 ½ inch diameter),
    peeled and cored
¼ cup sugar
1 tsp. cinnamon
2 Tbsp. raisins (optional)
1 tsp. water
1 egg

Sauce:
½ cup sugar
1 cup water
2 Tbsp. margarine
¼ tsp. cinnamon
2-3 drops red food coloring

Yield: 4 dumplings

Preheat oven to 400°F. Allow 1 crust pouch to sit at room temperature 15 to 20 minutes. Unfold pie crust; peel off plastic sheets. Cut crust into fourths. From curved edge of each pastry piece, cut a leaf-shape to use as garnish. Place an apple in center of each pastry piece. In small bowl, combine sugar, cinnamon and raisins; spoon one-fourth of the mixture into each apple cavity. Bring sides of pastry up to top of apple. Press edges well to seal. Garnish with pastry leaf. Place in lightly greased 9-inch square baking pan. Repeat with remaining apples. In small bowl, beat egg and water. Brush over dumplings. Bake 15 minutes. In small saucepan, combine all sauce ingredients. Bring to a boil, continue boiling for 2 minutes. Pour over partially baked dumplings; bake additional 25 to 30 minutes until golden brown. Spoon sauce over dumplings several times during baking.

Arla Stegall (Mrs. Robert)

233

BAVARIAN APPLE TORTE

½ cup butter or margarine
1 ⅓ cup sugar, divided
¾ tsp. vanilla, divided
1 cup flour
1 (8 oz.) pkg. cream cheese, softened
1 egg
4 cups apples, peeled and sliced
½ tsp. cinnamon
¼ cup sliced almonds

Yield: 8 servings

Preheat oven to 450°F. Cream butter, ½ cup sugar and ¼ teaspoon vanilla in a small bowl. Add flour and mix well. Pat into the bottom and 1 ½-inches up sides of a 9-inch springform pan; set aside. In another small bowl, combine cream cheese and ½ cup sugar. Add the egg and remaining ½ teaspoon vanilla; mix well. Spread in the bottom of prepared crust. Combine apples, remaining ⅓ cup sugar and cinnamon; toss well. Place in an even layer on top of the cream cheese mixture. Sprinkle with almonds. Bake 10 minutes, then reduce temperature to 400°F and continue baking 25 minutes. Serve warm or cold.

Jolene Jebsen (Mrs. Darrell)

RHUBARB DESSERT

A quick and easy family dessert, say our testers.

6 slices thin-slice bread
butter
4 cups rhubarb, cut in 1-inch pieces, divided
1 ½ cups sugar, divided

Yield: 8-9 servings

Preheat oven to 400°F. Spread butter generously on 6 slices of bread. Cut bread into small cubes. Butter a 9x9-inch pan. Layer one-half of bread, one-half of rhubarb and one-half of sugar. Repeat these three layers. Bake 40 minutes.

Marie Watt (Mrs. Russell)

234

FRUIT PIZZA

Crust:
1 (20 oz.) tube refrigerated
    sugar cookies

Filling:
1 (8 oz.) pkg. cream cheese,
    softened
½ cup sugar
1 tsp. vanilla

Fruit layer:
fresh fruit of your choice

Glaze:
1 ½ cups pineapple juice
½ cup sugar
¼ cup cornstarch

Yield: 12-15 servings

Preheat oven to 350°F. Lightly grease a 14-inch pizza pan. Cut the cookie roll into ⅛ to ¼-inch slices and arrange on pizza pan. Lightly dust fingers with confectioners sugar and press dough together to make a continuous crust. Bake approximately 10 minutes or until golden brown. While crust is baking, prepare glaze. Combine pineapple juice, sugar and cornstarch in a saucepan. Cook over medium heat until thickened, stirring constantly. Remove from heat and let cool completely. Cool crust. In a small bowl, combine cream cheese, sugar and vanilla until well blended. Spread onto crust. Arrange fruit, such as strawberries, raspberries, blueberries, bananas, kiwi, or peaches on top of filling. Spread cooled glaze over all. Serve immediately.

Variation: Crust: 1 (8 oz.) tube of refrigerated crescent rolls. Unroll and press flat into a rectangle on a cookie sheet. Bake per package instructions. Cool. Glaze: 1 cup orange juice, ½ cup sugar and 2 tablespoons cornstarch. Prepare glaze according to method above.

Jane Norris (Mrs. David)
Julie Schlesinger (Mrs. Michael)

THREE BERRY LEMON TART

Pastry:
1 ½ cups flour
3 Tbsp. sugar
½ cup butter
1 egg yolk
2 Tbsp. lemon juice
2 Tbsp. water

Filling:
3 eggs
¾ cup sugar
⅔ cup butter, melted
2 tsp. grated lemon rind
¾ cup lemon juice

Topping:
1 cup strawberries
1 cup black currants
1 cup raspberries

Glaze:
½ cup red currant jelly
1 Tbsp. cassis or other liqueur

Yield: 10 servings

Preheat oven to 450°F. Combine flour and sugar. With pastry blender, cut in butter until crumbly. Blend in egg yolk, lemon juice and water. Roll out or pat pastry ⅛-inch thick. Place into a 10-inch flan pan. Trim excess crust and prick pastry. Bake 5 minutes or until golden. Cool completely. Reduce oven temperature to 350°F. In another bowl, beat eggs and sugar together. Blend in butter, lemon rind and lemon juice. Pour into pastry shell and bake 20 to 25 minutes or until filling is set. Cool slightly. Place strawberries in center of tart. Surround with ring of currants and finish with outer circle of raspberries. In a small saucepan, heat jelly until it is melted; stir in cassis. Brush over fruit.

Sally Robertson (Mrs. James)

CANDY BAR CUT-UP

A light dessert or salad with a surprise in the dressing.

5 (2.07 oz.) Snickers® candy bars
1 (8 oz.) container frozen
    whipped topping, thawed
5-6 apples

Yield: 10 servings

Chill candy bars well and chop into small pieces. Mix with frozen whipped topping. For better results, do this a day ahead. Chop apples into small bite-size pieces, leaving peels on. Add apples to dressing just before serving. Serve in sherbet glasses.

Jane Norris (Mrs. David)

BLITZ TORTE

Crust:
½ cup margarine
½ cup sugar
4 egg yolks
1 cup flour, minus 1 Tbsp.
4 Tbsp. milk
2 tsp. baking powder
1 tsp. vanilla

Meringue:
4 egg whites
1 cup sugar
1 (3 oz.) pkg. slivered almonds

Filling:
2 eggs
2 Tbsp. cornstarch
4 Tbsp. sugar
2 cups milk
1 tsp. vanilla

1 (10 oz.) pkg. frozen strawberries
    or fresh strawberries

Yield: 8-10 servings

Preheat oven to 350°F. Cream margarine and sugar. Add egg yolks one at a time. Add flour and milk alternately. Add baking powder and vanilla. Lightly grease and line bottom of two 8-inch round cake pans with waxed paper. Spread batter evenly in both pans. Set aside. In a large bowl, beat egg whites adding sugar until stiff peaks form. Spread meringue on top of torte batter. Sprinkle with slivered almonds. Bake 20 minutes. Cool on wire racks. When cool, remove from pan. Place almond side up. To prepare filling, lightly beat eggs, add cornstarch, sugar and milk. Cook over medium heat until thickened, stirring constantly. Remove from heat and add vanilla. Cover with plastic wrap and cool until set. To assemble torte, spread filling on first layer, then place second layer on top. Chill until ready to serve. Cut into 8 to 10 slices and serve with strawberries spooned over each slice.

Cathy Frost (Mrs. Curt)

FROZEN CADILLAC TORTE

A very easy microwave dessert which can be frozen for later use.

Crust:
¼ cup butter or margarine
30 chocolate wafer cookies, crushed

Filling:
3 cups miniature marshmallows or
*   32 large marshmallows,*
*   cut into fourths*
¾ cup milk
¼ cup Irish cream liqueur
1 cup heavy cream
½ tsp. vanilla
½ cup miniature chocolate morsels

Yield: 8-9 servings

Place butter in a small microproof bowl and microcook on high about 45 seconds to melt butter. Add cookie crumbs and stir well to moisten. Pat evenly into bottom and sides of 8x8-inch pan or 9-inch pie pan. Cover and refrigerate. Combine marshmallows and milk in large microproof mixing bowl. Microcook uncovered on high 1½ to 2 minutes, or until marshmallows are melted, then cool slightly. Stir well and add liqueur. Let stand until cool. In separate bowl, whip cream with vanilla until soft peaks form. Fold whipped cream into cooled marshmallow mixture and turn into chilled crust. Sprinkle miniature chocolate morsels around edge of dessert to garnish. Cover and freeze until firm.

Variation: Flavor the marshmallow mixture with different liqueurs for a variety of pies. Grasshopper pie: ¼ cup creme de menthe and 2 tablespoons white creme de cacao. Brandy Alexander pie: ¼ cup dark creme de cacao and 2 tablespoons brandy.

Jean G. Brennecke (Mrs. Earl)

CHOCOLATE TRIFLE

A chocolate-lovers delight!

1 9x13-inch chocolate cake,
   baked and cooled
1/2 cup coffee-flavored liqueur
3 (3.4 oz.) pkgs. instant
   chocolate pudding
4 ½ cups milk
2 (8 oz.) containers frozen
   whipped topping, thawed
6 (1.4 oz) chocolate-covered
   toffee candy bars

Yield: 15 servings

Cut cake into 1-inch cubes. Pour coffee-flavored liqueur over cake slowly so it will soak in. Mix instant chocolate pudding and milk. Chill 15 minutes to set. Crush chocolate-covered toffee candy bars. In a large glass bowl, 12-inch diameter and 5-inches deep, layer one-half of cubed cake, one-half of pudding, one-half of whipped topping and one-half of crushed candy bars. Repeat layers. Chill in refrigerator 2 hours or overnight before serving.

Cathy Frost (Mrs. Curt)

ENGLISH TRIFLE-THE EASY ONE

1 (10 ¾ oz.) pkg. frozen pound cake
   or equivalent amount of
   lady finger cookies
¼ cup raspberry jam
¼ to ⅓ cup dry sherry per taste
3 cups homemade custard or
   1 (5 ⅛ oz.) pkg. vanilla pudding
   and pie filling
1 (8 oz.) container frozen whipped
   topping, thawed or 1 cup heavy
   cream, whipped
½ cup slivered almonds

Yield: 8 servings

Slice pound cake into approximately 16 thin slices. Spread cake or lady fingers with a thin layer of raspberry jam. Place in the bottom of a trifle dish or other clear bowl. Sprinkle sherry over the cake. Prepare homemade custard or pudding mix as directed and cool completely. Spread pudding over the cake; top with whipped topping; sprinkle with slivered almonds. Use Pastry Cream Filling recipe (p. 240) for homemade custard.

Pat Marble (Mrs. Edwin)

PASTRY CREAM FILLING

Use with recipe for English Trifle—The Easy One.

2 cups milk
2 tsp. vanilla
½ cup plus 2 Tbsp. sugar
·6 egg yolks
2 Tbsp. flour
2 Tbsp. cornstarch
1 cup heavy cream, softly whipped

Yield: 3 cups

Scald milk, vanilla and ½ cup sugar in a saucepan. In a bowl, beat egg yolks with 2 tablespoons sugar until thick. Sprinkle in flour and cornstarch and continue beating until well mixed. Beat one-half of hot milk into yolk mixture; stir. Return to remaining hot milk and bring to a boil whisking constantly as it scorches easily. Remove from heat and let cool completely. Fold in whipped cream gently. This is a good filling for fruit tartlets, cream puffs and napoleons.

Maureen Lyons (Mrs. Ken)

CREAM PUFF DESSERT

½ cup margarine
1 cup water
1 cup flour
4 eggs
1 (5.1 oz.) pkg. instant
    vanilla pudding
3 cups milk
1 (8 oz.) pkg. cream cheese,
    softened
1 (8 oz.) container frozen
    whipped topping, thawed
chocolate syrup

Yield: 12-15 servings

Preheat oven to 400°F (375°F if using glass pan). Place margarine and water in a saucepan and boil until margarine melts. Remove from heat. Add flour and beat vigorously until it forms a ball. Add eggs, one at a time and continue beating. Spray non-stick vegetable spray into a 9x13-inch baking pan; spread dough evenly in pan. Bake 30 minutes; cool completely. Blend pudding with milk; add cream cheese and mix well. Let stand 15 minutes. Spread over cooled crust. Top with frozen whipped topping; drizzle chocolate syrup over the top. Refrigerate several hours before serving.

Barbara Beichley (Mrs. Duane)

DIRT DESSERT

This is a fun dessert for children's parties.

**1 (20 oz.) pkg. chocolate
    sandwich cookies
½ cup butter or margarine,
    softened
1 (8 oz.) pkg. cream cheese,
    softened
1 cup confectioners sugar
3 ½ cups milk
2 (3.5 oz) pkgs. French vanilla
    instant pudding
1 (12 oz.) container frozen
    whipped topping, thawed**

Yield: 15-20 servings

Crush chocolate sandwich cookies in blender until it looks like dirt; set aside. Cream butter and cream cheese. Add confectioners sugar, milk and dry pudding mix; stir until smooth. Fold in whipped topping. Line bottom and sides of an 8-inch diameter flower pot with aluminum foil. Layer one-third of cookie crumbs, one-half of pudding, one-third of cookie crumbs, one-half of pudding and top with remaining cookie crumbs. Refrigerate or freeze. A plastic flower is a nice garnish. Serve in the flower pot with plastic spades for spoons. Kids love candy worms on top!

Variation: Use 2 (3.5 oz.) pkg. of chocolate instant pudding instead of the French vanilla flavor.

**Lenora Brown (Mrs. Stanley)
Marilyn Dodd (Mrs. Charles)
Jolene Jebsen (Mrs. Darrell)
Donna Roasa (Mrs. Darryn)**

SUNDAE IN A PAN

¾ cup margarine, divided
10 whole graham crackers, crushed
4 large bananas
½ gallon strawberry ice cream,
*   slightly softened*
½ cup semi-sweet chocolate morsels
1 cup confectioners sugar
¾ cup evaporated milk
½ tsp. vanilla
1 (8 oz.) container frozen
*   whipped topping, thawed*
maraschino cherries (optional)

Yield: 12-15

Melt ½ cup margarine; combine with graham cracker crumbs. Press into a 9x13-inch baking pan. Slice bananas over the crust. Slice strawberry ice cream into fourths and spread over the bananas; freeze. In a saucepan, melt chocolate morsels with ¼ cup margarine; add confectioners sugar and evaporated milk. Cook over low heat stirring constantly until thick; add vanilla. Cool completely and spread over ice cream; freeze again. Top with whipped topping and garnish with maraschino cherries, if desired. Freeze. Allow to thaw 10 minutes before cutting and serving.

Barbara Beichley (Mrs. Duane)

SUNSHINE SHERBET

1 ½ quarts (48 oz.) orange soda
1 (14 oz.) can sweetened
*   condensed milk*
1 (15 ¼ oz.) can crushed pineapple,
*   including juice*

Yield: 1 gallon

Mix ingredients well. Freeze in home ice-cream freezer according to directions.

Tanya Davison (Mrs. Dennis)

INDEX

A

All-Day Mushrooms 17
APPETIZERS
  Canapés
    All-Day Mushrooms 17
    Burrito Roll-Ups 15
    Crazy Corn Nachos 15
    Creamy Chicken-Filled Turnovers ...14
    Kitten's Biscuits 16
    Mexican Vegetable Pizza Squares ...17
    Party Wedges 16
    Tortilla Crisps 14
    Vegetable Pizza Squares 17
  Dips
    Caramel Apple Dip 20
    Cheesey Fruit Dip 21
    Cinnamon Fruit Dip 21
    Creamy Orange Dip 21
    Hot Cheese and Pepperoni Pleaser ..22
    The Big Dipper 22
  Pick Ups
    Asparagus Roll-Ups 18
    B.L.T. in a Bite 19
    Baked Mushrooms 18
    Cucumber Sandwiches 19
    Mandarin Chicken Bites 20
    Saucy Chicken Wings 19
  Snacks
    Apricot-Almond Granola 11
    Crunch-Coated Pecans 212
    Hiker's Birdseed 11
    Party Pretzels 12
    Peanut Butter Popcorn 13
    Sugar and Spice Cocktail Nuts 13
  Spreads
    Bacon-Almond Cracker Spread 23
    Baked Brie with Almonds and
      Chutney 24
    Beefed-Up Cheese Ball 23
    Hot Gouda Cheese 24
Apple Dumplings 233
Apple Harvest Coleslaw 39
Applets 209
APRICOT
  Apricot Bread Pudding 226
  Apricot Burritos 232
  Apricot-Almond Granola 11
Apricot Bread Pudding 226
Apricot Burritos 232
Apricot Glazed Ham 127
Apricot-Almond Granola 11

ASPARAGUS
  Asparagus Roll-Ups 18
  Asparagus and Pea Casserole 170
  Asparagus with Pasta 184
  Chilled Asparagus with Dijon
    Vinaigrette 42
  Fresh Asparagus Soufflé 93
  Perfect Baked Asparagus 170
Asparagus Roll-Ups 18
Asparagus and Pea Casserole 170
Asparagus with Pasta 184
Avocado Salad Dressing 37
Avocado and Bean Salad 37

B

B.L.T. in a Bite 19
Bacon and Egg Lasagna 84
Bacon-Almond Cracker Spread 23
Baked Beans with Fruit 181
Baked Brie with Almonds and Chutney ...24
Baked Brown Rice 187
Baked Brownie Pudding 225
Baked Corned Beef 133
Baked Mushrooms 18
Baked Pheasant Under Glass 125
Baked Potato Salad 175
BANANA
  Banana Breakfast Shake 8
  Banana Cake Supreme 217
  Golden Banana Loaves 57
  Whole Wheat Banana Bread 56
Banana Breakfast Shake 8
Banana Cake Supreme 217
BARBECUE
  Barbecued Ribs 161
  Chicken Fajitas 164
  Fajitas 165
  Grilled Chicken Bundles 163
  Grilled Turkey Breast 163
  Hamburger Pinwheels 162
  Honey Apple Pork Chops 160
  Jimmy's Marinade for Beef 167
  Jody's Chicken Breast 164
  Marinated Flank Steak 161
  Marinated Salmon 166
  Mock Filets 162
  Pork Chops Teriyaki 160
  Sauce for Marinating 166
  Spicy Bar-B-Que Sauce 168
  Teriyaki Marinade 167
  Thompson's Tangy Rib Sauce 168
  Western Lite Marinade 166

Barbecued Ribs 161
Bavarian Apple Torte 234
BEEF
  Beef and Spinach Roll 141
  Cavatini 147
  Chimichangas 137
  Hamburger Pinwheels 162
  Hawaiian Meat Loaf 145
  Hearty Chili Con Carne 144
  Italian Beef 33
  King Boreas Barbecue 34
  Lobster-Stuffed Tenderloin of Beef 139
  Marinated Flank Steak 161
  Mock Filets 162
  Pantry Casserole 147
  Peppered Beef Tenderloin 140
  Quick Lasagna 138
  Salisbury Steak and Mushroom
    Sauce 146
  Sicilian Meat Roll 143
  Tostado Casserole 138
  Trader's Pie 142
  Waikiki Meatballs 143
  Wild Rice Baron 148
Beef and Spinach Roll 141
Beefed-Up Cheese Ball 23
Beer Cheese Soup 27
Beets with Mandarin Oranges 171
Bernie's Broccoli Salad 43
Best-Ever Chicken Salad 85
BEVERAGES
  Banana Breakfast Shake 8
  Champagne Punch 9
  Christmas Tea 9
  Iced Margaritas 10
  Orange Sherbet Cooler 10
  Strawberry Smoothie 8
  Yellow Birds 10
Blitz Torte 237
Blueberry Crumb Coffee Cake 67
Brandy Alexander Brownies 190
BREADS
  Coffee Cake
    Blueberry Crumb Coffee Cake 67
    Lady Lee Coffee Cake 68
    Pineapple Bundt Coffee Cake 69
    Poppy Seed Bundt Cake 69
    Raspberry Cream Cheese
      Coffee Cake 71
    Sour Cream Coffee Cake &
      Honey Nut Topping 70
  Herb Bread 183
  Muffins
    Fruit and Honey Muffins 72

Glazed Jam Puffs 74
Magic Marshmallow Crescent Puffs . 75
Morning Glory Muffins 73
Refrigerator Wheat Germ Muffins 72
Rhubarb Muffins 74
Sugar and Spice Muffins 73
Quick
  Golden Banana Loaves 57
  Peach Bread 57
  Pumpkin Swirl Bread 58
  Scones with Strawberry Almond
    Butter 97
  Strawberry Bread 58
  Whole Wheat Banana Bread 56
  Whole Wheat Biscuits 56
Waffles
  Gingerbread Waffles 76
  Poppy Seed Waffles 76
Yeast
  English Muffin Bread 65
  Food Processor Whole Wheat
    Bread 64
  German Sour Cream Twists 59
  Jam and Cream Cheese Loaf 66
  Quick Cinnamon Rolls 61
  Sarah's Rolls 60
  Swedish Christmas Tea Ring 62
  Three Loaf White Bread 63
BROCCOLI
  Bernie's Broccoli Salad 43
  Broccoli Cauliflower Salad 44
  Broccoli Raisin Salad 43
  Cheesey Broccoli Salad 42
  Raw Vegetable Salad 44
Broccoli Cauliflower Salad 44
Broccoli Raisin Salad 43
Broccoli-Ham Casserole 127
Broiled Scampi 158
Brownie Bites 200
Brownie Pie 229
BRUNCH
  Bacon and Egg Lasagna 84
  Brunch Casserole 79
  Cheese Soufflé 94
  Crescent Sausage and Cheese
    Squares 81
  Egg and Sausage Breakfast 81
  Eggs Tahoe 82
  Frittata 83
  Ham and Egg Casserole 80
  Italian Zucchini Pie 83
  Oven Cheese Fondue 78
  Seafood Brunch 80

This is Strata 79
Brunch Casserole 79
Burrito Roll-Ups 15
Butterscotch Bars 194

C

Cabbage, Carrot and Caraway Soup 28

CABBAGE
Apple Harvest Coleslaw 39
Cabbage, Carrot and Caraway Soup 28
Cabbage Patch Salad 38
Cabbage and Blue Cheese Soup 28
Chinese Cabbage Salad 39
Hot Cabbage Salad 40
Sour Cream Coleslaw 38
Sweet and Sour Red Cabbage 171
Cabbage Patch Salad 38
Cabbage and Blue Cheese Soup 28
Calico Salad 47
Canadian Cheese Soup 26

CANDY
Applets 209
Candy in a Pan 210
Chocolate Covered Cherries 210
Coconut Candy 211
Creamy Nut Caramels 211
Crunch-Coated Pecans 212
Easy Candy 214
French Chocolates 212
Never Fail Fudge 213
Tiger Butter 213
Truffles 214
Candy Bar Cut Up 236
Candy in a Pan 210
Caramel Apple Dip 20
Caramel Pecan Dream Bars 195
Carousel Cookies 200
Carrots Vicchy 173

CASSEROLE
Broccoli-Ham Casserole 127
Cavatini 147
Challupas 122
Chicken Enchiladas Supreme 121
Chicken Stuffing Casserole 107
Chicken Tetrazzini 114
Chicken and Wild Rice Casserole 117
Mexican Chicken Casserole 121
Microwave Chicken and Rice 116
Microwave Pizza Casserole 134
Pantry Casserole 147
Party Ham Casserole 128
Pork Chop Casserole 132
Quick Lasagna 138
Reuben Casserole 134

Santa Fe Enchiladas 136
Spinach Lasagna 185
Stuffed Pasta Shells 185
Tex-Mex Turkey Enchiladas 123
Three Cheese Enchiladas 136
Tostado Casserole 138
Trader's Pie 142
Turkey Lasagna 122
Wild Rice Baron 148
Cauliflower Supreme Salad 45
Cavatini 147
Celebration Casserole 188
Challupas 122
Champagne Punch 9
Cheese Manicotti 184
Cheese Meatballs with
    Spaghetti Sauce 149
Cheese Soufflé 94
Cheese and Vegetable Soup 27
Cheesey Broccoli Salad 42
Cheesey Crab-Stuffed Baked Potatoes 92
Cheesey Fruit Dip 21
Cheesey Wild Rice Soup 30
Cherry Glaze 133

CHICKEN
Best-Ever Chicken Salad 85
Challupas 122
Chicken Artichoke Salad 86
Chicken Breasts Diane 106
Chicken Breasts Dijon 110
Chicken Breasts in Phyllo 119
Chicken Breasts with Sherry Butter 111
Chicken Enchiladas Supreme 121
Chicken Fajitas 164
Chicken Marengo 105
Chicken Mozzarella 112
Chicken Stuffing Casserole 107
Chicken Tetrazzini 114
Chicken and Snow Pea Salad 86
Chicken and Wild Rice Casserole 117
Creamy Chicken-Filled Turnovers 14
Crepes Almondine 91
Crouton Chicken 111
Easy Chicken Wellington 118
Easy and Elegant Chicken Breasts 109
Elegant Chicken Breast 116
Fajitas 165
Fancy Chicken Bake 107
Foil Baked Chicken and Canadian
    Bacon 114
Fruited Chicken Salad 85
Grilled Chicken Bundles 163
Herb Chicken Stir-Fry 117
Jody's Chicken Breast 164

Katie's Chicken 110
Lemon-Marinated Chicken 120
Make Ahead Chicken Bake 112
Mandarin Chicken Bites 20
Mexican Chicken Casserole 121
Microwave Chicken and Rice 116
Parmesan Chicken Bake 109
Poppy Seed Chicken 108
Quik-Chix Monterey Style 106
Ruby Chicken 113
Saucy Chicken Wings 19
Sherry Orange Chicken 104
Spinach-Stuffed Chicken Breasts 115
Stuffed Chicken Breast for Two 108
Chicken Artichoke Salad 86
Chicken Breasts Diane 106
Chicken Breasts Dijon 110
Chicken Breasts in Phyllo 119
Chicken Breasts with Sherry Butter 111
Chicken Enchiladas Supreme 121
Chicken Fajitas 164
Chicken Marengo 105
Chicken Mozzarella 112
Chicken Stuffing Casserole 107
Chicken Tetrazzini 114
Chicken and Snow Pea Salad 86
Chicken and Wild Rice Casserole 117
Chicken in a Ham Blanket 113
Chilled Asparagus with Dijon
    Vinaigrette 42
Chimichangas 137
Chinese Cabbage Salad 39
Choco-Caramel Cookie Bars 191
CHOCOLATE
    Baked Brownie Pudding 225
    Brandy Alexander Brownies 190
    Brownie Bites 200
    Brownie Pie 229
    Candy Bar Cut Up 236
    Candy in a Pan 210
    Choco-Caramel Cookie Bars 191
    Chocolate Bittersweets 203
    Chocolate Chip Cheesecake.............. 222
    Chocolate Covered Cherries.............. 210
    Chocolate Cream Cake 216
    Chocolate Meringue Drops 201
    Chocolate Raspberry Cheesecake 101
    Chocolate Steam Pudding 227
    Chocolate Trifle 239
    Chocolate Truffle Loaf with Raspberry
        Sauce 100
    Chunky Brownies 192
    Coca-Cola Cake 218
    Coconut Candy 211

Dirt Dessert 241
Double Chocolate Brownies 191
Double Chocolate Chip Cookies 201
French Chocolates 212
Frozen Cadillac Torte 238
Good 'N Soft Cookies 202
Great Grandmother's Chocolate
    Soufflé 228
Hershey Pennsylvania Chocolate
    Cream Pie 229
Never Fail Fudge 213
Oatmeal Fudgies 198
Quick Super Brownies 192
Rocky Road Fudge Bars.................... 193
Super Cookies 203
The Best Ever Chocolate Chip
    Cookie 202
Tiger Butter 213
Truffles 214
Turtle Cake 221
White Chocolate Cheesecake........... 102
Chocolate Bittersweets 203
Chocolate Chip Cheesecake 222
Chocolate Covered Cherries 210
Chocolate Cream Cake 216
Chocolate Meringue Drops 201
Chocolate Raspberry Cheesecake 101
Chocolate Steam Pudding 227
Chocolate Trifle 239
Chocolate Truffle Loaf with Raspberry
    Sauce 100
Christmas Tea 9
Chunky Brownies 192
Cinnamon Fruit Dip 21
Clam Chowder 31
Classic Italian Spaghetti Sauce 148
Classic Spinach Salad............................. 40
Coca-Cola Cake 218
Coconut Candy 211
Company Carrots 172
CONDIMENTS
    Herb Butter 183
    Herb Seasoning Mix 183
    Red Tomato Chutney 183
COOKIES
    Bars
        Brandy Alexander Brownies 190
        Butterscotch Bars 194
        Caramel Pecan Dream Bars........... 195
        Choco-Caramel Cookie Bars 191
        Chunky Brownies 192
        Double Chocolate Brownies 191
        Energy Bars 195
        Lemon Cheese Bars 196

Mixed Nut Bars 197
Mom's Chewy Cereal Bars 196
No Bake Butterscotch Bars 194
Oatmeal Bars 197
Oatmeal Fudgies 198
Peanut Butter Cup Bars 199
Quick Super Brownies 192
Raisin Cream Bars 198
Rhubarb Bars 199
Rocky Road Fudge Bars 193
Salted Nut Roll 190

Drop
Brownie Bites 200
Carousel Cookies 200
Chocolate Meringue Drops 201
Double Chocolate Chip Cookies ... 201
Good 'N Soft Cookies 202
Honolulu Cookies 205
Peanut Butter Chip Cookies 207
Sour Cream Cookies & Brown
    Butter Frosting 208
Super Cookies 203
Whole Wheat Oatmeal Cookies 208

Molded
Chocolate Bittersweets 203
Giant Sugar Cookies 204
Grandma's Caramel Cream
    Sandwich Cookie 205
The Best Ever Chocolate Chip
    Cookie 202
Thumbprint Cookie 209

Refrigerator
Iced Nut Roll Cookies 206
Refrigerator Crisp Oatmeal
    Cookies 207

Rolled
Gebackens 204
Corn Bacon Curry Bake 174
Crazy Corn Nachos 15
Cream Puff Dessert 240
Creamed Pheasant 126
Creamy Chicken-Filled Turnovers 14
Creamy Ham Salad 50
Creamy Nut Caramels 211
Creamy Orange Dip 21
Creole Pork Chops 131
Crepes Almondine 91
Crescent Sausage and Cheese Squares 81
Crouton Chicken 111
Crunch Veggie Gelatin 51
Crunch-Coated Pecans 212
Cucumber Sandwiches 19
Cucumbers with Sour Cream 45

D
Deep Dish Chicago Style Pizza 135
DESSERTS
Cakes
Banana Cake Supreme 217
Chocolate Cream Cake 216
Coca-Cola Cake 218
Harvest Apple Cake 216
Hummingbird Cake 219
Italian Cream Cake 220
Lemonade Cake 225
Royal Raspberry Cake 224
Turtle Cake 221
Whole Wheat Carrot Cake 222

Cheesecake
Chocolate Chip Cheesecake 222
Chocolate Raspberry Cheesecake .. 101
Strawberry Cheesecake 223
White Chocolate Cheesecake 102

Frozen
Sundae in a Pan 242
Sunshine Sherbet 242

Fruit
Apple Dumplings 233
Apricot Burritos 232
Bavarian Apple Torte 234
Candy Bar Cut Up 236
Fruit Pizza 235
Rhubarb Dessert 234
Strawberry Meringue Dessert 99
Three Berry Lemon Tart 236
Toffee Strawberry Continental 98
Great Grandmother's Chocolate
    Soufflé 228

Pies
Brownie Pie 229
Double Crust Lemon Pie 230
Hershey Pennsylvania Chocolate
    Cream Pie 229
Pineapple Cream Pie 231
Rhubarb Custard Pie 232
Sour Cream Lime Pie 231
Summer Heaven-Fresh Fruit Pie 230

Pudding
Apricot Bread Pudding 226
Baked Brownie Pudding 225
Chocolate Steam Pudding 227

Refrigerator
Chocolate Truffle Loaf with
    Raspberry Sauce 100
Cream Puff Dessert 240
Dirt Dessert 241
French Creme Mold 98

Pastry Cream Filling 240
Tortes
    Blitz Torte 237
    Frozen Cadillac Torte 238
Trifles
    Chocolate Trifle 239
    English Trifle 239
Dilled Tomatoes 46
Dirt Dessert 241
Double Chocolate Brownies 191
Double Chocolate Chip Cookies 201
Double Crust Lemon Pie 230
DRESSINGS
    Avocado Salad Dressing..................... 37
    Grandma's Potato Salad Dressing........ 36
    Parmesan Cheese Dressing................. 36
E
Easy Candy 214
Easy Chicken Wellington 118
Easy Fixin' Pheasant 124
Easy and Elegant Chicken Breasts 109
Egg and Sausage Breakfast..................... 81
EGGS
    Bacon and Egg Lasagna 84
    Brunch Casserole 79
    Crescent Sausage and Cheese
        Squares 81
    Egg and Sausage Breakfast.................. 81
    Eggs Tahoe 82
    Frittata 83
    Oven Cheese Fondue 78
    This is Strata 79
Eggs Tahoe 82
Elegant Chicken Breast 116
Em's Gnocci 182
Energy Bars 195
English Muffin Bread 65
English Trifle 239
ENTREES
    Beef
        Baked Corned Beef 133
        Beef and Spinach Roll 141
        Cavatini 147
        Cheese Meatballs with Spaghetti
            Sauce 149
        Chimichangas 137
        Classic Italian Spaghetti Sauce 148
        Deep Dish Chicago Style Pizza 135
        Hamburger Pinwheels 162
        Hawaiian Meat Loaf 145
        Hearty Chili Con Carne 144
        Lobster-Stuffed Tenderloin of Beef. 139
        Marinated Flank Steak 161

Microwave Pizza Casserole 134
Mock Filets 162
Mushroom Spaghetti Sauce 150
Pantry Casserole 147
Peppered Beef Tenderloin 140
Quick Lasagna 138
Reuben Casserole 134
Salisbury Steak and Mushroom
    Sauce 146
Santa Fe Enchiladas 136
Sicilian Meat Roll 143
Slow Cooker Italian Sausage 142
Tomato Meat Sauce 150
Tostado Casserole 138
Trader's Pie 142
Waikiki Meatballs 143
Wild Rice Baron 148
Cheese Manicotti 184
Cheese Soufflé 94
Pork
    Apricot Glazed Ham 127
    Broccoli-Ham Casserole 127
    Creole Pork Chops 131
    Honey Apple Pork Chops 160
    Marinated Pork Loin 130
    Old Fashioned Pork and Beans 131
    Orange-Glazed Pork Tenderloins .. 129
    Party Ham Casserole 128
    Pork Chop Casserole 132
    Pork Chops and Sour Cream 132
    Pork Tenderloin Diane 128
    Pork and Apple Sauté 129
    Slow Cooker Italian Sausage 142
    Tangy Glazed Pork Loin 130
Poultry
    Baked Pheasant Under Glass 125
    Challupas 122
    Chicken Breasts Diane 106
    Chicken Breasts Dijon 110
    Chicken Breasts in Phyllo 119
    Chicken Breasts with Sherry
        Butter 111
    Chicken Enchiladas Supreme 121
    Chicken Fajitas 164
    Chicken Marengo 105
    Chicken Mozzarella 112
    Chicken Stuffing Casserole 107
    Chicken Tetrazzini 114
    Chicken and Wild Rice Casserole . 117
    Chicken in a Ham Blanket 113
    Creamed Pheasant 126
    Crepes Almondine 91
    Crouton Chicken 111
    Easy Chicken Wellington 118

Easy Fixin' Pheasant 124
Easy and Elegant Chicken Breasts .. 109
Elegant Chicken Breast 116
Fajitas 165
Fancy Chicken Bake 107
Foil Baked Chicken and Canadian
    Bacon 114
Grilled Chicken Bundles 163
Grilled Turkey Breast 163
Herb Chicken Stir-Fry 117
Jody's Chicken Breast 164
Katie's Chicken 110
Lemon-Marinated Chicken 120
Make Ahead Chicken Bake 112
Mexican Chicken Casserole 121
Microwave Chicken and Rice 116
Microwave Chop Suey 124
Old Scotsman's Pheasant 126
Parmesan Chicken Bake 109
Pheasant Parmigiana 125
Poppy Seed Chicken 108
Quik-Chix Monterey Style 106
Ruby Chicken 113
Sherry Orange Chicken 104
Spinach-Stuffed Chicken Breasts ... 115
Stir-Fry Turkey Fajitas 123
Stuffed Chicken Breast for Two 108
Tex-Mex Turkey Enchiladas 123
Turkey Lasagna 122
Three Cheese Enchiladas 136

F

Fajitas 165
Fancy Chicken Bake 107
FISH
    Hot Tuna Salad Rolls 92
    Low-Cal Gourmet Fish 152
    Marinated Salmon 166
    Microwave Salmon Loaf 155
    Monkfish with Grapes and Cashews .. 152
    Orange Roughy and Rice 153
    Parmesan Orange Roughy 153
    Portuguese Sole 154
    Salmon Avocado Mousse 90
    Salmon Croquettes 154
    Salmon Quiche 155
    Tuna Bake 156
    Tuna Oriental 156
Foil Baked Chicken and Canadian
    Bacon 114
Food Processor Whole Wheat Bread 64
French Chocolates 212
French Creme Mold 98
Fresh Asparagus Soufflé 93

Frittata 83
Frozen Cadillac Torte 238
Frozen Date Salad 96
Frozen Peach Salad 53
Fruit Pizza 235
Fruit and Honey Muffins 72
Fruited Chicken Salad 85

G

Garden Linguine 88
Gebackens 204
German Sour Cream Twists 59
Giant Sugar Cookies 204
Gingerbread Waffles 76
Glazed Jam Puffs 74
Golden Banana Loaves 57
Good 'N Soft Cookies 202
Grandma's Caramel Cream Sandwich
    Cookie 205
Grandma's Potato Salad Dressing 36
Great Grandmother's Chocolate
    Soufflé 228
Grilled Chicken Bundles 163
Grilled Turkey Breast 163

H

HAM
    Apricot Glazed Ham 127
    Broccoli-Ham Casserole 127
    Chicken in a Ham Blanket 113
    Creamy Ham Salad 50
    Ham Mousse 90
    Ham and Egg Casserole 80
    Party Ham Casserole 128
Ham Mousse 90
Ham and Egg Casserole 80
Ham-Flavored Cornbread Dressing 182
Hamburger Pinwheels 162
Harvest Apple Cake 216
Hawaiian Meat Loaf 145
Healthy Heroes 34
Hearty Beef Soup 30
Hearty Chili Con Carne 144
Herb Bread 183
Herb Butter 183
Herb Chicken Stir-Fry 117
Herb Seasoning Mix 183
Hershey Pennsylvania Chocolate
    Cream Pie 229
Hiker's Birdseed 11
Holiday Cranberry Salad 53
Honey Apple Pork Chops 160
Honolulu Cookies 205
Hot Cabbage Salad 40
Hot Cheese and Pepperoni Pleaser 22

Hot Gouda Cheese 24
Hot Tuna Salad Rolls 92
Hummingbird Cake 219

I

Iced Margaritas 10
Iced Nut Roll Cookies 206
Isola's Shrimp Curry 157
Italian Beef 33
Italian Cream Cake 220
Italian Salad 87
Italian Zucchini Pie 83

J

Jam and Cream Cheese Loaf 66
Jellied Horseradish Creme 140
Jimmy's Marinade for Beef 167
Jody's Chicken Breast 164

K

Katie's Chicken 110
King Boreas Barbecue 34
Kitten's Biscuits 16

L

Lady Lee Coffee Cake 68
Layered Cauliflower Casserole 173
Layered Vegetable Salad 97
Layered Vegetable and Cheese
    Casserole 180
Lemon Cheese Bars 196
Lemon-Marinated Chicken 120
Lemonade Cake 225
Lobster-Stuffed Tenderloin of Beef 139
Low-Cal Gourmet Fish 152

M

Magic Marshmallow Crescent Puffs 75
Make Ahead Chicken Bake 112
Mandarin Chicken Bites 20

MARINADES

    Jimmy's Marinade for Beef 167
    Sauce for Marinating 166
    Teriyaki Marinade 167
    Western Lite Marinade 166
Marinated Flank Steak 161
Marinated Fresh Fruit Salad 53
Marinated Pork Loin 130
Marinated Salmon 166
Marinated Vegetable-Pasta Salad 49
Meat and Vegetable Fettucine Salad 89
Mexican Chicken Casserole 121
Mexican Corn Chowder 32
Mexican Vegetable Pizza Squares 17

MICROWAVE

    Chicken in a Ham Blanket 113
    Frozen Cadillac Torte 238
    Microwave Chop Suey 124

Microwave Pizza Casserole 134
Microwave Salmon Loaf 155
Reuben Casserole 134
Santa Fe Enchiladas 136
Tuna Oriental 156
Microwave Chicken and Rice 116
Microwave Chop Suey 124
Microwave Pizza Casserole 134
Microwave Salmon Loaf 155
Mike's Potatoes 175
Minestrone 29
Mixed Nut Bars 197
Mixed Vegetable Salad 47
Mock Filets 162
Mom's Chewy Cereal Bars 196
Mom's Easy Vichyssoise 33
Monkfish with Grapes and Cashews 152
Morning Glory Muffins 73
Mushroom Spaghetti Sauce 150
Mushroom Spinach Florentine 177
Mustard Sauce 133

N

Napa Cabbage, Carrot and Snow Pea
    Sauté 172
Never Fail Fudge 213
New Potato Salad Vinaigrette 46
No Bake Butterscotch Bars 194
Northwest Salad 52
Nutty Wild Rice Salad 48

O

Oatmeal Bars 197
Oatmeal Fudgies 198
Old Fashioned Pork and Beans 131
Old Scotsman's Pheasant 126
Orange Carrots 171
Orange Cooler Salad 52
Orange Roughy and Rice 153
Orange Sherbet Cooler 10
Orange Tapioca Salad 54
Orange-Glazed Pork Tenderloins 129
Orange-Glazed Sweet Potatoes 178
Oven Cheese Fondue 78
Overnight Salad 41

P

Pantry Casserole 147
Parmesan Cheese Dressing 36
Parmesan Chicken Bake 109
Parmesan Orange Roughy 153
Party Ham Casserole 128
Party Pretzels 12
Party Wedges 16

PASTA

    Asparagus with Pasta 184

Cheese Manicotti 184
Garden Linguine 88
Italian Salad 87
Marinated Vegetable-Pasta Salad 49
Meat and Vegetable Fettucine Salad 89
Pasta Salad Italiano 87
Perfect Pasta Primavera 186
Rotini Salad 50
Shrimp Mostaccioli 158
Spinach Lasagna 185
Stuffed Pasta Shells 185
Summer Pasta Salad 49
Tortellini Salad 89
Pasta Salad Italiano 87
Pastry Cream Filling 240
Peach Bread 57

PEANUT BUTTER
Easy Candy 214
Peanut Butter Chip Cookies 207
Peanut Butter Cup Bars 199
Peanut Butter Popcorn 13
Tiger Butter 213
Peanut Butter Chip Cookies 207
Peanut Butter Cup Bars 199
Peanut Butter Popcorn 13
Pearl Onions and Peas in Mustard
Sauce 174
Pecan Sweet Potatoes 178
Peppered Beef Tenderloin 140
Perfect Baked Asparagus 170
Perfect Pasta Primavera 186

PHEASANT
Baked Pheasant Under Glass 125
Creamed Pheasant 126
Easy Fixin' Pheasant 124
Old Scotsman's Pheasant 126
Pheasant Parmigiana 125
Pheasant Parmigiana 125
Pineapple Bundt Coffee Cake 69
Pineapple Cream Pie 231
Pineapple Sauce 145
Polynesian Rice Salad 48
Poppy Seed Bundt Cake 69
Poppy Seed Chicken 108
Poppy Seed Waffles 76

PORK
Barbecued Ribs 161
Creole Pork Chops 131
Honey Apple Pork Chops 160
Marinated Pork Loin 130
Old Fashioned Pork and Beans 131
Orange-Glazed Pork Tenderloins 129
Pork Chop Casserole 132

Pork Chops Teriyaki 160
Pork Chops and Sour Cream 132
Pork Tenderloin Diane 128
Pork and Apple Sauté 129
Tangy Glazed Pork Loin 130
Pork Chop Casserole 132
Pork Chops Teriyaki 160
Pork Chops and Sour Cream 132
Pork Tenderloin Diane 128
Pork and Apple Sauté 129
Portuguese Sole 154

POTATO
Baked Potato Salad 175
Cheesey Crab-Stuffed Baked Potatoes . 92
Mike's Potatoes 175
New Potato Salad Vinaigrette 46
Orange-Glazed Sweet Potatoes 178
Pecan Sweet Potatoes 178
San Diego Beach-Baked Potatoes 93
Provolone-Cheddar Vegetable Soup 26
Pumpkin Swirl Bread 58

Q
Quick Cinnamon Rolls 61
Quick Lasagna 138
Quick Spinach 176
Quick Stove Top Rice Pilaf 187
Quick Super Brownies 192
Quik-Chix Monterey Style 106

R
Raisin Cream Bars 198

RASPBERRY
Chocolate Raspberry Cheesecake 101
Chocolate Truffle Loaf with Raspberry
Sauce 100
French Creme Mold 98
Northwest Salad 52
Raspberry Cream Cheese Coffee Cake . 71
Red, Red Salad 51
Royal Raspberry Cake 224
White Chocolate Cheesecake 102
Raspberry Cream Cheese Coffee Cake 71
Raw Vegetable Salad 44
Red, Red Salad 51
Red Tomato Chutney 183
Refrigerator Crisp Oatmeal Cookies 207
Refrigerator Wheat Germ Muffins 72
Reuben Casserole 134
Rhubarb Bars 199
Rhubarb Custard Pie 232
Rhubarb Dessert 234
Rhubarb Muffins 74

RICE
Baked Brown Rice 187

Celebration Casserole 188
Cheesey Wild Rice Soup 30
Nutty Wild Rice Salad 48
Polynesian Rice Salad 48
Quick Stove Top Rice Pilaf 187
Rice Casserole 187
Superb Wild Rice 188
Rice Casserole 187
Rocky Road Fudge Bars 193
Rotini Salad 50
Royal Raspberry Cake 224
Ruby Chicken 113

S

SALADS
Fruit
Candy Bar Cut Up 236
Frozen Peach Salad 53
Holiday Cranberry Salad 53
Marinated Fresh Fruit Salad 53
Orange Tapioca Salad 54
Spiced Peaches 95
Watermelon Cherry Compote 54
Meat
Best-Ever Chicken Salad 85
Chicken Artichoke Salad 86
Chicken and Snow Pea Salad 86
Creamy Ham Salad 50
Fruited Chicken Salad 85
Hot Tuna Salad Rolls 92
Molded
Crunch Veggie Gelatin 51
Frozen Date Salad 96
Ham Mousse 90
Northwest Salad 52
Orange Cooler Salad 52
Red, Red Salad 51
Salmon Avocado Mousse 90
Pasta
Creamy Ham Salad 50
Italian Salad 87
Marinated Vegetable-Pasta Salad 49
Meat and Vegetable Fettucine
  Salad 89
Pasta Salad Italiano 87
Rotini Salad 50
Summer Pasta Salad 49
Tortellini Salad 89
Rice
Nutty Wild Rice Salad 48
Polynesian Rice Salad 48
Vegetables
Apple Harvest Coleslaw 39
Avocado and Bean Salad 37

Bernie's Broccoli Salad 43
Broccoli Cauliflower Salad 44
Broccoli Raisin Salad 43
Cabbage Patch Salad 38
Calico Salad 47
Cauliflower Supreme Salad 45
Cheesey Broccoli Salad 42
Chilled Asparagus with Dijon
  Vinaigrette 42
Chinese Cabbage Salad 39
Classic Spinach Salad 40
Cucumbers with Sour Cream 45
Dilled Tomatoes 46
Hot Cabbage Salad 40
Layered Vegetable Salad 97
Mixed Vegetable Salad 47
New Potato Salad Vinaigrette 46
Overnight Salad 41
Raw Vegetable Salad 44
Sour Cream Coleslaw 38
Spinach Salad Supreme 41
Strawberry-Spinach Salad 96
Tomatoes Provencale 95
Salisbury Steak and Mushroom Sauce ... 146
Salmon Avocado Mousse 90
Salmon Croquettes 154
Salmon Quiche 155
Salted Nut Roll 190
San Diego Beach-Baked Potatoes 93
SANDWICHES
Cucumber Sandwiches 19
Healthy Heroes 34
Hot Tuna Salad Rolls 92
Italian Beef 33
King Boreas Barbecue 34
Shrimp Salad Sandwiches 91
Santa Fe Enchiladas 136
Sarah's Rolls 60
SAUCE
Cheese Meatballs with Spaghetti
  Sauce 149
Cherry Glaze 133
Classic Italian Spaghetti Sauce 148
Jellied Horseradish Creme 140
Mushroom Spaghetti Sauce 150
Mustard Sauce 133
Pineapple Sauce 145
Red Tomato Chutney 183
Spicy Bar-B-Que Sauce 168
Tarragon Caper Sauce 140
Thompson's Tangy Rib Sauce 168
Tomato Meat Sauce 150
Sauce for Marinating 166
Saucy Chicken Wings 19

Scones with Strawberry Almond Butter ... 97
Seafood Brunch 80
Sharing Vegetable Soup 29
SHELLFISH
    Broiled Scampi 158
    Cheesey Crab-Stuffed Baked Potatoes . 92
    Isola's Shrimp Curry 157
    Lobster-Stuffed Tenderloin of Beef 139
    Seafood Brunch 80
    Shrimp Mostaccioli 158
    Shrimp Salad Sandwiches 91
    Stir-Fried Almond Shrimp and
        Peppers 157
Sherry Orange Chicken 104
Shrimp Mostaccioli 158
Shrimp Salad Sandwiches 91
Sicilian Meat Roll 143
SIDE DISHES
    Em's Gnocci 182
    Ham-Flavored Cornbread Dressing ... 182
Slow Cooker Italian Sausage 142
SOUFFLÉ
    Cheese Soufflé 94
    Fresh Asparagus Soufflé 93
    Great Grandmother's Chocolate
        Soufflé 228
    Spinach Soufflé 94
SOUPS
    Beer Cheese Soup 27
    Cabbage, Carrot and Caraway Soup 28
    Cabbage and Blue Cheese Soup 28
    Canadian Cheese Soup 26
    Cheese and Vegetable Soup 27
    Cheesey Wild Rice Soup 30
    Clam Chowder 31
    Hearty Beef Soup 30
    Hearty Chili Con Carne 144
    Mexican Corn Chowder 32
    Minestrone 29
    Mom's Easy Vichyssoise 33
    Provolone-Cheddar Vegetable Soup 26
    Sharing Vegetable Soup 29
    Three Bean Chili Chowder 32
    Viking Stew 31
Sour Cream Coffee Cake & Honey Nut
    Topping 70
Sour Cream Coleslaw 38
Sour Cream Cookies & Brown Butter
    Frosting 208
Sour Cream Lime Pie 231
Spiced Peaches 95
Spicy Bar-B-Que Sauce 168
SPINACH
    Beef and Spinach Roll 141

Classic Spinach Salad 40
Mushroom Spinach Florentine 177
Quick Spinach 176
Spinach Lasagna 185
Spinach Salad Supreme 41
Spinach Soufflé 94
Spinach Spoon Bread 176
Spinach-Stuffed Chicken Breasts 115
Strawberry-Spinach Salad 96
Stuffed Pasta Shells 185
"Viola" Spinach Pudding 176
Spinach Lasagna 185
Spinach Salad Supreme 41
Spinach Soufflé 94
Spinach Spoon Bread 176
Spinach-Stuffed Chicken Breasts 115
Squash Casserole 177
Stir-Fried Almond Shrimp and Peppers .. 157
STIR-FRY
    Herb Chicken Stir-Fry 117
    Isola's Shrimp Curry 157
    Lemon-Marinated Chicken 120
    Napa Cabbage, Carrot and Snow Pea
        Sauté 172
    Stir-Fried Almond Shrimp and
        Peppers 157
    Stir-Fry Turkey Fajitas 123
    Waikiki Meatballs 143
Stir-Fry Turkey Fajitas 123
STRAWBERRY
    Blitz Torte 237
    Scones with Strawberry Almond
        Butter 97
    Strawberry Bread 58
    Strawberry Cheesecake 223
    Strawberry Meringue Dessert 99
    Strawberry Smoothie 8
    Strawberry-Spinach Salad 96
    Toffee Strawberry Continental 98
Strawberry Bread 58
Strawberry Cheesecake 223
Strawberry Meringue Dessert 99
Strawberry Smoothie 8
Strawberry-Spinach Salad 96
Stuffed Chicken Breast for Two 108
Stuffed Pasta Shells 185
Sugar and Spice Cocktail Nuts 13
Sugar and Spice Muffins 73
Summer Heaven-Fresh Fruit Pie 230
Summer Pasta Salad 49
Sundae in a Pan 242
Sunshine Sherbet 242
Super Cookies 203
Superb Wild Rice 188

Swedish Christmas Tea Ring 62
Sweet and Sour Red Cabbage 171

T

Tangy Glazed Pork Loin 130
Tarragon Caper Sauce 140
Teriyaki Marinade 167
Tex-Mex Turkey Enchiladas 123
The Best Ever Chocolate Chip Cookie ... 202
The Big Dipper 22
This is Strata 79
Thompson's Tangy Rib Sauce 168
Three Bean Chili Chowder 32
Three Berry Lemon Tart 236
Three Cheese Enchiladas 136
Three Loaf White Bread 63
Thumbprint Cookie 209
Tiger Butter 213
Toffee Strawberry Continental 98
Tomato Meat Sauce 150
Tomatoes Provencale 95
Tortellini Salad 89
Tortilla Crisps 14
Tostado Casserole 138
Trader's Pie 142
Truffles 214
Tuna Bake 156
Tuna Oriental 156

TURKEY
  Grilled Turkey Breast 163
  Microwave Chop Suey 124
  Stir-Fry Turkey Fajitas 123
  Tex-Mex Turkey Enchiladas 123
  Turkey Lasagna 122
Turkey Lasagna 122
Turtle Cake 221

V

Vegetable Medley 179
Vegetable Pizza Squares 17
VEGETABLES
  Asparagus and Pea Casserole 170
  Baked Beans with Fruit 181
  Baked Potato Salad 175
  Beets with Mandarin Oranges 171
  Carrots Vicchy 173
  Company Carrots 172

Corn Bacon Curry Bake 174
Garden Linguine 88
Layered Cauliflower Casserole 173
Layered Vegetable and Cheese
  Casserole 180
Mike's Potatoes 175
Mushroom Spinach Florentine 177
Napa Cabbage, Carrot and Snow Pea
  Sauté 172
Orange Carrots 171
Orange-Glazed Sweet Potatoes 178
Pearl Onions and Peas in Mustard
  Sauce 174
Pecan Sweet Potatoes 178
Perfect Baked Asparagus 170
Perfect Pasta Primavera 186
Quick Spinach 176
Spinach Spoon Bread 176
Squash Casserole 177
Sweet and Sour Red Cabbage 171
Vegetable Medley 179
"Viola" Spinach Pudding 176
Zucchini Casserole 181
Zucchini Parmesan 179
Viking Stew 31
"Viola" Spinach Pudding 176

W

Waikiki Meatballs 143
Watermelon Cherry Compote 54
Western Lite Marinade 166
White Chocolate Cheesecake 102
Whole Wheat Banana Bread 56
Whole Wheat Biscuits 56
Whole Wheat Carrot Cake 222
Whole Wheat Oatmeal Cookies 208
Wild Rice Baron 148

Y

Yellow Birds 10

Z

ZUCCHINI
  Italian Zucchini Pie 83
  Zucchini Casserole 181
  Zucchini Parmesan 179
Zucchini Casserole 181
Zucchini Parmesan 179

NO RESERVATIONS REQUIRED

P.O. Box 365 • Marshalltown, Iowa 50158

Please send me _____ copies of
   "No Reservations Required" @ $16.00 each $_____

Add postage & handling @ $3.00 for first book $_____

Additional books postage & handling @ $1.00 each $_____

                        Total enclosed $_____

Make checks payable to Assistance League of Marshalltown

Mail Cookbooks to:

Name_____

Address_____

City_____State_____Zip_____

NO RESERVATIONS REQUIRED

P.O. Box 365 • Marshalltown, Iowa 50158

Please send me _____ copies of
   "No Reservations Required" @ $16.00 each $_____

Add postage & handling @ $3.00 for first book $_____

Additional books postage & handling @ $1.00 each $_____

                        Total enclosed $_____

Make checks payable to Assistance League of Marshalltown

Mail Cookbooks to:

Name_____

Address_____

City_____State_____Zip_____